PARADIPLOMACY IN ACTION

THE CASS SERIES IN REGIONAL AND FEDERAL STUDIES
ISSN 1363-5670
General Editor: John Loughlin

This series brings together some of the foremost academics and theorists to examine the timely subject of regional and federal issues, which since the mid-1980s have become key questions in political analysis and practice.

The Political Economy of Regionalism
edited by Michael Keating and John Loughlin

The Regional Dimension of the European Union: Towards a Third Level in Europe? *edited by Charlie Jeffery*

Remaking the Union: Devolution and British Politics in the 1990s
edited by Howard Elcock and Michael Keating

Paradiplomacy in Action: The Foreign Relations of Subnational Governments
edited by Francisco Aldecoa and Michael Keating

PARADIPLOMACY IN ACTION
The Foreign Relations of
Subnational Governments

Editors

FRANCISCO ALDECOA
MICHAEL KEATING

FRANK CASS
LONDON • PORTLAND, OR.

First published in 1999 in Great Britain by
FRANK CASS PUBLISHERS
Newbury House, 900 Eastern Avenue, London IG2 7HH

and in the United States of America by
FRANK CASS PUBLISHERS
c/o ISBS, 5804 N.E. Hassalo Street
Portland, Oregon 97213-3644

Website: www.frankcass.com

Copyright c 1999 Frank Cass & Co. Ltd.

British Library Cataloguing in Publication Data

Paradiplomacy in action : the foreign relations of
subnational governments. – (The Cass series in regional and
federal studies; v. 4)
1. Administrative and political divisions 2. Diplomacy
3. International relations 4. Negotiation – International
cooperation 5. Central-local government relations
I. Aldecoa, Francesco II. Keating, Michael, 1950–
320.8

ISBN 0 7146 4971 6 (cloth)
ISBN 0 7146 8018 4 (paper)
ISSN 1363-5670

Library of Congress Cataloging-in-Publication Data:

Paradiplomacy in action : the foreign relations of subnational
governments / edited by Francisco Aldecoa and Michael Keating.
        p.   cm. – (The Cass series in regional and federal studies,
ISSN 1363-5670 : 4)
    Includes bibliographical references and index.
    ISBN 0-7146-4971-6 (cloth). – ISBN 0-7146-8018-4 (pbk.)
    1. Subnational governments–Foreign relations. I. Aldecoa,
Francisco. II. Keating, Michael, 1950– . III. Series.
JZ4059.P37   1999   99-20579
327.1–dc21   CIP

This group of studies first appeared in a special issue of Regional & Federal Studies
(ISSN 1359-7566) Vol.9, No.1 (Spring, 1999)
published by Frank Cass and Co. Ltd.

Printed in Great Britain by
Antony Rowe Ltd, Chippenham, Wiltshire

Contents

Introduction

FRANCISCO ALDECOA AND
MICHAEL KEATING

The international activities of regions have attracted considerable political and scholarly attention in recent years. This has perhaps been most notable in Europe, where the protagonism of regions within the EU and the alliances among regions have generated a substantial literature, but the phenomenon has also marked federal states such as the USA, Australia and Canada. The motives, strategies and resources of substate governments in the international arena differ considerably, as the contributions to this volume show. So do the responses of sovereign states to what many of them still regard as an intrusion into their exclusive domain.

This activity is not new, as several of the contributions show, yet its resurgence in the late twentieth century is normally attributed to the effects of globalization and the rise of continental trading regimes such as the European Union (EU) and the North American Free Trade Agreement (NAFTA). These have served to erode the old distinction between domestic and international affairs and focused attention on the need for regions and cities to position themselves for global competition. From this perspective, there is a strong functional logic in regions' external projection, which is related to economic needs, to the spillover of their domestic competences into the international arena and in some cases to the need to manage ethnic or nationalist conflicts at their borders, with the security issues that these pose. Yet functionalism itself does not explain everything and we need to add political explanations derived from the goals and strategies of substate elites, building or promoting their region or, in some cases, preparing the way for national independence.

Responses on the part of national states also differ. In general it would be reasonable to say that states do not welcome the intrusion of substate actors into an area which is traditionally their reserved domain. Some see any external representation of regions as a threat to national sovereignty and integrity. On the other hand, state foreign policy has itself been transformed away from classical diplomacy and foreign ministries have themselves lost their monopoly of external action as large areas of domestic policy have been internationalized. States are therefore learning to live with a new dispensation in which they share roles with their regions and need to co-operate abroad. In some cases, matters are more sensitive than others, and a variety of patterns of conflict and co-operation emerge from the contributions.

There are sharp differences in the interpretation of these activities. Does this activity represent a new paradigm for international relations, in which state borders are penetrated by a multiplicity of actors and the old models of interstate relations are challenged? Does it force us to reconsider the traditional distinction between international relations and comparative politics? Several of the contributions address this issue, seeking to distinguish a field of 'paradiplomacy' carried out by non-state actors and to be distinguished from the classical diplomacy of states. This is itself controversial. Aguirre, in the final chapter, expresses considerable reservations about the term, and others have complained of its vagueness or asked whether it represents a coherent field of activity. We are aware of this problem and have adopted the term in our title as an indication of the general field, while leaving authors free to use, interpret or criticize it as they see fit. A similar problem concerns the actors involved, which include regions, cities, stateless nations and ethnic groups and a variety of sectoral and political interests. Again, we have striven for a broad and open approach, going for the term 'subnational' to refer to public authorities at the regional level, below the sovereign state, in the full knowledge that many of these regard themselves as national, if not fully sovereign actors. Most of the contributions deal with the activities of governments at this level and this, rather than the work of social movements and non-governmental organizations, is the focus of the project, although again we do not rule out the latter where they come into the picture.

It was to discuss these issues and to compare the experiences of regions in various parts of the world that we launched this project, with a seminar in Bilbao in September 1997. What emerged is a phenomenon of growing importance in a wide variety of settings. Michael Keating starts with a discussion of the motives, opportunities and strategies of regions in going international, placing the phenomenon in the context of globalization, free trade and the interpenetration of domestic and international spheres of action. Brian Hocking considers the ways in which non-central governments (NCGs) can constitute themselves as actors in the international arena alongside states, warning against the easy tendency to assimilate them to conventional international actors, whether states or corporations. Noé Cornago offers a wide-ranging review of the role of paradiplomacy in the redefinition of national security, notably in the field of ethnic conflict, citing examples from Europe, Asia, the former Soviet Union and the Americas. European integration further erodes the distinction between internal and external policy and creates a new set of institutions and policy arenas at the continental level which have drawn massive attention from subnational governments of all types.

The next three chapters examine paradiplomacy in Europe. Kepa

Sodupe looks at the way in which the European Union promotes and manages inter-regional co-operation through its policies and programmes. Francisco Aldecoa presents the case for plurinational diplomacy as a means for managing nationality conflicts in multinational states, themselves embedded in the European Union. This involves a surrender by the state of its monopoly in defining the national interest and carrying it through but also a recognition on the part of national minorities of their membership in the state. José Luis de Castro goes beyond the European Union to look at the role of the Council of Europe and its Congress of Local and Regional Powers of Europe and assesses its role in promoting regional co-operation and representation.

Paradiplomacy has always been a sensitive issue in federal states, where the division of powers, giving exclusive external competence to the federation, often clashes with the desire on the part of the federated units to project their domestic responsibilities abroad. The next three chapters examine this phenomenon in non-European cases. John Kincaid reviews the history and experience of international action by US states, showing how this is rooted in early constitutional practice and has been revived and expanded in an era of globalization. John Ravenhill covers the case of Australia, tracing the evolution from conflict to a more co-operative relationship. The case of Quebec is particularly sensitive since Quebec governments have long sought an external presence not merely for functional purposes but as a recognition of their national personality. This has come into conflict with Canadian policy as Canada, emerging from the British connection, has sought to constitute itself as a nation and to reserve the right of representation abroad. Louis Balthazar discusses the conflicts and difficulties to which this has given rise.

Alexander Ugalde presents a historical case, that of the Basque nationalist movement in its early years and during the period of Basque self-government under the Second Republic, highlighting the strategies, links and institutions used by the Basques to project themselves abroad. This reminds us that the phenomenon of paradiplomacy is not new and provides material for comparison with the strategies of national minorities in contemporary Europe.

Concluding the collection, Iñaki Aguirre questions the evolution of the 'paradiplomacy' paradigm, asking whether this adequately captures the phenomenon we are currently witnessing. Rather than seeking to extend the concept of diplomacy, he suggests, we might better think about a 'postdiplomatic' world, truly recognizing the new and complex realities.

While there is no common conclusion to the collection, some themes recur throughout the volume. First is the recognition that subnational involvement in external affairs is not a matter of transient fashion but does represent a change in the practice of diplomacy. Second, this will give rise to conflicts with states and to rivalries among regions within them. Third, these conflicts are not necessarily intractable, and the external roles of states and regions are not necessarily incompatible. Rather there are multiple opportunities for co-operation and shared roles. Fourth, this requires some change in attitude on the part of states and regions, to accept the new realities of shared powers and interdependence. Practices in this field are changing and evolving and there is a learning process involved.

We are grateful to the University of the Basque Country for financial support of our 1997 seminar and to the participants for their commentaries and criticisms.

Regions and International Affairs: Motives, Opportunities and Strategies

MICHAEL KEATING

THE RISE OF PARADIPLOMACY

Recent years have seen an increasing involvement of regional governments in the international arena (Duchacek *et al.*, 1988; Hocking, 1997), a phenomenon sometimes known as paradiplomacy. The reasons lie both in changes at the level of the state and international system, and in political and economic developments within regions themselves. Globalization and the rise of transnational regimes, especially regional trading areas, have eroded the distinction between domestic and foreign affairs and by the same token have transformed the division of responsibilities between state and subnational governments. Globalization itself has economic, cultural and political dimensions. Free movement of capital and the rise of the multinational corporation have eroded the ability of states to manage national economies, and have indeed made it ever more difficult to talk of national economies at all. Modern communications technology and the dominance of a global culture originating largely in the United States have eroded national cultures and the role of states in promoting and protecting them. The consequent loss of autonomy and capacity on the part of states has given rise to speculation about the end of sovereignty (Camilleri and Falk, 1992) as understood in the last 200 years or so.[1] Transnational regimes[2] have arisen in defence (NATO), in trade (NAFTA and the European Union), and in human rights (European Convention on Human Rights) and in Europe there is a project for building a political union above the sovereign states. Many of these provisions impinge on issues that are the responsibility of subnational governments or have a particular incidence in specific territories, drawing regions into the international arena.

At the same time, there has been a restructuring of territorial politics within states, with the rise of new actors and issues. Functional restructuring is in some respects eroding the importance of territory. Globalization of the economy, mobility of capital and communications and transportation technology have severed many of the links between place and production, allowing a freer choice of location and reducing the dependence of firms on the proximity of raw materials or waterways. The new communications media may erode the connection between culture and territory, by importing global culture, as well as by making it possible for cultural communities to exist without physical proximity. Politics too can be detached from territory, as transnational social and political movements or groups defined by ethnicity or gender compete with traditional forms of mobilization. Some observers have taken this so far as to talk of the 'end of territory' (Badie, 1995). Yet this is only part of the story, since there has also been a reinvention of territory as a functional requirement and as a political principle, within the new global order (Keating, 1998). Functionally, the most important effects are in economic and cultural matters. In the face of global change, the importance of territory as an ingredient in economic restructuring is now widely recognized (Storper, 1995; Amin and Thrift, 1994; Dunford and Kafkalas, 1992). The impact of global forces is mediated by the characteristics of specific territories, while the successful insertion of regions into the global economy depends very much on their capacity to engage in social co-operation and produce public goods. In a revival of the old idea of industrial districts, the qualities of specific places are now seen to be key factors in competitiveness, while the old idea of comparative advantage, according to which each region found its place in the global division of labour, has given way to the idea of competitive advantage, in which absolute advantages accrue to regions with the appropriate characteristics (Storper, 1995). This inter-regional competition is partly imposed by functional changes in the global economy; but it is partly the invention of political entrepreneurs who use the theme to consolidate their own regions and enhance their political standing within them. Regions are thus pitched into a neo-mercantilist competition for advantage in global and continental markets. Culture may also be globalizing in some respects, but local and minority cultures are also reviving, and territory is seen increasingly as the basis on which to protect and develop them.

To these functional reasons are added political impulses to re-territorialization. The weakening of the nation-state in the face of global pressures has enhanced the importance of territorial fault lines within multinational states such as Canada, Spain, Belgium or the United Kingdom. New forms of nationalism have emerged, less tied to the construction of a state in the classic sense, and more concerned with building a capacity for collective action, in government and civil society, in the face of the global market (Keating, 1997). In other places, we see a new regionalism (Keating, 1998) defined by its global and market context, or the rise of cities as actors. Development coalitions have emerged in these territorial spaces, seeking to manage the insertion of their territories into the global market, while controlling the socially disintegrative effects of that market. Territory thus becomes a key factor in the relationship between society and the global market and in the constitution of arenas for political debate and systems of collective action. Regionalism and minority nationalism, often associated in the past with protectionism, are now as likely to be committed strongly to free trade and especially in Europe, to continental integration, seeing this as a new space within which to develop and project their social and economic programmes.

An important factor in this is the decline of the state's capacity for territorial management, and the undermining of the exchange relationship in which states delivered protection from the market and favourable spending policies, in exchange either for loyalty to the state (in multinational states) or support for the government in power. In the nineteenth century, the state's contribution to the exchange usually comprised trade and tariff policies, which could be adjusted to the needs and demands of various regions as well as sectors and social groups. In the twentieth century, the high point of territorial exchange was represented by the regional policies of the 1960s and 1970s, presented as a non-zero-sum arrangement whereby developing or declining regions could benefit from the diversion of investment their way, booming regions could benefit from the relief of congestion and the national economy could gain from the use of idle resources in the periphery. Tariff policies are now limited by global and continental trading regimes. Diversionary regional policies are also limited by international trading rules (especially in Europe) and are of decreasing effectiveness in a global economy where firms can choose to locate outside the state boundaries altogether if they do not get their preferred location. National governments have accordingly put more emphasis on national competitiveness and less on regional balance, leaving sub-state governments to fill the gap. This decline in the mediating role of the state exposes regions more directly to the effects of the global economy, and forces them to seek opportunities to operate within it and within the emerging transnational regimes. This coincides with the new thinking on economic development, which places less emphasis on central state policies and more on factors rooted in the regions themselves. So the old dyadic exchange between the state and the regions, with the state mediating regions' relations with the global market, has given way to a more complex set of relationships, in which regions operate within the state, but also within transnational regimes and the global economy. Ohmae (1995) has made a lot of this point but takes it beyond all reasonable limits in linking the rise of the regional economy to the decline of the nation-state in a purely functionalist and determinist manner. To understand the phenomenon properly, we need to look at the regions themselves and the political incentive structure they face.

WHY DO REGIONS GO ABROAD?

Looking at the new paradiplomacy from the perspective of the regions themselves, we can discern three sets of motivations for them to go into the international arena: economic, cultural and political. Economically, regions seek investment, markets for their products, and technology for modernization. In a world of increasing mobility, they also promote themselves as tourist destinations. Inward investment is a means for obtaining employment and growth, as well as moving into new economic sectors, but it carries with it the risk of dependency and insecurity, as capital can move out as easily as it moves in. So it is often balanced by policies to build up the local business sector, especially in small and medium-sized firms. Markets and export promotion are of more importance for local small firms, which lack international connections or the knowledge and resources to establish them. Technology transfer is similarly of importance for small firms, which lack their own research and development capacity or the connections to tap into research and development circuits. Regions also seek, by collaboration among small and medium-sized firms in different places, to exploit the same complementarities and synergies that characterize successful industrial districts, again enhancing market competitiveness. As well as promoting inward investment, some regions try to increase the internationalization of their economies and the development of local firms and to develop markets through outward investment. A more altruistic style of external activity is the programmes of assistance to regions in developing countries mounted in some parts of Europe, notably in the Basque Country and in Fländers.

Some regions have sought to build a distinct model of development based on close linkages between government and private business, the assertion of a common territorial interest and the subsequent insertion of the region into the global economy. This neo-corporatist strategy is underpinned by a shared culture and identity and a political project aimed at securing effective functional autonomy for the region, by securing local control of both the political and the economic levers. While keeping economic control in local hands was usually associated in the past with protectionism, it is now allied with a strategy for inserting the regional economy into global markets without being dominated completely by them. The most elaborate such model is found in Quebec, where it has been labelled Quebec Inc. or 'market nationalism' (Courchene, 1990) and is claimed to give Quebec an advantage in facing the challenge of globalization by exploiting the productive potential of social concertation, while responding better to social demands (Latouche, 1993). This strategy can be traced back to the Quiet Revolution of the 1960s, and was later imitated by Fländers. An active external policy is a fundamental part of it.

Regions with their own language or culture also seek resources and support in the international arena, especially where their own state government is unsympathetic or the homeland of the language is in another state. So, for example, Quebec governments have sought collaboration with France and other francophone countries to gain support for their own cultural development and language promotion. It has gained the right to select its own immigrants and uses this to favour people from francophone countries. Catalonia has promoted its language in departments of Spanish language in universities and academies abroad, and has sought a place for non-state languages in European institutions. Alliances among cultural regions have been forged to lobby state and transnational institutions, for example in the European Bureau for Lesser Used Languages (Price *et al.*, 1997). These seek to promote the use of minority languages in European and international institutions and to secure exemptions for cultural industries in world and continental trade negotiations. International consortia are also used to project and export the cultural production of regions in world markets in a variety of ways, from exchanges of artists and performers to participation in satellite broadcasting syndicates.

Regions have a variety of political reasons for entering the international arena. Those with nationalist aspirations seek recognition and legitimacy as something more than mere regions. For example, at the time of the 1992 Olympic Games, the Catalan government placed advertisements in English-speaking newspapers asking rhetorically 'Where is Barcelona?' The text corrected readers' assumption that it was merely in Spain, by explaining that it was in a distinct nation called Catalonia.[3] External projection may also serve by a reverse effect to help nation-building at home, by showing local leaders in international contexts. Even in regions without nationalist movements, the international arena can be used as a platform for internal region-building, as well as for the projection of the regional politicians themselves. Regions, especially those with distinct historical and cultural identities, may also use diasporas to enhance their political influence in other countries and to mobilize resources. The role of the Irish diaspora has been important at various times in the Northern Ireland conflict and the peace process. The Basque diaspora in America provides an arena for the Basque movement. In other cases, regionally concentrated minorities may look to a motherland for support. So Quebec looks to France for political support in developing its distinct social and political model and, in the case of sovereigntists, for eventual recognition of an independent Quebec. There may be some tendencies developing for chicanos in the southern United States to look to Mexico for support as they assert their distinct place in American society. Territorial minorities across central Europe look to ethnic motherlands for support and assistance in their conflicts with their own states. There may even be efforts to rediscover and revitalize old connections and identities, as in some parts of central Europe where the German heritage is being refurbished as an asset in the new European market. More focused political campaigns seek to influence public or elite opinion in key foreign countries. In the summer of 1997 British Columbia aired radio commercials in Washington State, giving its side of the fisheries dispute. Quebec has gone to the United States to combat hostility from environmentalists and sympathizers of native peoples towards its hydroelectric schemes, whose viability depends on power exports to the US market. Canadian provinces have also sought to combat hostility in Europe and the United States to their logging and trapping practices. Quebec leaders make regular trips to Wall Street to reassure holders of provincial debt that their bonds will be secure. Nationalist leaders seek to reassure both political and economic opinion-makers in the United States that Quebec independence would not be a threat to them.

THE OPPORTUNITY STRUCTURE

Paradiplomacy is part of a broadening of the universe of international affairs, in which states are no longer the sole actors. Regions operate alongside firms, trade unions, social movements and transnational organizations like Greenpeace or Oxfam. This universe is complex, fragmented and unstructured. The global market is particularly complex and many regions have had great difficulty in finding ways to operate within it. For example, many subnational governments in the 1980s sent out missions to attract inward investors with little thought as to how to make an effective pitch, whom to target, or even where to go. This 'scattergun' approach has generally now given way to more selective strategies.

Transnational regimes present another point of access, but this depends on the nature of the regime. NAFTA has important implications for regional development across North America (Conklin, 1997) but presents few opportunities for influence other than through states. The European Union, by contrast, presents a range of such opportunities and these were enlarged and formalized by the Treaty on European Union (Maastricht Treaty). Hence there is a massive amount of regional activity in Europe (Jones and Keating, 1995: Petschen, 1993; Pintarits, 1995; De Castro, 1994; Hooghe, 1996). Regions have established offices in, and sent missions to, Brussels; by 1996, there were 115 such offices (*Europa Magazine*, 1, 1996). Regional lobbying might also coincide with sectoral pressures, where there is an important firm located in the region, allowing approaches through more than one channel. The Committee of the Regions, established by the Maastricht Treaty, gives regional and local governments a formal consultative role alongside the Economic and Social Committee, enabling them to comment on Commission proposals and Council deliberations as well as issues of general concern to regions. Maastricht also provided a mechanism for some regional input by allowing regions in some instances to stand in for their respective states in the Council of Ministers. This clause, which so far has been interpreted as applying only to the three federal states of Germany, Austria and Belgium, does not allow regions to represent themselves individually since the regions must first agree among themselves and, where national issues impinge, with the national government, on what their position will be. It does, however, represent an important breach in the principle that only national governments are represented in Europe, since where purely regional matters are concerned, it is the regions that speak for the state. Regions have also been drawn into direct contact with European policy-makers through the partnership arrangements for managing the structural funds, which bring together European, national and regional officials.

These opportunities for regions to act in Europe remain limited and states are still the dominant actors. Some regions have sought to expand on their role by promoting the concept of a Europe of the Regions. This rather vague expression has been interpreted in a variety of ways. One, rather utopian, vision sees nation-states – caught between Europe and the regions– fading away, to give rise to a new territorial dispensation, in which economic or cultural units below the existing states will be the principal actors. A more limited concept sees regions emerging as a 'third level' in Europe (Bullman, 1994) with a recognized status within European institutions, but still nested within states. A still weaker concept is that of Europe with the Regions, in which the regional dimension of European policies will be increasingly recognized, and opportunities for collaboration and consultation will be developed. The problem with systematizing this is the sheer variety of regions and regional demands. Some regions, with nationalistic leaders, see Europe as permitting them to operate almost like states, escaping the national framework. So Fländers, for example, has set itself the goal of moving from being a 'third-level' player to being a 'second-level' actor, more like the existing states than the mere regions. For this purpose it has come up with yet another concept, that of 'Europe of the Cultures', in which those regions with their own cultures or languages[4] would have a special status. German Länder, for their part, are highly integrated into the national policy-making system and the domestic concessions made to them in the 1990s made them less eager to pursue the Europe of the Regions idea. These concessions included the right to represent the state in the Council of Ministers on regional matters, and a constitutional change requiring Bundesrat consent to any further transfer of powers to Europe. So their preference has been for the 'third-level' strategy, allowing them to act both within the German domestic arena and in Europe. The Maastricht Treaty represented the high-water mark of regional ambitions in the EU. The Amsterdam Treaty gave them nothing very substantial in addition. Demands to strengthen the European level and the position of the regions in it by making the principle of subsidiarity justiciable and giving the regions access to the European Court of Justice to pursue it and other concerns, were not taken up. Some observers have therefore concluded that the 'third level' strategy has run out of steam (Jeffery, 1996).

Another set of opportunities is provided in the inter-state system, with linkages to national governments. Generally, this is difficult, since national governments do not see much to be gained in return, and the state government of the region concerned is likely to see this as a threat to its own diplomatic position. Cases such as the relationship between Quebec and France, where a state considers itself the motherland of the regional population and has a strategic interest in cultivating the link, are the exception. Fländers has nonetheless indicated that henceforth its privileged partners will be states rather than regions.

More common are links and partnerships among subnational governments in different states. These take the form both of multi-purpose or general associations of regions, and of alliances between specific regions. The main multi-purpose associations in Europe are the Council of Local Authorities and Regions of Europe, the Congress of Local and Regional Authorities of Europe, which comes under the aegis of the Council of Europe, and the Assembly of European Regions (AER), which covers the whole of Europe but whose main focus is on the European Union. The AER has played an important role in formulating policies and demands for regional representation in the negotiations leading to the Maastricht and Amsterdam treaties. Universal associations like these can play a role in establishing the presence of regions as institutional actors, but they suffer from the heterogeneity of their membership and the very different understanding of what constitutes a region in different European states.

A more focused effort is provided by groups of regions with a narrower geographical or sectoral focus, able to identify common interests and formulate proposals. These started to appear in Europe in the 1970s, the first being the Association of European Frontier Regions (Balme, 1996). In 1973, the Conference of Peripheral Maritime Regions (CPMR) was set up on the initiative of the Breton CELIB. This was followed by the Association of Regions of Industrial Technology (formerly Tradition). These lobby national governments and the European Commission on common problems, and mount inter-regional collaboration programmes such as the Atlantic Arc initiative of the CPMR. The most celebrated sectoral initiative is the Four Motors of Europe, founded as an alliance of Baden-Württemberg, Lombardy, Rhone-Alpes and Catalonia, four advanced regions which felt neglected by the Commission's emphasis on declining areas (Kukawka, 1996; Morata, 1996). The aim is to establish trans-European networks for research, innovation and production, applying in the single market the lessons learned from territorially-bound industrial districts. The initiative has gained a high political profile and its promoters claim great things for it, although outside observers have often been more reserved, noting that much of the activity is symbolic and pointing to the practical difficulties of co-operation across regions with such different administrative structures, levels of development,[5] and systems of innovation (Borras, 1993). Many other partnerships exist, across Europe and North America, and extending into Asia, focused on economic and cultural collaboration. The reality of these often depends on the enthusiasm of individuals and their willingness to follow them through. The Ontario government has a series of agreements, including an association with the Four Motors of Europe, but some remain empty shells as new governments have failed to pick up on the initiatives of their predecessors. One important focus, with specific implications, is on exchanges among university researchers, teachers and students, but this requires a capacity to follow through on the broad principles and the presence of individuals within the universities themselves who are willing and able to pursue matters.

By far the most common type of inter-regional co-operation is the cross-border initiative. Indeed there is not a single border in western Europe that does not have one. There appears to be a strong functional logic to this, especially where economic or cultural regions are bisected by state boundaries, some of them of quite recent origin. The European Single Market programme, and the INTERREG scheme launched by the European Commission to accompany it, produced a wave of initiatives. NAFTA also produced some interest in cross-border working in North America, but without the impetus provided in Europe by Commission funding. Typically, cross-border initiatives have a functional basis, focused on common problems and opportunities, notably in economic development, promotion, infrastructure, environment or culture. They are most successful where there are complementary assets and resources on either side of the border, and common interests in realizing them. This is most likely to be the case in environmental policy and infrastructure provision. In matters of economic development, it is more difficult, since regions are usually in competition for investment and markets and politicians lack the incentives to take risks which might not benefit their own populations. This can even affect common infrastructure projects, a typical example being the existence of two airports, one on each side of the frontier and neither large enough to serve the needs of growth. Yet neither side is willing to close its own airport to permit the development of the other one to the critical size. Another factor is the compatibility of legal and administrative systems on each side of the border, and the existence of governments with the powers and resources to undertake common projects. Success is also critically dependent on individual politicians and the way in which they use cross-border working to project an image of dynamism and build political capital. So there are complex games at multiple levels. At one level is the economic and functional context, which points variously to collaboration and the pursuit of common interests, or to competition. Then there is the level of state politics and government, where gatekeepers exist who want to maintain the monopoly of international contacts and channel them through state capitals. The next level is that of regional political entrepreneurs who, by contrast, see cross-border collaboration as a means of escaping central state control, pooling resources and, in the European case, gaining access to EU programmes and funding. The INTERREG programme is significant here in that, as a programme of community initiative, it escapes national control, unlike most of the structural fund initiatives. Finally, there is the micro-political level represented by local actors, often technical or general bureaucrats, and the personal networks that develop among them. These are very difficult for states to control, based as they are on informal links and unwritten communication. Again, cross-border collaboration can be a means for officials on both sides of the border to increase their autonomy from central state control by pooling resources and sharing information.[6]

The combination of these factors means that cross-border co-operation is much better developed in Europe than in North America. In North America, the tradition of inter-regional competition is much more entrenched, affecting states and provinces as well as cities, and there is not a lot of political capital to be gained from co-operating across the border. Politicians on the borders are often suspicious of free trade and are protectionist in sentiment, in contrast to European politicians who are often enthusiastic Europhiles. Cross-border initiatives in economic development and technology transfer are of most use to small and medium sized firms, while the large motor corporations that dominate US–Canadian trade can fend quite well for themselves. Language issues apart, there is often more compatibility between the various European welfare states and attitudes to government than there is among the three countries of North America, making co-operation in joint programmes easier. Finally, in Europe there is the presence of the European Union and its programmes for cross-border initiatives which provide resources to help costs, provide political support against often sceptical national governments, and give guidance and programme assistance for mounting schemes.

STRATEGIES AND STYLES

The strategies adopted by regions in their external relations are shaped by their motivations and the opportunity structures facing them. Paradiplomacy is not the same as conventional state diplomacy, which is about pursuing a defined state interest in the international arena. It is more functionally specific and targeted, often opportunistic and experimental. There is certainly a strong functional logic to the activity, and we have noted how it has expanded with globalization and the need for regions to operate in the global market. Yet it is not functionally determined, and political considerations play the main role in deciding on strategy and initiatives. This can be seen by contrasting the cases of Ontario and Quebec. The latter has pursued an active external policy as part of a strategy of nation-building, and has embraced free trade as part of this vision. Ontario, by contrast has been until the present government very reticent about free trade, and its external policy is not nearly as well developed as is that of Quebec, despite its even greater degree of insertion into the North American and global economies. Paradiplomacy is also characterized by a high degree of involvement of civil society and the private sector. This varies according to political and institutional factors. In Germany, where there are strong regional governments, these have tended to take it upon themselves to define a regional interest and determine how it should be pursued. In Catalonia, by contrast, there is a stronger role for private associations, often acting in collaboration with, or as agents for, the regional government. Quebec external policy has come to be pursued increasingly in collaboration with business and social interests (Balthazar, 1991), though this may have changed under the Parti Québécois, which has a more specific political agenda.

Relations with the host state vary greatly according to constitutional and political factors. The most permissive constitutional regime is in Belgium, where regions and language communities have full external competence in matters under their purview. They are restricted only in being unable to sign treaties with states with which Belgium does not have diplomatic relations. Since federalization has meant the abolition of national ministries in devolved matters, indeed, Belgium is reliant on the communities and regions for a presence not only in the EU but in organizations like the OECD and UNESCO. Canadian provinces also have a wide legal scope to act abroad, though there is a difference of opinion between the Quebec government, which regards the agreements it has signed abroad as full binding treaties, and the Canadian federal government, which sees them merely as accords. In Germany, the Länder can act abroad, but with fairly strict constitutional limits. Elsewhere in Europe, states try to maintain strict control. In France, the doctrine of state unity abroad is so entrenched that the constitutional court even refused to allow a constituency system for elections to the European Parliament, on the grounds that only the whole nation, and not individual parts of it, can be represented externally. As is usual in France, this doctrine is softened in the application by all manner of expedients. In Spain and Italy, states have interpreted the constitution in a very restrictive way although, in the last year or two a court ruling (in Spain) and a constitutional amendment (in Italy) have explicitly permitted regions to open offices in Brussels. The United Kingdom has no written constitution, and so British local governments have been among the most active in Europe.

Political relationships also vary. In Quebec, relationships with the federal government are, not surprisingly, worse when the nationalist Parti Québécois (PQ) is in power. Yet paradiplomacy is emphasized rather more by governments of the Quebec Liberal Party, which see it as an instrument of stateless nation-building, without requiring difficult constitutional changes. The PQ, for its part, gives priority to the achievement of independence, which will permit a full external diplomatic presence. So it was a PQ government that recently closed most of Quebec's offices abroad. Relations in Spain depend on the relationship of the political parties, notably the relationships with the central government of the dominant moderate nationalist parties of Catalonia and the Basque Country. Where they are in alliance with the central government, as under the Socialists 1993–96 and the conservative Popular Party after 1996, conflict is moderated and co-operation is enhanced. More generally, Catalan representatives abroad have sought co-operation with Spanish diplomacy rather than confrontation, in order to increase effectiveness. The Catalan government has also sought to distinguish its own role from that of traditional diplomacy.[7] In Belgium, the potential for conflict is reduced by the tendency for governing coalitions to be reflected at national and regional/community level. Since 1995, however, these have been elected separately, and as from the next elections the national and regional/community elections will no longer be held on the same day, so a divergence of political opinion can be expected. In Germany, there has been some tendency recently for the stronger Länder to operate increasingly outside the framework of co-operative federalism and to seek their own presence in the exterior. In the United Kingdom, relationships between central and sub-state governments are highly partisan and governments are suspicious of anything that might give opposition forces a platform. There was great tension under the late Conservative administration, a centralizing and increasingly anti-European government facing a periphery that was increasingly assertive and pro-European. Forced by functional necessities to establish a bureau to represent Scottish interests in Brussels, the government insisted that its mission should be economic rather than political representation and that Scotland Europa should provide a shelter for Scottish interest groups rather than articulating a 'Scottish interest' itself. The 1998 devolution legislation, however, allows the Scottish Parliament to establish a political presence in Brussels.

Foreign ministries have, not surprisingly, looked askance at regional activities abroad, seeing them as a breach of the united diplomatic front, and they go to immense lengths to control them. The French–Belgian cross-border regional collaboration teams were given an extremely top-heavy committee structure, including the French ambassador in Brussels, to bring them into the diplomatic fold. In the early 1980s, the British Foreign Office waged a war against the inward investment activities of the Scottish Development Agency and its offices abroad. Eventually a compromise was reached whereby they were subsumed in a new agency, Locate in Scotland, coming under more direct control from the Scottish Office which, as a ministry of the central government, was more easily controlled.

THE LIMITS OF PARADIPLOMACY

Paradiplomacy is a rather recent phenomenon and subject to a great deal of trial and error, as regions experiment to see what works and what is cost-effective. Some regions have been adding the costs and benefits, and are coming to realize that a great deal of what they have been doing is of doubtful value. There has in consequence been some retrenchment. Ontario and Quebec have closed most of their overseas offices and some European regions have closed their missions in Brussels. The efforts to institutionalize a third level in the EU did not ultimately succeed (Jeffery, 1996). Immense practical problems have emerged in efforts to secure inter-regional collaboration and co-operation, including the realities of territorial competition, differing constitutional and legal provisions, and the resistance of politicians and officials who have a continued stake in the existence of borders and central control. Paradiplomacy has not, therefore, proved state-transforming, except where states are already disintegrating for other reasons, as in Belgium or perhaps Canada. In those cases where regions encapsulate a sense of distinct national identity and a nation-building project, external projection is qualitatively different from those cases where it is motivated only by functional considerations. In the former, paradiplomacy is used in a highly political manner, either to prepare the ground for eventual independence, or as an element in stateless nation-building, a strategy to acquire as much as possible of the substance of national independence, without worrying too much about the formal status.

Paradiplomacy, while for the most part unspectacular, does represent an important and new dimension both to regionalism and to international relations, further evidence of the breakdown of the distinction between domestic and international affairs and between national and regional matters. As political leaders and publics are able increasingly to adopt multiple identities and roles in different contexts, they are more able to span the old state–international divide. Policy making is increasingly a matter of complex networks that cannot be contained neatly within political institutions, spanning both the public and private divide and international borders. It becomes more important, therefore, for politicians and officials to be able to operate in different arenas, and to link up powers, resources and opportunities found among them. This does not in itself imply that regions will become more important. There are many territorial and sectoral interests seeking expression in the international arena. The very forces of globalization that are drawing regions into the international arena may serve to disarticulate the region as a system of action, as different elements are drawn differentially into distinct global networks. Links between sectoral and territorial lobbies may be broken. Even local business interests may, as they are drawn into the global market, lose their territorial identity, while the neo-corporatist connections that underlie, for example, the Quebec model of development, may be under strain in the global market place. Regions will only be important to the extent that they have institutions and leadership capable of arriving at a definition of the regional interest, articulating this and devising policies to pursue it. This capacity varies, so that in some cases we find powerful regional governments pursuing a defined interest; in others there are competing versions of the territorial interest, often pitching a development coalition based on the region against one focused on a big city or metropolitan area;[8] in other cases again, there is no articulated territorial interest. So, for all the functionalist determinism of observers like Ohmae (1995), it is politics that ultimately counts.

ACKNOWLEDGEMENT

This paper was written while I was visiting scholar the Rockefeller Foundation Study and Conference Center at Bellagio, Italy, in August 1997.

NOTES

1.   I do not refer here to the 'Westphalian state' since I do not share the view that the present state system dates from 1648. The only European state to retain its Westphalian borders in 1997 is Portugal. The state system as we know is it largely the product of the second half of the nineteenth century and of the Versailles settlement of 1919. For a historical critique of the Westphalian fallacy, see Osiander (1994). The reason for emphasizing this point is to stress that state borders have long been permeable in many respects, and remained so until

the First World War and the collapse of the international trading system in the 1930s.

2. I use this term rather loosely to avoid entering the scholastic debate on the existence or meaning of 'international regimes.'

3. This type of ignorance is not confined to large states. Many Catalans and Basques, including nationalists, are insensitive to the *multinational* nature of the United Kingdom, referring to it as 'England.'

4. Effectively this means minority nations, but this terminology is not used. The concept also includes independent states which are small nations, such as Ireland and Denmark.

5. Each claims to be the most advanced region within its own state but, on a European scale, there are big differences between Baden-Württemberg and Catalonia.

6. Information is an important power resource here. In one set of interviews, French local officials revealed that, deprived of information by Paris, they went to their Flemish colleagues, who are in a more powerful position, and obtained the data from them.

7. Jordi Pujol has said that Catalonia has 'una presencia internacional, y no digo una politica exterior; me gustaria que quedara clara esta precision', *El Pais*, 15 Dec. 1993.

8. For example, the rivalry between the Generalitat of Catalonia and the city of Barcelona (Morata, 1996).

REFERENCES

Amin, A. and N. Thrift (1994), 'Living in the Global', in A. Amin and N. Thrift (eds), *Globalization, Institutions, and Regional Development* (Oxford: Oxford University Press).

Badie, B. (1995), *La fin des territoires. Essai sur le désordre international et sur l'utilité social du respect* (Paris: Fayard).

Balme, R. (1996), 'Pourquoi le gouvernement change-t-il d'échelle?', in R. Balme (ed.), *Les politiques du néo-régionalisme* (Paris: Economica).

Balthazar, L. (1991), 'Conscience nationale et contexte internationale', in L. Balthazar, G. Laforest and V. Lemieux (eds), *Le Québec et la restructuration du Canada, 1980–1992. Enjeux et perspectives* (Sillery, Quebec: Septentrion).

Borras, S. (1993), 'The "Four Motors of Europe" and its Promotion of R&D Linkages: Beyond Geographic Contiguity in Inter-Regional Agreements, *Regional Politics and Policy*, Vol.3, No.3, pp.163–76.

Bullman, U. (ed.) (1994), *Die Politik der dritten Ebene. Regionen im Europa der Union* (Baden-Baden: NOMOS).

Camilleri, J. and J. Falk (1992), *The End of Sovereignty? The Politics of a Shrinking and Fragmenting World* (Aldershot: Edward Elgar).

Conklin, D. (1997), 'NAFTA: Regional Impacts', in M. Keating and J. Loughlin (eds), *The Political Economy of Regionalism* (London and Portland, OR: Frank Cass), pp.195–214.

Courchene, T. (1990), *Quebec Inc. Foreign Takeovers, Competition/Mergers Policy and Universal Banking* (Kingston, Ont.: School of Policy Studies, Queen's University).

De Castro Ruano, J-L. (1994), *La emergente participación política de las regiones en el proceso de construcción europea* (Vitoria: Instituto Vasco de Administraction Publica).

Duchacek, I., D. Latouche and G. Stevenson (1988), *Perforated Sovereignties and International Relations* (New York: Greenwood).

Dunford, M. and G. Kafkalas (1992), 'The Global–Local Interplay, Corporate Geographies and Spatial Development Strategies in Europe', in M. Dunford and G. Kafkalas (eds), *Cities and Regions in the New Europe* (London: Belhaven).

Hocking, B. (1997), 'Regions and International Relations' in M. Keating and J. Loughlin (eds), *The Political Economy of Regionalism* (London and Portland, OR: Frank Cass).

Hooghe, L. (ed.) (1996), *Cohesion Policy and European Integration* (Oxford: Clarendon).

Jeffery, C. (1996), 'Farewell the Third Level? The German Länder and the European Policy Process', *Regional and Federal Studies*, Vol.6, No.2, pp.56–75.

Jones, B. and M. Keating (eds) (1995), *The European Union and the Regions* (Oxford: Clarendon).

Keating, M. (1997), 'Stateless Nation Building. Quebec, Catalonia and Scotland in the Changing State System', *Nations and Nationalism*, Vol.3, No.4, pp.689–717.
Keating, M. (1998), *The New Regionalism in Western Europe: Territorial Restructuring and Political Change* (Aldershot: Edward Elgar).
Kukawka, P. (1996), 'La Quadrige européen ou l'Europe par les régions', in R. Balme (ed.), *Les politiques du néo-régionalisme* (Paris: Economica).
Latouche, D. (1993), '"Quebec, See Canada": Quebec Nationalism in the New Global Age', in A-G. Gagnon (ed.), *Quebec. State and Society*, 2nd edn. (Scarborough: Nelson Canada).
Morata, F. (1996), 'Barcelone et la Catalogne dans l'arène européenne', in R. Balme (ed.), *Les politiques du néo-régionalisme* (Paris: Economica).
Ohmae, Kenichi (1995), *The End of the Nation State. The Rise of Regional Economies* (New York: Fress Press).
Osiander, A. (1994), *The States System of Europe, 1640–1990. Peace-making and the Conditions of International Stability* (Oxford; Clarendon).
Petschen, S. (1993), *La Europa de las regiones* (Barcelona: Generalitat de Catlunya).
Pintarits, S. (1995), *Macht, Demokratie und Regionen in Europa. Analysen und Szanarien de Integration und Desintegration* (Marburg: Metropolis).
Price, A., C. O'Torna and A. Wynne Jones (1997), *The Diversity Dividend. Language, Culture and Economy in an Integrated Europe* (Brussels: European Bureau for Lesser Used Languages).
Storper, M. (1995), 'The Resurgence of Regional Economies, Ten Years Later: The Region as a Nexus of Untraded Interdependencies', *European Urban and Regional Studies*, Vol.2, No.2, pp.191–221.

Patrolling the 'Frontier': Globalization, Localization and the 'Actorness' of Non-Central Governments

BRIAN HOCKING

The growing extranational involvement of regional and local governments – I shall refer to them collectively as non-central governments (NCGs) – has provided an increasing focus of interest from a variety of disciplinary perspectives, providing a good deal of analytical and empirical material from which to draw conclusions regarding the meaning and significance of this phenomenon. And as one might expect, diversity is accompanied by disagreement. Indeed, NCG internationalization has provided sustenance for very different approaches to understanding world politics, from realist to post-modern analyses, from arguments concerning neo-medievalism (Anderson and Goodman, 1995) to territorial 'debordering' (Brock and Albert, 1995). The fact that such differing approaches exist alongside one another poses interesting questions about the nature of what is being described. Frequently, however, the processes of NCG internationalization have been isolated from their broader contexts, imposing on them assumptions derived from the concerns and language of foreign policy, and focusing on the boundaries separating actors rather than the linkages binding them together. This is reinforced by a tendency to locate NCGs within the traditional, and increasingly uninformative, categories of state and non-state actor rather than seeking to appreciate their defining characteristics.

As with other entities, the analysis of the qualities inherent in non-central governments (NCGs) as actors in world politics – their 'actorness' – helps us to move beyond evaluations of their role and significance rooted in these assumptions of separateness, discontinuity and exclusivity.[1] If it is the case that, as Rosenau has suggested, we are confronted by an ever widening 'frontier' where domestic and foreign policy meshes into a seamless web and in which differing 'spheres of authority' jostle one another for advantage, then NCGs can, by virtue of their actorness, be seen as patrolling the edges of this territorially imagined and yet partially deterritorialized space (Rosenau, 1997). First, in a policy-oriented sense, it is obvious that the actions of many NCGs now cross the frontier imposed by assumptions rooted in traditional conceptions of foreign policy. The constitutions of federal states are, for reasons we shall come to later, no longer reliable guides to the role and place in world politics of the various levels of national political authority. But everywhere, it seems, foreign policy is being disaggregated and reconstructed as policy makers respond to domestic and international pressures, adapting the machinery of government in the quest to manage change. The difficulties inherent in this process are reflected in many official documents which grapple with the implications of the changing domestic-international order. In a recent report on Dutch foreign policy, for example, the Netherlands government seeks to distinguish between what it terms 'internationalized domestic policy' and 'activities abroad', or what one might conceive of as 'pure' foreign policy. In the process, it is forced to acknowledge that such categories are not watertight and that, 'If domestic policy is gaining an increasingly international dimension, foreign policy is gaining an increasingly national dimension' (The Hague, 1995: 46–7). Moreover, NCGs operate along the frontier in another, more literal, sense in that a good deal of their international activity involves cross-border links with other regional and local actors. Just as firms have engaged in the construction of strategic alliances for reasons of cost and competitiveness, so regions, localities and cities develop international linkages and their own brand of strategic alliance aimed at strengthening their position in the global economy.

The internationalization of NCGs also pushes us towards analytical frontiers, those connected with making sense of the processes of which it is a manifestation. At one level, of course, this is a dimension of the familiar problem of overcoming conventional disciplinary boundaries such as those separating comparative politics and international relations. But understanding the expanding arenas of NCG activity pose interesting questions as to the meaning of concepts fundamental to the emergence of the states system such as internationalization and foreignness, as well as the definition of international actorness and the relationships between differing categories of actor.

CONTEXTS: THE GLOBAL AND THE LOCAL

Inevitably, any discussion of this kind has to be located within the broader debate regarding the changing structures and processes of political, social and economic life and which focus on the contested concept of globalization. The interaction between globalization and localization, it is now well-recognized, does not represent some unfathomable paradox but reflects the competing pressures and tensions created by a broader and more integrated global economy (Taylor et al., 1995). Indeed, the search for a terminology to reflect the linkages between forces of integration and fragmentation which appear to confront us in varying contexts has produced some less than felicitous expressions such as 'fragmegration' and 'glocalization'. Certainly, regions and localities are increasingly affected by global forces. As with other actors, including national governments, this reduces their autonomy but does not mean that they have no scope for policy initiative and response. Common to these developments, however analysts have sought to describe them, is the recognition of a symbiotic relationship between cohering and fragmenting forces, constituting 'a local–global dialectic, where local events constitute global structures which then impinge on local events in an iterative continuum'(ibid.: 9).

Against this background, it is possible to view the desire for local and regional authorities to gain access to the international environment as one reflection of 'subgroupist' tendencies generated by globalizing forces, an expression of alienation represented by a turning inwards towards the closer and the more familiar. More positively, expressions of locally-based concerns on global issues from human rights to nuclear proliferation have become a familiar part of the political landscape. Again, the local is not the antithesis of the global but is itself one dimension of the processes of globalization as groups and individuals seek to exploit linkages between policy arenas and use the region or locality as one route to influence.

The frequent failure to recognize the nature of the global–local dialectic combined with the strong tendency to regard the relationships between actors in zero-sum terms, reflect conflicting interpretations of globalization, its effects on world politics and on the nation-state itself.[2] This impacts directly on the NCG issue. Indeed, the argument that NCG international involvement is one facet of the 'decline of the state' has been part of its fascination. Ohmae, on the one hand, sees the 'region-state' eclipsing the nation-state (Ohmae, 1995). Others remain sceptical. One Canadian economist, for example, argues that, on average, trade between a given Canadian province and US state is 20 times smaller than trade between any two Canadian provinces (Rodrik, 1997). Moving beyond zero-sum analyses of central–regional relationships, La Palombara, suggests that:

> even as national governments decide to share some of their sovereignty with their internal regions, their own scope of power can actually grow and not decrease. In fact, the most striking aspect of the powers of nations in this century is that they have continued to grow, notwithstanding such regional devolutions (La Palombara, 1994: 89–99).

The growth of clusters of regional economic activity – such as Silicon Valley – have, arguably, strengthened US national identity, not threatened it. But taking a more general perspective, rather than resulting in the dominance of any one actor, the erosion of policy boundaries both in terms of issues and the arenas in which these are pursued has, in many circumstances, created a multi-layered policy milieu which ties together governmental and non-governmental actors in mutual dependencies (Linklater and MacMillan, 1995; Hocking and Smith, 1997). Business and government, it is argued, are now linked in a triangular set of diplomatic interactions as the former seeks to develop strategic alliances and the latter pursues the Holy Grail of competitiveness and increased market shares (Strange, 1996). Beyond this, however, we are witnessing growing levels of interaction as various categories of actor, focusing on a multitude of issues and interests, form what Seyom Brown (1995) has termed a 'global polyarchy', 'in which conflicts are prosecuted and resolved primarily on the basis of *ad hoc* power plays and bargaining among combinations of these groups – combinations that vary from issue to issue'. In one sense, this is a recognition of the limitations inherent in actorness in an increasingly complex policy environment and the need to draw on the resources of others, whether these assume the form of knowledge and policy expertise or legitimacy. If there has been a 'power shift' in world politics, underpinned by new economic forces and the growing influence of 'new' actors such as non-governmental organizations (NGOs), it is more subtle than sometimes suggested, and mapping it is proving to be a contentious exercise (Matthews, 1997).

One consequence of this is that the nature of diplomacy itself is changing as the traditional representative of the state – the diplomat – is frequently required to act as a facilitator, assembling coalitions of actors in the attempt to manage problems which are beyond the capacity of government alone.[3] If it is the case that a defining quality of the state is its hierarchical, bureaucratic structures, then the state is finding it necessary to co-opt, or tap into, looser, more fluid, networks whose qualities of actorness are different from its own.

Furthermore, in some senses, the *behaviour* of actors is becoming similar. The conventional image of NGOs is being redefined as their officials engage in processes and arenas which are, in many senses, closely related to those of conventional intergovernmental diplomacy. Regions and cities, as Cable notes, are able to act like national governments in borrowing in international capital markets: 'The cost of their market borrowing is now set globally by highly integrated bond and bank credit markets. *Regions today differ from countries only in ways that are quite subtle* (Cable, 1996: 135, my italics).' That having been said, however, subtle differences often generate significant effects.

NON-CENTRAL GOVERNMENTS AND ACTORNESS

As suggested earlier, employing the terminology of foreign policy has often seemed to pre-judge the nature of NCG internationalization. Thus many of the terms coined during the 1980s to describe it – such as paradiplomacy and protodiplomacy – are suggestive of a second-order set of activities, pale imitations of 'real' diplomacy, and help to disguise the distinctiveness of what is being examined. This reinforces the need to apply criteria of international actorness which not only move beyond those traditionally associated with the state – sovereignty, territory, population and recognition – but also those which privilege the capacity to pursue a 'foreign policy' as the key dimension of international activity.[4] Such alternative criteria include:[5]

- aims and motivations
- extent and direction of involvement
- structures and resources
- levels of participation
- strategies

The purpose of such a typology is to move us beyond profitless debates as to who are and who are not significant actors in world politics. Most usually these are rooted in arguments regarding both the nature of actor participation and the qualities deemed necessary for 'acting internationally'. This has been particularly confusing in the case of regions and the authorities presiding over them, given the fact that several of these qualities are shared by states and regions – particularly territoriality and sovereignty. Confusion is reinforced by hyperglobalist assertions to the effect that regions, responding to ever-increasing flows of capital, technology and information, are eclipsing the nation-state as they redefine their location within a highly integrated global economy. Equally, however, to suggest that NCGs are simply one manifestation of a proliferating range of interests cutting across what have hitherto been regarded as discrete political arenas denies us the opportunity to examine what is characteristic in their extranational actions and presence and places them in the grab-all category of 'non-state' actor. With this in mind, let us consider what lessons we have learned regarding NCG actorness.

Aims and Motivations

If we have learned anything from the substantial literature on NCG internationalization it is that broad generalizations have only limited validity. To a considerable degree, this is because NCGs' aims in developing an international presence is the product of complex domestic and externally-generated forces. As Latouche has suggested in the case of Quebec, in evaluating the external interests of NCGs, 'we are operating at the margin of both the domestic and international spheres, a location where what is "inside" and what is "outside" becomes difficult to assess.' Thus an understanding of Quebec's motivations in the international arena:

> must take into account not only the internal articulation of its own state-building process (and the specific configuration of forces which give it life) but also its position within the overall Canadian statist space. We must consider Quebec's federal and regional components, the place of Canada within the international system, and the evolving nature of this system (Latouche, 1988: 34).

Similar points, with appropriate adjustments, can be made for most state/provincial/regional governments. Not infrequently, then, a clear understanding of the motivations for specific modes of NCG international activity needs to relate domestic to international forces and the interactions between the two.[6] Mushrooming overseas offices have been taken as indicative of the 'foreign policy' ambitions of local and regional authorities, often neglecting the fact that their functions are limited in scope, have little to do with foreign policy as traditionally conceived and, in resource terms, often amount to little more than a part-time professional consultant.

The complexity of this domestic–international interface has revealed several dimensions to the involvement of NCGs in the web of world politics. First, they can be purposive actors or *initiators*, seeking to pursue local/regional policy goals outside their national setting. Second, they can act as *channels* through which other actors, particularly non-governmental organizations (NGOs) can articulate their own concerns – in the environmental sphere, for example – thereby using the locality or region as a base for global strategies. Third, they may become *targets* of international activity where their own policies and activities affect the interests of other international actors.

In terms of policy initiation, it is clearly the case that the twin objectives of trade promotion and investment attraction have been key factors in understanding the growing NCG international presence over the last 20 years or so as regions and localities found themselves buffeted by international economic forces. In the US, for example, the 1980s witnessed a growing concern with trade promotion as the costs and benefits of competing for direct foreign investment were questioned. In this context, the enhanced European regional presence in North America – as represented by the Regional Mission for the Co-ordination of International Trade with Brittany (MIRCAB) and North Rhine-Westphalia's Foreign Trade Institute – came to be regarded as a model in terms of flexibility of approach and success in forging co-operative ventures with national authorities and the private sector (Northdurft, 1992). The centrality of trade and investment-related motivations has constituted the defining image of international presence even for the largest players such as California:

> California is so big, and its problems so immense, that it needs its own foreign policy. In an era when economics commands foreign relations, this does not mean embassies and armies, but it does mean more trade offices and state agents in foreign countries, its own relations with foreign nations and a governor and legislature willing to represent the state's interests independently of Washington (Goldsborough, 1993: 89).

But the changing nature of the global economy and the role of the state within it, more specifically the re-shaping of the trade agenda as it has moved from a primary concern with tariffs to more domestically sensitive non-tariff barriers (NTBs) and regulatory issues, together with the shift towards knowledge-based industries as the engines of growth, have both re-focused the concerns of NCGs and given their role an added significance within national economic strategies. Regions and cities, it is now recognized, can become 'nodes of competitive advantage' and thus key elements in the strategies through which national governments can respond to the pressures of a global economy (Courchene, 1995). This reflects the fact that the growing significance of knowledge in economic growth has blurred the distinction between social and economic policy. As Gertler and Wolfe (1997) have noted, it is regional governments and cities which are often the critical players in areas such as education and vocational training – now central factors in economic success. Thus the National Council of State Legislatures' report on the implications of the Single European Market for the US states stressed that its key lesson was the need to create a coherent economic development strategy into which a variety of elements – education, workforce training and basic and specialized infrastructure – are woven together (Roberts, 1991).[7]

The concern with competitiveness is reflected in another manifestation of internationalization, the creation of 'super-regions' or cross-border strategic alliances between regional governments (Keating and Loughlin, 1997; Ammon, 1996; Delamaide, 1995). In response to the recognition of new global economic challenges, some regional authorities have supplemented their domestic strategies by creating strategic alliances with other regions focused on scientific and technological collaboration, in the belief that by creating such networks, each can benefit. Probably the most publicized example is that of the Four Motors of Europe promoted by a former premier of Baden-Württemberg in Germany. Here, the concept of

regions as 'engines of growth' within national economies was extended to
the international level through the proposition that networks of regions
located in different countries could generate even greater growth (Gertler
and Wolfe, 1997: 6–8). In the late 1980s, stimulated by the creation of the
Canada–US Free Trade Agreement on the one side of the Atlantic and the
prospect of the Single Market on the other, an agreement was signed
between Baden Württemberg and Ontario. In Spain, Galicia has sought to
develop links with the Southern Cone Common Market (Mercosur),
facilitated by the 1995 EU-Mercosur framework agreement (Fraga Iribarne,
1998). At the city level, and also stimulated by the emergence of the Single
Market, the Californian city of San Jose established a series of partnerships
with five European cities with the aim of mutually reinforcing their
economic development.[8]

These developments have encouraged processes of 'relocation' on the
part of regions and cities as they define their interests in relation to
international economic forces, gearing themselves 'more to the challenges
emanating from the international sector than to the dictates of their national
economies' (Courchene, 1995: 2). In the European context, Kresl has noted
the effects of closer integration on the role of cities such as Amsterdam and
Lyon as they become 'gateways' within the global economy, redefining
their role in the European and global, as distinct from the national,
economic space (Kresl, 1992). In the Canadian context, the impact has been
felt in the weakening of East–West in favour of North–South economic
linkages. As noted above, however, the consequences of such relocation are
disputed. Far from eroding the role of the state, responses to the challenges
of economic competitiveness and the demands of operating in multiple
arenas may, on the one hand, result in co-ordinated strategies designed to
maximize co-operation between central and regional governments and, on
the other, the decision to limit NCG international involvement, relying on
national governments as interlocutor.

The second, and closely allied motivation for international access and
presence lies in the increasingly fluid nature of policy-making environments
and the enhanced capacity of, and need for, actors to intervene in them at a
variety of levels through a multiplicity of channels. The fact that many
issues, particularly on the environmental agenda, cannot be resolved
without the co-operation of several jurisdictions from the subnational to the
international, presents both challenges and opportunities to NCGs. Where
central governments seek to exclude regional authorities from policy
processes – and even attempt to restrict their powers on the grounds that a
given issue falls into the 'foreign policy' category – then the latter may well
respond by seeking out an international route to action and influence,
developing alliances with other regions and/or gaining access to relevant

international forums.[9] Similarly, the changing trade agenda and the deepening of global and regional economic integration impinge more and more on the concerns of NCGs. This reinforces their role as initiators – as when to the intense annoyance of Washington, the Texas Agricultural Commission intervened directly in Brussels over the EU's ban on the import of hormone-treated beef from the US (Hocking and Smith, 1997: 114).

The significance of the quest for international access and presence will, of course, be determined by the characteristics of the immediate international environment whether this be, for example, the North American Free Trade Area or the European Union. Here, the capacity of national governments to act as gatekeepers, or the primary channels, for contact between public and private interests within their borders has been reduced by the changing nature of the European policy arena in the wake of the Single European Act and the Maastricht Treaty (Van Schendelen, 1993; Rometsch and Wessels, 1996). A major motivating force is the desire to gain access to European structural funds. As one of the poorest regions of the former East Germany, Brandenburg regards obtaining maximum financial help from Brussels as a primary objective (Kramer, 1997). But, as in other locations, the expansion of policy areas dealt with by Brussels cuts across policy responsibilities assigned to local and regional authorities, ranging from education and culture to agriculture and environmental issues. In turn this creates an increasingly complex three-way relationship between regions, national governments and Brussels, which offers regional governments the opportunity to use the Brussels link to manage their relationships with their national capitals.[10]

Extent and Direction of Involvement

Involvement is a critical dimension of actorness in the sense that it explains the degree of international presence exhibited by NCGs, the direction that it takes and the opportunity to exert influence. Clearly, there are a number of factors which condition the extent of involvement such as bureaucratic resources, geography (transborder linkages offer some North American and European regions opportunities for involvement denied to the Australian states), location in policy environments (EU, NAFTA, Mercosur), the degree of asymmetry within federal systems and the powers assigned to NCGs. Thus the nature of the Spanish, German and Belgian political systems affords contexts for action very different from the hitherto highly centralized states of Britain and France. Although, for example, some observers see the French region of Rhônes-Alpes developing the kind of regional economic dynamism of Catalonia or certain German Länder, others suggest that the lack of a clear identity, distinctive language and aspirations to statehood make such comparisons far-fetched (Owen, 1997).

At a more general level, however, two dimensions of NCG involvement have become apparent over recent years. The first of these is *continuity* of involvement and is reflected in the development of structures and procedures at both national and international levels through which regional and local concerns can be channelled. The idea that NCG involvement is something that is exceptional and episodic has, in many policy contexts, disappeared. In their study of British Columbia's international involvement, Cohn and Smith trace an evolutionary pattern 'from an incremental and largely ad hoc policy phase to a rational policy phase, to a strategic policy phase, and finally to an emerging globalist policy phase' (Cohn and Smith, 1996).

At the same time, patterns of NCG international involvement have become more unpredictable as their status as *targets* and *channels* for others' actorness has increased. In the more expansive and fluid policy agendas transcending the domestic–international divide, NCGs have become policy targets for multinational enterprises and NGOs. In part, this reflects the growing importance of regulatory policies noted earlier and the fact that regional and local authorities are significant sources of such policies. The long-running battle between international firms and US states, particularly California, over their attempts to tax the global profits of multinationals is one notable instance where a policy perceived within a largely domestic framework was to become an issue attracting the attentions of governmental and non-governmental actors around the world. In the area of competition policy, the payment of state aid by the government of Saxony to Volkswagen was firmly opposed by Brussels which threatened to seek a court injunction against Bonn (*Financial Times*, 31 July 1996).

Outside the economic policy sphere, human rights and environmental issues have focused the attention of a range of actors on NCG policies. Since the 1980s, the Australian state governments of Western Australia and Queensland have attracted the attention of, among others, the World Council of Churches and Amnesty International over their treatment of their Aboriginal populations. Kramer notes the use made by a growing number of NGOs concerned with Third World development issues of the five Eastern German Länder governments and parliaments to promote their cause (Kramer, 1997: 24). On the environmental front, Greenpeace and other environmental groups have targeted British Columbia (both its forest industries and government agencies) over forest management practices (Hocking, 1996).

Added complexity is created where NCG international activity generates responses from other actors which are both unexpected and potentially harmful. One current example is offered in the development of NCG sanctions policies directed towards foreign governments, usually on human rights grounds – a not uncommon phenomenon in Canada and the USA, for example. The international coverage given to Massachusetts in passing a law which imposes restrictions on government agencies purchasing goods or services from firms (US or foreign) that have economic dealings with Burma has not only begun to exercise the international business community (the US–ASEAN Business Council, for example) but also the EU and the WTO (de Jonquieres, 1997; *Financial Times*, 11 March 1997). This appears to be one instance of a growing trend with, according to some estimates, more than 30 states, counties and cities having enacted – or proposing to enact – sanctions laws directed to countries as diverse as Indonesia and Switzerland. Against this background, EU protests are intended, in the words of a spokesperson – to 'nip a rather nasty trend in the bud' (Buckley,1997).

The second perspective on the extent of NCG involvement might be termed *issue scope*. Here, I have in mind the assumption that NCGs are concerned with what has traditionally been defined as 'low policy' as distinct from 'high policy' represented by the military security agenda. In one sense, as suggested earlier, this is true given the dominance of economic motivations to an understanding of NCG involvement. The difficulty arises where this leads to the conclusion that NCG activities are therefore of negligible significance. Such a view was not shared by the Swiss government who came to regard the campaign directed towards the Swiss banks over Nazi gold and the funds of Holocaust victims – in which US city and state governments played a critical role – as a direct assault on the status and identity of Switzerland on the world stage (Hall, 1998; Authers, 1998). Here, the point is that security itself has been re-defined, reflecting the fact that drugs, climate change, BSE ('mad cow disease') are themselves now 'high politics' – and, moreover, are problems in which subnational levels of government are often involved. Security ('human security') in this sense may be dissociated from traditional notions of national security, endowing regional and local responsibilities with additional significance (see Mathews, 1997: 51).

A third perspective on the extent of NCG involvement is provided in the form of the demands of global governance. Taking the environment as but one example (international trade is another) it is clear that, as Boardman has noted in the context of the Australian and Canadian federal systems, the states/provinces are the foundations of environmental policy with considerable jurisdictional overlap between central and regional levels of government (Boardman, 1990). The implications of this are that the effectiveness or otherwise of international environmental agreements can, at least in part, be explained by attitudes and policies at NCG level (Kux, 1994:46–7). Put another way, if it is the case – as Porter and Brown have suggested – that success in environmetnal regime building is determined in large part by the politics of 'veto coalitions', then explaining the composition of those coalitions may need to look below the national and embrace the subnational levels of government (Porter and Brown, 1991).

Structures and Resources

Clearly, aims and involvement will be determined in large part by the structural characteristics of NCGs and the resources that they are able to muster in pursuit of international interests. Again, diversity is a key factor. Wealthy regions with political clout in their national settings – California, Baden-Württemberg, Bavaria, Ontario, New South Wales – have far greater resources for acting internationally than do their smaller, less well-endowed equivalents. But resources are not measured purely in monetary terms. One resource that NCGs often do possess is bureaucratic expertise in specific policy areas (such as fisheries) which central government may not be able to match – or, indeed, in which it may be totally deficient.

However, the real competitive advantage that NCGs located in federal or quasi-federal states enjoy in the arenas of world politics is rooted in 'status ambiguity' reflecting their qualities as both 'sovereignty-bound' and 'sovereignty-free' actors (Rosenau, 1997: 36). As repositories of shared sovereignty with central government, combined with territoriality, they have a claim to presence in the international system which stands independent from their status in international law. And for their own political reasons, foreign governments (such as France in the case of Quebec) may accord them a special status. Moreover, because of their position within their national settings, they enjoy structured channels of access to national decision-making processes, including those with a marked international content. Unlike non-governmental actors, they may also be afforded privileged access to national diplomatic networks and international negotiations.

At the same time, their status ambiguity may afford them advantages associated with NGOs. Apart from possessing policy-relevant knowledge and expertise, NCGs can employ modes of behaviour unavailable to national governments. Thus Ontario (in the case of the Canada–US acid rain dispute) and British Columbia (the salmon 'war') both appeared in US courts, an avenue of action not available to sovereign governments. More generally however, NCGs enjoy a degree of legitimacy as the direct representatives of local interests untainted by the failings of national policy-makers. This is helped by the fact that they can often afford to take firm positions on issues (such as labour standards in Third World countries) which national governments will need to balance against broader international policy considerations.

This can, of course, turn against them. One of the strengths of the Greenpeace international campaign directed towards BC's forest industries was its success (at least in its early phases) in portraying the BC government as the 'Brazil of the North', allied with forest companies in despoiling one of the world's greatest repositories of temperate rainforest. Interestingly, two forms of legitimacy were set against one another – one (territorially based) deriving from the economic interests of regional constituencies within BC, not least those working in the forest industries, and the other (non-territorial and knowledge-related) represented by Greenpeace and allied NGOs, supported by an international audience.

Levels of Participation

Arguably, the most significant aspect of NCGs' actorness, linked closely to their status ambiguity, is represented by the variety of networks in which they can operate. Here, it is important to recognize the ways in which the traditional categorizations of networks – subnational, governmental, intergovernmental, transgovernmental and transnational – have become less clearly defined and the interactions and dependencies between them more pronounced. As Risse-Kappen has argued in the context of transnational relations, the empirical evidence suggests that separating international processes into categories such as 'transnational' – and particularly debates focused on the relative significance of categories of actor – are unhelpful to an understanding of when and how non-state actors are successful and unsuccessful in achieving their policy objectives. Appreciating this, he suggests, requires an analysis of the interactions between non-state actors on the one side and domestic and international structures of governance on the other (Risse-Kappen, 1995).

If it is the case that state and international structures determine the degree of success enjoyed by non-state actors, it is also the case, as argued earlier, that the ability of governments to achieve their goals is also dependent to an increasing extent on developing relationships with other categories of actor, and even on demonstrating some of their behavioural characteristics. Arguably, the most interesting, significant and challenging aspects of the various tests confronting policy-makers, whether they be agents of government, business or NGOs, is to identify the levels at which they can operate most effectively and the development of strategies that cross what are, in many cases, artificial boundaries.

This points once again to the problem of analyzing NCG international activity within a foreign policy paradigm with its strong emphasis on the dominance of intergovernmental networks. One of the most significant lessons that recent experience has taught us is that the hybrid actorness of NCGs offers them considerable scope to operate in various networks either simultaneously or sequentially. This is one of the main reasons why NCGs find themselves involved in the international arena and why they may find it desirable or profitable to adopt a diversity of routes to the exercise of influence.

This is not to say that governmental and intergovernmental networks are insignificant to an understanding of NCG international involvement. Indeed, in cases where their resources are meagre and their power *vis-à-vis* central government is limited, then influence through governmental and intergovernmental channels may offer the best route to the achievement of goals. But the porosity of agendas and arenas together with the relatively complex character of NCG actorness means that, in many instances, understanding their international presence requires a recognition of the availability and utility of other channels. Obviously, the more profuse these are, the more complex are the permutations of action that can be woven together. This becomes most marked in the case of the EU where the image of 'multilevel governance' rests on the capacity of regions to exploit the opportunities offered by the networks – governmental, intergovernmental and supranational – within which they are located (Marks, Hooghe and Blank, 1996).

Strategies

Underlying this complexity, however, a distinction can be made in terms of the routes to international action available to NCGs. On the one hand, they can adopt *mediating strategies*, using the channels of influence available to them through their access to national policy-making processes. These can also offer channels of access to intergovernmental networks in areas of policy relating to NCG responsibilities. On the other, there are *primary strategies* whereby NCGs muster their resources for direct international action thereby establishing a presence in relevant international arenas. The second strategy often reflects situations where regional authorities feel that their interests are not reflected in national policy leading them to lobby and/or to establish coalitions of interests across the various networks (Groen, 1994). Strategic choices of this kind are not, of course, available to all. Ironically, NCGs on the periphery of national political systems may have the greatest motivation to seek a direct presence in the international system while lacking the resources to achieve it. But, at the same time, as the policy environment has become more complex and as actors, both governmental and non-governmental find themselves linked by mutual dependencies, the distinctions between these two strategic orientations have become less marked.

And even where NCGs do possess the necessary resources, in the form of financial and bureaucratic strength for example, the choices may not be straightforward. As Groen's studies of BC international involvement suggest, cases such as the Canada–US softwood lumber dispute and the driftnet fishery issue, although they provide examples of transnational coalition-building, also demonstrate how the objective of such activity may be to pressure the national government either to change its policy stance or to demonstrate a degree of involvement previously absent. The fishery issue demonstrates both the tension between levels of government on the issue but at the same time, the potential synergy between NCG and national action:

> BC's subnational work brought together international expertise which might not otherwise have come to Ottawa's attention. In return, Canada's standing as a sovereign nation capable of submitting ecumenical legal positions provided the vehicle for the international representation of BC's concerns (Groen, 1994: 78).

This underscores the need to consider the linkages and continuities between levels of international action as well as the discontinuities. Indeed, as suggested above, the one may help to determine the other. For it is important to recognize that the decision as to where and when to act in various arenas is one that confronts both NCG and national policy-makers (as well as non-state actors). As Paarlberg has suggested, this issue of *sequencing* is critical to policy outcomes as it determines the range of available options (Paarlberg, 1995). One of the key changes that we are witnessing in world politics, and one that is critical to an understanding of NCG international strategy, is the erosion of traditional sequencing patterns in the management of international policy. This comes from internal pressures as NCGs seek to respond directly to pressures bearing down on them from the global economy and externally from other actors, such as the WTO, as agenda change embraces subnational interests and policies. Consequently, from a national perspective, the NCG 'problem' can no longer be defined as one of domestic implementation of foreign policy decisions but of continuous involvement which demands enhanced communication.

This highlights the centrality of a concept not unfamiliar in debates on the management of international policy – that of co-ordination. Traditionally thought of in terms of a problem for national foreign policy managers, the need to pursue linked diplomatic strategies at both domestic and international levels has greatly expanded its scope. Indeed, the co-ordination problem is one that stretches throughout all levels of policy formulation. Just as national administrations confront the need to cope with situations where a coherent response on international issues is both of growing importance and harder to achieve, so similar challenges are felt at the NCG level. In the wake of the ruling by a General Agreement on Tariffs and Trade (GATT) panel that US state regulations giving preference to home-produced over imported alcoholic drinks violated GATT rules, federal officials found it difficult to establish communication channels with state governments. In some instances, state governors were unaware of the ruling (Hocking and Smith, 1997: 113). The growing need for close federal–state co-operation in trade policy has been underscored in a report prepared for the National Governors' Association:

> if states are unprepared to effectively participate in trade policy discussions, it is the nation as a whole that will pay the price of lost market opportunities. In the event that state practices are found in violation of trade agreements, it is the federal government...that may be obligated to compensate the aggrieved trading partner (Colgan, 1992: 9).

Not surprisingly, then, one of the key strategic issues that these developments has posed is the growing need for effective structures and processes for communication between central and non-central governments on issues which challenge established allocations of function and responsibility in dealing with cross-boundary policy issues.

These may take the form of procedural agreements between levels of government, as have developed in Germany, Belgium and Spain regarding EU affairs (Rometsch, 1996; Morata, 1996) as well as bureaucratic 'linkage mechanisms' located in the foreign ministry, other government departments and within the broader domestic political structures. Such developments have to be seen in the context of institutional adaptation in response to the erosion of policy boundaries. Thus the issue of integrating NCG representatives into systems of national diplomatic representation (provincial officers located in Canadian embassies and a more unified Australian federal and state trade presence in London, for example) is one facet of a broader process whereby the character of national diplomatic services is under close scrutiny with limited experiments in shared facilities and 'co-location' of missions. In the EU context regions, particularly the German Länder, have succeeded in strengthening their input into the policy processes both at the national level and in Brussels. In the wake of the Maastricht Treaty, they have established a conference of European ministers (*Europaministerkonferenz*) which has the task of articulating Länder views to both Bonn and Brussels (Rometsch, 1996: 90–1; see Jeffrey, 1994). As with other forms of international activity, however, this imposes costs in terms of the need to ensure effective co-ordination at regional, national and European levels if influence is to be maximized.

EVALUATING ACTORNESS

It follows from the above that making sense of NCG international involvement requires us to abandon preoccupations with the foreign policy paradigm and the belief that understanding the internationalization of regions and localities can best be understood in terms of its language (of which the term 'paradiplomacy' is one example) and its assumptions. NCGs are, to a greater or lesser extent depending on the range of factors outlined above, part of the web of increasingly complex multilayered policy environments constituting world politics. These are marked by dependencies between actors, often conflictual but also based on the recognition of mutual need and the possibilities of linked strategies spanning a variety of networks. It is in a context such as this that the qualities of actors are significant, revealing their motives for extranational involvement, the extent of this involvement and the forms that it takes. And from the evidence of the above, the nature of these qualities and their consequences is more subtle than is frequently suggested.

The most general but often overlooked point is diversity. Too frequently, discussions of the growing internationalization of substate regions have assumed a coherence in the patterns underpinning regional internationalization where none exists. This is such an obvious point that it hardly seems worth making, but even a cursory examination of the literature of the last 20 years reveals how frequently it is ignored. From this follows another obvious but often overlooked point, namely that substate territorial actors are no more unitary actors than are nation-states, posing the question as to who is the actor in this context with all the levels of analysis problems with which we are familiar. Understanding NCG qualities reveals the often fragmented nature of their international involvement. This may result from the actions of regional tax authorities, trade and investment ministries, pension fund commissioners, port authorities, legislators acting on behalf of human rights NGOs or regional political leaders recognizing the value of presence in the international arena to processes of region-building. It is important to remember here that operating in multilayered policy milieus reflects, and is capable of generating, conflict within the region as well as between region and central governments (not to mention between regions). Put another way, it is as dangerous to assume a clearly articulated regional interest as it is a clear and coherent national interest.

Equally, it has been suggested that by no means all regional/local international activity is purposive and sought after. Increasingly, NGOs and multinational business enterprises (MNEs) have their own reasons for internationalizing regional policies and the growing integration of the global economy enhances the degree to which local and regional policies are of concern to other actors. Interest in local protectionist policies (as in the case of the EU and the US states) is long established but is being joined by other issues – local sanitary and phytosanitary regulations, for example – which cut deep into the powers of NCGs. In turn, this relates to a further point: the unevenness and variability of international involvement. Too often it is suggested that internationalization is a one-way street whose ultimate goal and result is the detachment of the region from its national setting. The available evidence suggests that this is far from the case. Not only is it apparent that the desire of regions to incur the costs of extranational activity is dependent on the fluctuations of fortune imposed by geopolitical and geoeconomic forces, but these fluctuations (along with other factors) can strengthen, rather than weaken, the links between locality, region and the political centre.

Inevitably, this leads us to the core issue: meaning and significance. Firstly, at the national level we are confronted once more by the 'foreign policy' question. One of the points which has already been made but which bears restatement, is that the conflation of a web of motivations for international involvement under the label regional 'foreign policy' is both unhelpful and misguided. At the same time, this is not to deny that significant implications for the way in which national governments define and conduct foreign policy can flow from regional and local international involvement. As noted above, in Europe, North America and elsewhere, the internationalization of NCGs in their various forms can make the conduct of a coherent and sustainable foreign policy more difficult just as, in certain contexts, it also offers the opportunity to devolve aspects of that policy. However, it complicates the management of international policy in ways that reflect the specific qualities of regions and their location in policy networks. In a number of contexts, especially the re-defined trade policy agenda, the real problem for national policy makers often lies in encouraging participation in shaping policy, not limiting it.

Meaning and significance can also be approached from the interests and concerns of the global community. Increasingly, the processes of global governance in their various forms are bound up with actions within national communities as well as between national governments. In areas such as environmental regulation, for example, substate interests and policies can be highly significant in determining international outcomes.

Moving to the regional level itself, it has to be remembered that developing an international presence is a strategic or tactical decision. Often, that strategy is directed towards gaining access to money (inward investment or structural funds in the EU context) or to arenas of influence. And strategies may be modified or abandoned. Returning to the point just made, examining the international involvement of regions over the last two decades illustrates its volatility. The goal for a very limited number of regional governments may be detachment – the establishment of a foreign policy within an independent state. For the most part, however, access to the international arena enhances choices for exercising influence and achieving policy goals. But this is far from arguing that the key to understanding the real significance of NCGs in the arenas of world politics derives from their ambitions to establish ersatz foreign policies. In part, this is because the foreign policy 'model' at the national level is being radically redefined due to enhanced global integration and developing international-level regionalism. Moreover, experience of interviewing NCG officials in several very different settings suggests that it is only comparatively rarely that they define their actions in 'foreign policy' terms. Certainly, this seems evermore inappropriate within the EU arena. Even in the USA, where the analysis of state and 'municipal' foreign policy has become a minor industry in recent years, one recent study notes that city governments 'rarely take positions on issues of foreign affairs, and city officials experience little constituency pressure to do so...they rarely translate [global economic] interests into formal policy positions communicated to federal and state officials' (Kincaid, 1997; Hobbs, 1994). Far less is it the case that the main significance of NCG international involvement relates to the popular declinist scenarios which consign the state to ever-diminishing significance. To argue in this fashion is to ignore the subtleties of subnational–national–international interactions which create fluctuating relationships between levels of political activity.

CONCLUSION: BEYOND FOREIGN POLICY

In attempting to draw out some conclusions from what is now a substantial literature on NCG international involvement, I have set this against the broader backcloth of a changing policy milieu conditioned by the linked effects of globalization, regionalization and localization. The key point is that NCG international activity has to be seen in the context of the analytical assumptions applied to it as well as in the light of the policy issues around which it has coalesced. Looking at the former, it is clear that one of the problems confronting us in trying to make sense of what is happening in the increasingly densely textured patterns of world politics is the continuing urge to stress the separateness of different categories of actor and to view the relationships between them in zero-sum terms – epitomized by often sterile debates as to the relative power of different categories of actor. In this sense, discontinuities and conflict predominate where the erosion of agenda and policy arena boundaries suggest the importance of continuities and linkage and the merging of networks of participation in world politics. The problem is reinforced by the rhetoric of globalization where a regional international involvement is adduced as further evidence of the decline of the state.

These and associated influences have conditioned our understanding of the role and significance of NCGs in world politics and discouraged the posing of questions free of assumptions regarding the end state of NCG international presence. Not surprisingly this, in turn, has generated contradictions where the evidence fails to conform to the images being imposed upon it. The problem is not the absence of a foreign policy dimension to NCG international activity for, as suggested above, there is one, but that it provides only partial explanations, almost inevitably skewing the issue towards a national policy maker perspective. Not surprisingly, from this angle, the international presence of NCGs is a problem to be managed by developing strategies which will fluctuate between containment and engagement, with an increasing emphasis on the latter as the centre recognizes the need to deploy a multifaceted diplomacy at both international and domestic levels.[11]. Underlying this, however, there remains an aura of inappropriateness, a lack of legitimacy in NCG international activity. As the preceding discussion has sought to demonstrate, such activity does not fit into the neat explanatory boxes to which many have attempted to confine it. To recognize this is neither to exalt nor diminish its significance but to identify its place within broader developments in world politics. Ultimately, however, it is to acknowledge that this significance is not rooted in its foreignness but, rather in its location in the frontierland where changing perceptions and definitions of foreignness and domesticity render the understanding of actorness at once important but increasingly difficult.

NOTES

1. I am not claiming that the notion of 'actorness' as employed in this article is in itself a novel one for it has been the subject of considerable discussion within the international relations literature. See, for example, the typology developed by Michael Smith in Hocking and Smith (1995) pp.84–9.

2. Among the extensive literature see, S. Strange, *The Retreat of the State: the Diffusion of Power in the World Economy*, Cambridge, Cambridge University Press, 1996; p.184; P. Hirst and G. Thompson, *Globalization in Question: The International Economy and the Possibilities of Governance*, Cambridge, Polity Press, 1996; L. Weiss, *The Myth of the Powerless State: Governing the Economy in a Global Era*, Cambridge, Polity, 1998; and V. Cable, 'Globalisation: Can the State Strike Back?' *The World Today*, May 1996; pp.133–7.

3. I have termed this form of activity 'catalytic diplomacy'. See Hocking, 1995.

4. Thus, for example, Chris Hill (1993) regards the three elements of actorness as an individual identity, autonomous decision-making capacity and *a structural capability to pursue a foreign policy* (my italics).

5. These criteria are adapted from those developed by Michael Smith in Hocking and Smith (1995).

6. I have discussed these at some length in Hocking (1993).

7. Similar themes can be found in publications from the National Governors' Association: for example, *America in Transition*.

8. These were Dublin, Barcelona, Rouen, Stuttgart and Milan. Among other things, San Jose

offered to assist Irish firms wishing to establish links with firms in Silicon Valley and the Irish Development Agency offered assistance in educating local businesspeople about the Single Market Programme.

9. See, for example, Kux's description of the role of regions in the context of the Alpine Convention, pp.14–17.
10. See, for example, Newhouse's (1997) comments on Catalonia, Madrid and Brussels, 1997.
11. In this context, a considerable literature has developed around the concept of 'two-level games' involving negotiations at both domestic and international levels. See Evans et al. (1993).

REFERENCES

Ammon, G. (1996) L'Europe des Regions (Paris: Economica).

Anderson, J. and J. Goodman (1995) 'Regions, States and the European Union: Modernist Reaction Or Postmodern Adaptation?', Review of International Political Economy, Vol.2, No.4, pp.600–631.

Authers, J. (1998) 'Tangled Negotiations on the Road to $1.25bn Accord', Financial Times, 14 August.

Boardman, R. (1990) Global Regimes and Nation States: Environmental Issues in Australian Politics (Ottawa: Carleton University Press).

Brown, S. (1995) New Forces, Old Forces and the Future of World Politics (post-Cold War edition) (New York: HarperCollins).

Buckley, N. (1997) 'Brussels Worried By Law on Burma', Financial Times, 24 June.

Cohn, T.H. and P.J. Smith (1996) 'Subnational Governments as International Actors: Constituent Diplomacy in British Columbia and the Pacific Northwest' BC Studies, Vol.110 (Summer).

Colgan, C.S. (1992) Forging a New Partnership in Trade Policy Between the Federal and State Governments (Washington, DC: National Governors' Association).

Courchene, T.J. (1995) 'Glocalization: The Region/International Interface', Canadian Journal of Regional Science, Vol.18, No.1.

Delamaide, D. (1995) The New Superregions of Europe (New York: Plume).

Evans, P.B., H.K. Jacobson, and R.D. Putnam, (eds) (1993) Double-Edged Diplomacy: International Bargaining and Domestic Politics (Berkeley: University of California Press).

Fraga Iribarne, M. (1998) 'Regional Government in Europe: Legal and Constitutional Implications', British Council European Senior Civil Servants Seminar: How Europe Is Working: Constitutional Issues and Accountability (Worcester, Oxford).

Gertler, M.S. and D.A. Wolfe (March 1997) 'Region State Networking: Ontario and the Four Motors for Europe'. Paper presented to the 38th International Studies Association Convention, Toronto.

Goldsborough, J.O. (1993) 'California's Foreign Policy', Foreign Affairs, Vol.72.

Groen, J.P. (1994) 'British Columbia's International Relations: Consolidating A Coalition-Building Strategy', BC Studies, Vol.102 (Summer).

The Hague, Ministry of Foreign Affairs (September 1995) The Foreign Policy of the Netherlands: A Review, pp.46–7.

Hall, W. (1998) 'Happy 150th – and Cheer Up, Swiss Told', Financial Times, 1–2 August.

Hill, C. (1993) 'The Capability–Expectations Gap, Or Conceptualising Europe's International Role', Journal of Common Market Studies, Vol.31, No.3.

Hobbs, H.H. (1994) City Hall Goes Abroad: the Foreign Policy of Local Politics (Thousand Oaks, CA: Sage).

Hocking, B. (1995) Beyond 'Newness' and 'Decline': The Development of Catalytic Diplomacy. Discussion Paper No.10, Diplomatic Studies Programme, University of Leicester.

Hocking, B. (1996) 'The Woods and the Trees: Catalytic Diplomacy and Canada's Trials as a 'Forestry Superpower', Environmental Politics, Vol.5, No.3.

Hocking, B. (1993), Localizing Foreign Policy: Non-Central Governments and Multilayered Diplomacy, London, Macmillan, Ch.2

Hocking, B. and M. Smith (1995) World Politics: An Introduction to International Relations (2nd edition) (Hemel Hempstead: Prentice Hall/Harvester Wheatsheaf).

Hocking, B. and M. Smith (1997) *Beyond Foreign Economic Policy: The United States, the Single European Market and the Changing World Economy* (London: Pinter).

Jeffery, C. (1994) *The Lander Strike Back: Structures and Procedures of European Integration Policy-Making in the German Federal System.* Discussion Papers in Federal Studies, University of Leicester.

Johnston, R.J., M.J. Taylor and M.J. Watts (eds) (1995) *Geographies of Global Change: Remapping the World in the Late Twentieth Century* (Oxford: Blackwell).

De Jonquieres, G. (1997) 'Business Worried By US States' Sanctions' *Financial Times*, 11 March.

Keating, M. and J. Loughlin (eds) (1997) *The Political Economy of Regionalism* (London and Portland, OR: Frank Cass).

Kincaid, J. (1997) *American Cities in the Global Economy: a Survey of Municipalities on Activities and Attitudes* (Washington, DC: National League of Cities).

Kramer, R. (1997) *Transfederal Relations of the Eastern Lander. The Case of Brandenburg.* University of Birmingham, Institute of German Studies, IGS Discussion Paper Series Number 97/9.

Kresl, P.K. (1992) 'The Response of European Cities to EC 1992', *Journal of European Integration*, Vol.15, Nos 2&3.

Kux, S. (1994) *Subsidiarity and the Environment: Implementing International Agreements* (Europainstitut, University of Basel).

La Palombara, J. (1994) 'International Firms and National Governments: Some Dilemmas', *The Washington Quarterly*, Vol.17, No.2, pp.89–99.

Latouche, D. (1988) 'State Building and Foreign Policy at the Subnational Level' in D. Duchacek, D. Latouche and G. Stevenson (eds) *Perforated Sovereignties and International Relations* (New York: Greenwood Press).

MacMillan, J. and A. Linklater (eds) (1995) *Boundaries in Question: New Directions in International Relations* (London: Pinter).

Marks, G., L. Hooghe and K. Blank (1996) 'European Integration from the 1980s: State Centric v Multi-Level Governance', *Journal of Common Market Studies*, Vol.34, No.3.

Matthews, J.T. (1997) 'Power Shift', *Foreign Affairs*, Vol.76, No.1, pp.50–66.

National Governors' Association (1989), *America in Transition: The International Frontier: Report of the Task Force on Foreign Markets*, Washington, DC.

Morata, F. (1996) 'Spain', in Rometsch and Wessels, pp.143–7.

Newhouse, J. (1997) 'Europe's Rising Regionalism', *Foreign Affairs*, January/February.

Northdurft, W.E. (1992) *Going Global: How Europe Helps Small Firms Export* (Washington, DC: Brookings).

Ohmae, K. (1995) *The End of the Nation State: The Rise of Regional Economies* (London: HarperCollins).

Owen, D. (1997) 'Pulling Together at the Heart of Europe', *Financial Times Survey: Rhone-Alpes*, 20 May, p.1.

Paarlberg, R.L. (1995) *Leadership Abroad Begins at Home: US Foreign Economic Policy After the Cold War* (Washington, DC: Brookings).

Porter, G. and J.W. Brown (1991) *Global Environmental Politics* (Boulder, CO: Westview).

Risse-Kappen, T. (1995) 'Structures of Governance and Transnational Relations: What Have We Learned?' in T. Risse-Kappen (ed.) *Bringing Transnational Relations Back In: Non-State Actors, Domestic Structures and International Institutions* (Cambridge: Cambridge University Press).

Roberts, B. (1991) *Competition across the Atlantic: the States Face Europe '92* (Denver, CO, National Council of State Legislatures).

Rodrik, D. (1997) 'Sense and Nonsense in the Globalization Debate', *Foreign Policy*, Vol.107, (Summer), pp.21–2.

Rometsch, D. (1996) 'The Federal Republic of Germany', in Rometsch and Wessels, pp.82–91.

Rometsch, D. and W. Wessels (eds) (1996) *The European Union and Member States: Towards Institutional Fusion?* (Manchester: Manchester University Press).

Rosecrance, R. (1996) 'The Rise of the Virtual State', *Foreign Affairs*, Vol.75, No.4, pp.45–61.

Rosenau, J.N. (1997) *Along the Domestic–Foreign Frontier: Exploring Governance in a Turbulent World* (Cambridge: Cambridge University Press).

Strange, S. (1992) 'States, Firms and Diplomacy', *International Affairs*, Vol.68, No.1, pp.1–15.

Taylor, P.J., M.J. Watts and R.J. Johnston, 'Global Change at the End of the Twentieth Century' in R.J. Johnston, P.J. Taylor and M.J. Watts (eds), *Geographies of Global Change: Remapping the World in the Late Twentieth Century* (Oxford: Blackwell, 1995).

Van Schendelen, M.P.C.M. (1993) *National Public and Private EC Lobbying* (Dartmouth: Aldershot).

Diplomacy and Paradiplomacy
in the Redefinition of International Security:
Dimensions of Conflict and Co-operation

NOÉ CORNAGO

The ability to conduct diplomatic relations used to be considered as one of the primary attributes of state sovereignty. Indeed, it may seem that the basic condition for the extension of diplomatic relations throughout the world was the existence of independent states able to develop political relations among themselves. Nevertheless, the origins of diplomacy were the multiple practices of public and private communication among different political entities which have existed since ancient times. Certainly, these practices underwent different historical transformations through modernity before becoming conventionally redefined as an exclusive attribute of the sovereign nation-states. Nowadays, conventional study of diplomacy tends to exclude a wide range of practices, such as non-governmental and non-central governments' involvement in international affairs, in spite of their increasing relevance (Watson, 1982; Barston, 1988; Anderson, 1993; Berridge, 1995). However, the widely held view of diplomacy as an exclusive attribute of sovereign states is more an institutionalized political discourse than the product of empirical evidence (Hamilton and Langhorne, 1995; Hocking, 1993a; Cornago, 1999).

This article aims to reflect upon the place of paradiplomacy in the redefinition of international security, as well as on the problem of the articulation of diverse forms of subnational foreign action with state diplomacy (Hocking, 1993). In this article paradiplomacy can be defined as non-central governments' involvement in international relations through the establishment of permanent or ad hoc contacts with foreign public or private entities, with the aim to promote socioeconomic or cultural issues, as well as any other foreign dimension of their constitutional competences. This single definition will allow us to use an operational definition in the context of this work, avoiding the terminological controversies associated with the word. On the basis of very different experiences, we will try to show the value of certain forms of paradiplomacy as an instrument for the reduction of the transnational dimensions of ethnic conflict. Later, different forms of paradiplomacy are considered as an instrument, limited but worthy of consideration, for the promotion of confidence and regional security. We will also look at the most complex expression of the subnational dimension of international security, that which is posed by the difficulties of the centralized management of some of the most important issues on the new security agenda, as far as it affects the area of responsibility and competence, of regional governments. This situation requires us to rethink the conventional methods of diplomacy, and recognize the subnational dimension of international security. Although this question is beginning to receive attention (Luke, 1994; Rosenau, 1994) it has been neglected in the literature on the redefinition of international security (such as Dewitt, Haglund and Kurtland, 1993; Klare and Thomas, 1994; Lynn-Jones and Miller, 1995). Certainly, this is a complex reality, which we hope to outline, in an effort to stimulate a reflection on the value of paradiplomacy in the present conditions of world security.

FROM THE INTERNATIONALIZATION OF ETHNIC CONFLICT AS A PARTISAN STRATEGY TO PARADIPLOMACY AS AN INSTRUMENT OF ETHNOTERRITORIAL POLITICS

In the following pages we will analyze the place of paradiplomacy in the management of those situations in which the existence of national minorities divided between two or more states, or the possibility of internationalization of ethnic conflict, raise ethnopolitical problems in foreign policy. The proliferation of conflicts in post-colonial societies, ethnic claims in industrialized countries, and fear of the proliferation of ethnic conflict in the post-communist arena are among the central questions of world politics. These problems were tackled in very different ways for decades: from genocide, displacement of population or forced assimilation in totalitarian or ethnic domination regimes, to the recognition of cultural rights and a certain autonomy, federalization, or the right to exercise full sovereignty. These varied experiences have highlighted the need to promote peaceful forms of ethnic conflict management (Coakley, 1992; McGarry and O'Leary, 1993; Silva and Samarashinge, 1993; Safran, 1994).

However, in recent years ethnic conflicts have moved to the centre of international politics, as state borders are unable to contain them. This is due to the increasing governmental concern about ethnopolitical problems, but also to the work done by various non-governmental organizations and the growing pressure of public opinion. In this way, a question which has generally been considered to belong to domestic affairs has gradually been gaining an important international relevance (Schechterman and Slamm, 1993; Broen, 1993; Gurr and Harff, 1994).

Although the internationalization of ethnic conflicts can contribute to finding solutions through mediation or international negotiation, the literature on this issue usually highlights the fact that it more frequently serves to escalate tension, serving partisan strategies and foreign intervention. Internationalization can certainly encourage ethnic demands, increasing the capacity for mobilization and establishing new logistic and sanctuary opportunities. It can also exacerbate the feeling of differentiated identity and relative deprivation with respect to dominant ethnic groups (Silva and May, 1991; Mildarsky, 1993). While none of these should be underestimated, there are other very different facets of this problem which have only recently begun to receive attention. These are the situations where the extension of national minorities across borders has led to the trying out, with more or less success, and in the presence of determined conditions of institutional stability, of paradiplomacy as an instrument for the reduction of ethnic tensions Europe gives us. The complex relations between Carinthia and Slovenia, and between Tyrol and Bolzano are two examples of this. Of course, these are not the only European cases where border relations have an undoubted ethnopolitical profile. It is enough to remember the relations between Alsace and Baden-Württemberg; Flanders and its neighbouring Dutch provinces; the Danish minority of Schleswig-Holstein; the relations between Catalonia and Langedoc Rousillon; or the co-operation between the Basque Country, Aquitane and Navarre. Although these relations have developed during the last few decades without great political controversy, it is enough to imagine one of the affected states imposing difficulties on such subnational contacts, to reveal their political relevance.

In the case of the Slovenian minority, the difficulties emerging in the last few decades have been due not so much to the position of the Austrian central government as the regional government of Carinthia itself. Its opposition to the cross-border contacts of the Slovenian minority and the adoption of discriminatory measures even managed to complicate bilateral relations between Austria and Yugoslavia during the 1970s and 1980s (Cohen, 1986). The fears of the Belgrade government of reawakening the nationalist conscience of its own ethnic groups led it to act with prudence in those years, but the problem persists in independent Slovenia. In the light of the recent Balkan war, it is interesting to remember the experience of Yugoslavia in the field of interregional co-operation. Foucher, one of the most important representatives of the new French geopolitics, in a book published in 1991 – just before the outbreak of the Yugoslavian conflict – made a wholly geopolitical analysis of the organization of interregional co-operation in the Alpine Arc, in which, along with regions from Austria, Italy, Hungary and Switzerland, Slovenia and Croatia, also participated at that time. Bosnia Herzegovina and Montenegro had applied for consultative status, without success up till that point. After considering the formal objectives of such initiatives, and their role in the promotion of regional concertation, Foucher stated that, beyond all of this, 'the Slovenian and Croatian strategy of secession would begin with discrete infranational procedures, overcoming an ideological barrier,' adding that 'this association has been energetically criticized by Serbia, where it has been interpreted, not without reason, as a *Catholic coalition* directed against the integrity of the federation' (Foucher, 1991: 524).

The problem of the Austrian Tyrol and the German speaking minority of Bolzano has similar characteristics but has evolved very differently. In this case barriers to cross-border contacts were imposed in the post-war period by the Italian government. Its promises to grant autonomy to Bolzano were diluted by the creation of the Trentino-Alto Adigio region. The discontent of the Austrian minority led to Austria bringing up the issue in the United Nations in the early 1970s. This pressure, together with the incipient emergence of terrorism, finally persuaded the Italian government to recognize, at the end of that decade, special rights for the minority of Bolzano, and to develop without formal recognition, a regime of tolerance towards the strengthening of links between the Tyrolese people on both sides of the border (Pelinka 1990; Morrow, 1992). This new context, as well as improving relations between Austria and Italy, led to the configuration of one of the most unusual expressions of the ethnopolitical dimension of foreign affairs: the periodic holding of joint meetings of provincial chambers belonging to different states (Pelinka, 1990; Alcock, 1992; Alcock, 1994).

Although it is undoubtedly difficult to find examples in which the ethnopolitical dimension of paradiplomacy were so institutionalized, the experiences mentioned so far help to understand the contrast between the slow development of minority protection by the international regime (Thornberry, 1991; Bokatola, 1992; Eide, 1993; Miall, 1994) and the innovative developments in ethnoterritorial policy made by the states themselves. These innovations contrast with the reticence of the states, in a context where claims for ethnic recognition seem to be on the increase, to clarify the scope of the right to self-determination. In any case, it is becoming widely accepted that the exercise of self-determination does not necessarily lead to the obtaining of full state sovereignty, and that the demands that justify it can often be satisfied by the recognition of cultural and self-government rights (Hannum, 1990; Heraclides, 1991; Buchanan, 1991; Halperin and Schaeffer, 1992; Tomuschat, 1993; Cassese, 1994). As we have pointed out, the states' reticence to incorporate such developments into international law contrasts with the ever more frequent practice, where war scenarios are not on the agenda, to accommodate ethnic demands using diverse measures of ethnoterritorial policy, with more or less success. Even though states have until now rejected formal international recognition of the right to self-government of ethnic minorities (Thornberry, 1991) this has not prevented them from experimenting with various forms of ethnic accommodation through the extension of different degrees of self-government (Montville, 1990; McGarry and O'Leary, 1993). This evolution coincides with the growing perception of a certain loss of appeal to numerous ethnonationalist movements of immediate claims of full sovereignty or independence (Keating, 1996).

With this realization of the need to try out new approaches to the ethnic question comes an incipient international recognition of the role that certain types of subnational foreign action can play in the development of new ways of dealing with ethnic conflicts and transnational protection of minorities. Of great importance in this area is the work of the Council of Europe, which has never hesitated to promote the adoption of instruments to encourage various forms of subnational foreign action in favour of regional peace building and the protection of minorities (see Castro, this volume). In the same way, the Organization for Security and Co-operation in Europe (OSCE) has suggested that communication between people belonging to national minorities should be allowed, beyond borders and without interference from the public authorities. Even the universal regime of the protection of minorities proposed by the United Nations has recognized, in article 2.4 of Resolution 47/135 of the General Assembly, that the members of minorities have the right to maintain contacts with neighbouring groups across borders, as long as these contacts are free and peaceful (Thornberry, 1994; Schumann, 1994; Dalton, 1994).

Such instruments might seem irrelevant for cases of extreme conflict, where the transnational dimension of ethnic problems has led, as in central Asia or certain points in Eastern Europe, to the very threshold of war (Cuthbertson and Leibowitz, 1993; Liebich and Reszler, 1993). However, we should not undermine the transnational dimension in the administration of ethnic problems even in the more complicated situations. The Chinese authorities, for example, are becoming more favourable to promoting paradiplomatic relations by some of its regions, not only through the promotion of informal relations across the border, but also by authorizing its governors to sign inter-regional co-operation agreements. Such is the case of the relations between Yunnan and the north of Burma, or Guangxi and Vietnam. This last phenomenon, it has to be said, is being interpreted in many different ways, but its importance is undeniable. For some, it is a strategic attempt by China to extend its sphere of influence through peaceful means; for others it is an attempt to normalize relations with its neighbouring countries. Whatever it is, its political relevance seems undeniable (Maung, 1994; Womack, 1994). The most notable case is the one which deals with the efforts of the Xinjang region, with its Muslim majority, to strengthen its links with the neighbouring republics of Central Asia in the context of the so-called Great Islamic Circle. The repeated violent repression of any hint of ethnic rebellion makes it clear what the limits of ethnoterritorial claims are in China. However, before this, in 1987, Xingjiang was able to sign protocols of co-operation with each of the then Soviet republics of Kazakstan, Tajikistan, Kyrgystan and Turkmenistan – agreements which, despite dealing with economic issues, had a great symbolic value of self-affirmation of identity for their promotors in Xinjiang facing the Han majority (Christophersen, 1993; Dreyer, 1994). No international regime of protection of minorities can be universal without the participation of Chinese authorities, and these are much more willing to encourage the paradiplomatic activity of its provinces than to accept any international on-the-ground inspection (Segal, 1992; Thual, 1994; Zheng, 1994). This extensive network of international contacts by the Chinese provinces is not the result of an improbable tolerance of the desire for international projection in its provinces by the central authorities. On the contrary, it is a reality which is perfectly integrated into the Chinese foreign policy strategy to open up to the international economy. The extension of paradiplomatic relations almost completely avoids controversies which dialogue with the great Chinese diplomacy usually produces in the West (Goodman and Segal, 1995).

Some of the recent developments in the administration of ethnic conflict in the Russian federation, within its borders – Tatarstan, Yakutia, Tyva, Northern Osetia or Chechenia – as well as in its relations with neighbouring republics, can help us to understand the value of paradiplomacy in this context. Some of these conflicts have led to the outbreak of war or the development of a climate of extreme tension, but in others there has been an attempt to use other forms of reconciliation, for example, the development of tolerance towards foreign action on the part of the central government, or the search for ways around the problem on the part of the regional governments. This is an idea that the Soviet Union itself had timidly tried out in the past (Hauslohner, 1981; Roeder, 1991; Batt, 1998). Furthermore, Bashkartasan, Tartarstan, Chuvasia, among other components of the Russian federation, have stood out in the development of a very active international presence in recent years (Melvin, 1995). Of special interest is the case of Tatarstan. The bilateral agreement in 1994 between the Moscow authorities and Tatarstan, even though it was clouded with ambiguities, recognized the right of Tatarstan, which has no international borders, to develop its own international relations in certain fields, in particular in the area of foreign trade. This model, which served as a model for the agreement which brought the Chechenian war to an end, might also contribute to the reduction of tension in other critical spots of the post-

Soviet arena, like Ukraine or the Crimea (Lapidus and Walker, 1993; Blum, 1994). A similar reflection can be made of the tolerance of the Russian authorities towards the links between the authorities of Sakhalioblast in Russia with the neighbouring Hokkaido in Japan (Zinberg, 1995).

We are not suggesting that the development of a certain tolerance towards minority cross-border or international contacts constitutes a solution to ethnic conflicts, which had until now passed unnoticed. We can claim, more modestly, that ethnoterritorial policy and management of ethnic conflicts is beginning to take into account, in the most disparate of contexts, the transnational dimension and, consequently, the value of different forms of paradiplomacy as political instruments to be used, in one form or another, in the administration of these problems, and not just as tools of partisan strategies for the internationalization of ethnic conflicts. This development is wholly coherent with others as we will now analyse, in the use of paradiplomacy as an instrument for the promotion of regional concertation.

PARADIPLOMACY AS AN INSTRUMENT FOR THE PROMOTION OF REGIONAL CONCERTATION

We will now look at one of the most important, but least noticed, subnational dimensions in the redefinition of international security, the use of paradiplomacy as an instrument for the promotion of regional concertation. This phenomenon is not new, but, in the present circumstances it is taking on a special interest. In fact, paradiplomacy as an instrument for the promotion of regional concertation, with all its limitations, has constituted one of the most relevant facets of the work of the Council of Europe since its creation (see Castro in this volume). Its pioneering impetus to the institutional recognition of the political importance of regional governments and its support for the development of inter-regional co-operation are clear evidence of this. Such initiatives are, however, not the only precedent. However modest it may have been, the practice of twinning between towns and regions came after the Second World War as a result of the need to find new channels of reconciliation between the peoples of states which had fought against each other. This practice evolved through time, and during the Cold War, expressing the desire to reduce tensions through the establishment of co-operation between groups belonging to different military alliances.

Later, the process of European integration contributed significantly to the strengthening of interregional co-operation, even though on a formal level this initial peace-building objective was kept at a distance. This process can be said to have two motives: to bring together these co-operation initiatives with the objective of integration itself through the setting up of various European programmes; and the need to establish regional peace-building measures, although the reduction of inter-state tensions reduced the need for this element (Biucchi and Gaudard, 1981; Luben, 1991; Balme, 1996). The complex administration of the cross-border relations between Ireland and the United Kingdom in Northern Ireland constitutes the most relevant exception in this area (Bew and Meehan, 1994; Tannam, 1995). However, everything seems to point to the fact that in a future European Union extended to Eastern Europe this issue could take on great importance. The European Union itself, in the framework of its policy towards Eastern Europe, has been encouraging various initiatives for the establishment of local and regional networks of inter-regional and cross-border co-operation (Maillot, 1990). The idea is to ease the transition to the free market economy and economic integration, but it also promotes regional security and peace building. Such initiatives, which come about as a result of the extraordinary geopolitical transformations of recent years, coincide with the parallel work of the Council of Europe, and of the Organisation for Co-operation and Security in Europe, in the promotion of paradiplomacy for regional co-ordination. In recent years, both organizations have been highlighting the role that interregional co-operation can play in the framework of new attempts at co-ordination and re-establishment of confidence in Central and Eastern Europe (Schumann, 1994; Dalton, 1994; Castro, this volume).

Of course, this promotion work cannot be effective without the backing of the states in question. Apart from the numerous early precedents at the time of the collapse of the communist regimes of Eastern Europe (Kruszewski, 1986) a recent example serves to illustrate this question. We refer to the creation of the Carpates Euroregio in February 1993, an initiative of the foreign ministers of Poland, Hungary and the Ukraine, adopted in a formal, signed agreement in the presence of the Secretary of the Council of Europe himself. It brought together different regional governments from the concerned states, who had repeatedly expressed a desire to try out interregional and cross-border co-operation. Although the initial ministerial agreement included a formal invitation for Romania to participate, the Iliescu government later rejected the invitation, in an attempt to prevent Satu Mara, Bihor and Maramures – in violation of the Romanian constitution – from participating in a new initiative for which they had shown so much interest. This event caused certain controversy in the neighbouring foreign ministries, and even led to a resolution of condemnation from the Assembly of European Regions, but the Romanian government was behaving this way to express its distrust of the way in which Hungary was able to take advantage of paradiplomacy to ensure its influence in Romania (Zsolti Pataki, 1994). More recently, and with the need to give impetus to the improvement of bilateral relations in phase of pre-adhesion to the European Union, Hungary and Romania signed a Treaty of Friendship in September 1996. This treaty, with the backing of the European Union, the Council of Europe and the OSCE, aims to promote closer relations of co-operation across the border as well as the protection of the Hungarian minority in Romania (Ghebali, 1996; Toledano, 1996).

Elsewhere, in the most disparate of geopolitical and institutional contexts, new forms of paradiplomacy are being recognized as instruments for the promotion of regional concertation. Cross-border co-operation of various sorts constitutes one of the fundamental dynamics in the new attempts at regional co-ordination in Asia and Latin America. As far as Central Asia is concerned, it can be said that the fear shared by Moscow and Beijing authorities of the spread of Islam in the new republics of Kazakstan, Uzbekistan, Turkmenistan, Tajikistan and Kyrgystan, because of the influence of Turkey, Iran, Afghanistan or Pakistan (Banuazizi and Weiner, 1994; Malik, 1994) has led both governments to develop forms of transborder co-operation through trade and tourism, as well as the creation of infrastructures, shaping a new climate of bilateral co-operation (Bondaresky and Ferdinand, 1994; Ferdinand, 1994). China and Russia have also progressed recently, considering the fact that they are experiencing tensions along their borders, in the promotion of regional concertation through the setting up of contacts between substate authorities on both sides of the border (Moltz, 1995; Godron, 1996; Trenin, 1998).

In South East Asia, Laos and Thailand have been experimenting with cross-border co-operation, and this has generally favoured the cohabitation of the population, and improved diplomatic relations (Thayer, 1995). In the Indian subcontinent there have also been similar proposals, but with less success. The Indian administration's failure to deal with its ethnic problems has always had important repercussions on its foreign policy. In the last few years there have been discussions about the need for constitutional reform which, strengthening the competences of the regional governments, could also allow controlled decentralization of certain aspects of foreign relations. In this way, it has been suggested that the very existence of ethnic ties across borders, in the case of Kashmir, Punjab and Assam, could be turned into new forms of ethnoterritorial accommodation which would favour economic development and regional co-ordination, allowing the border regions to sign cross-border co-operation or foreign trade agreements with its neighbours (Muni, 1989; Chaudhuri, 1993; Mawdsley, 1997).

We should also look at the incipient foreign activity of the subnational bodies of Latin America, where various regional governments in the 1980s started to experiment with different modes of paradiplomatic activity as instruments of economic development and regional concertation. In recent years initiatives of cross-border co-operation have multiplied, spreading out across the subcontinent (Bolognessi-Drosdoff, 1990; Herzog, 1992). Disputes over borders – such us those between Peru and Ecuador, or Honduras and Nicaragua – popular nationalism, and political authoritarianism prevented development in this area for decades. However, learning from the failures of the past, Latin American central governments increasingly see substate foreign action as a valuable instrument for the promotion of economic integration and regional concertation (González Posse, 1990; Tokatlian and Barrera, 1991). Participation of the regions in the formulation of foreign policy in the countries of Latin America is a process which is constantly developing, in tune with the claims for democratization and the new regional integration (Bernal Meza, 1990). In regimes with authoritarian characteristics, or in those countries where the regulatory capacity or sovereign control over territory has been eroded due to drug trafficking or guerilla warfare, the autonomous regions have seen that their capacity to act abroad is restricted. In states which today enjoy a certain political and institutional stability, particularly Argentina, Brazil and Uruguay, and in the framework of new processes of integration, this regional autonomy has been strengthened, giving a new profile to inter-American relations (Bernal Meza, 1990; Valenciano, 1995; Oliveros, 1995).

Similar proposals have also been discussed in Africa where, with the backing of the United Nations, the European Union and the World Bank, promotion of cross-border co-operation in strategies of economic development, administration of common resources, and management of ethnic conflict, is being studied. In contrast with the analyses which merely highlight the institutional weakness of the African states (Jackson, 1990) some authors emphasize the importance which different popular strategies of survival have achieved, in a context of deep economic and social crisis, through different forms of transborder activity in different modes of informal economy (Constantin, 1994). The recognition of this situation, and its possible institutional development, is beginning to be included in the design of the international co-operation programmes who, starting from the potential of bordering regions, aim to give impetus to preventative diplomacy and economic development in Africa, using various forms of cross-border co-operation (Asiwaju and Nugent, 1996).

Although it is important not to overestimate the possibilities offered by these initiatives, an institution as important, yet apparently modest, as cross-border relations has had a marked impact on the history of diplomacy. The use of more institutionalized forms paradiplomacy can be considered as one of the most illuminating expressions of the contemporary conditions for good border relations (Ercmann, 1987; Martinez, 1986; Rumley and Minghi, 1991). Moreover, a good diplomatic method for dealing with international disputes should be the deployment of different strategies of preventive diplomacy. Those strategies can be of a very different nature, according to their diverse objectives, but paradiplomacy, like other forms of the so-called second-track diplomacy, may be a good tool in this field (Lund, 1996; Diamond and McDonald, 1993).

PARADIPLOMACY, THE SUBNATIONAL POLITICAL AGENDA AND THE NEW DIMENSIONS OF SECURITY

One of the most surprising aspects of the transformation of contemporary international relations is the way in which the agenda of those responsible for state security has begun to acquire, in the last few years, an unexpected similarity with the conventional preoccupations of many regional governments responsible for the administration of border regions. The literature on relations of co-operation and conflict on the most disparate borders of the planet – with its classic attention to such issues as the administration of ports and rivers, living conditions for workers along the border, contraband, or collaboration in the event of natural disaster – seems, in one way, to anticipate many of the areas which have become, in recent years, part of the new agenda of international security: the administration of ecological resources and common spaces, the control of migration and the movement of refugees, the persecution of international organized crime, the impact of speculation on national economies, or the prevention of serious disasters.

A distinguished group of specialists has developed the analogy between the co-operation among local bodies and international co-operation among states. Indeed, they point out that we find ourselves faced with different scales of collective and horizontal solutions of important issues in a context where, unlike the conventional political process characteristic of domestic politics, there is no hierarchical or vertical decision-making power, or system of control which guarantees its implementation and compliance. From this perspective, inspired by the theories of rational choice, and the new economic institutionalism, the problems that are posed, for example, by the administration of irrigation or forest resources between neighbouring communities are relevant to the study of the great issues of international co-operation, such as the global commons (Keohane and Ostrom, 1994).

We are dealing here with a stimulating approach, but from the perspective of our work it presents an important limitation. When it comes to specifying the differences between the two spheres, its proponents try to exclude, by definition, any kind of subnational co-operation which, like cross-border or interregional co-operation, crosses the territorial limits of state jurisdiction – in other words any kind of international subnational co-operation or paradiplomatic activity. This means the exclusion from its consideration of the sphere of cross-border international co-operation as well as any other form of interregional co-operation. We on the contrary consider that, above and beyond the heuristic value of the establishment of such analogy, the local and global spheres of international co-operation are logically related to each other. Whether or not we are dealing with similar situations, or those which can be said to be comparable, local and global co-operation over such issues as the administration of natural resources, the fight against drug trafficking, migration control or interethnic relations must be understood, above all, as different manifestations of the same issues in international society.

One of the areas in which this has been shown most clearly is the international protection of the environment. In Europe, subnational initiatives for cross-border ecological co-operation have not met with reticence from the states, which prefer to encourage it with support for various organisms of interregional co-operation. Sometimes, however, subnational management of ecological resources can be a much more controversial issue. Between Mexico and the United States, for example, the administration of shared ecological resources across the border was, in the 1970s and 1980s, just as complex as the treatment of problems more usually related to national security, like clandestine immigration or drug trafficking. It has even been pointed out that the administration of these problems has been able to promote relations of *clientelism* between governments on both sides of the border (Mumme, 1984). More recently, the concerns about the repercussions which the recent free trade agreements might have on the environment have led to renewed interest by the federal authorities in paradiplomatic relations in the region (Thorup, 1993; Dunn, 1995).

On other occasions however, the problem is reversed, with the subnational governments being concerned about attitudes of their respective central governments (Hansen, 1984). This has been the case in various substate initiatives which have come about between the United States and Canada to co-operate against the ecological deterioration of their regional ecosystems, as a result of what is seen to be insufficient federal action. The lack of federal reaction to the effects of two consecutive oil slicks along the Pacific coast led the governments of British Columbia, Alaska, Washington, Oregon and California to create in 1988 a special unit or Task Force to bring together human, technical and financial resources to tackle the ecological disaster along their coasts. This co-operation was later institutionalized in spite of warnings from the federal authorities (Smith, 1993). A similar co-operation has developed between New York, Pennsylvania, Ohio, Illinois, Wisconsin, Minnesota, Ontario and Quebec – due to the lack of interest on the part of the federal governments – to give impetus to the adoption of measures of control against acid rain and the general ecological deterioration of the Great lakes. The subnational complaints against federal attitudes coincides, as in other similar situations (Hocking, 1996) with the evaluation of the issue of NGOs active in the area (Dyment, 1993; Allee, 1993; Manno, 1994). Mexico, in the last few years, has also been obliged to reconsider the effects of trade liberalization on its national security (Rochlin, 1995). The process of liberalization in North America has had the effect of reinforcing the feeling of territorial alienation of the southern states, particularly in the state of Chiapas, while activity on the northern border is increasing spectacularly (Cleaver, 1994; Zermeño, 1995; Dietz, 1995). We could easily go on to offer other examples, like the effects on Galicia of the changes in the Atlantic fishing regime, the impact of terrorism on tourism in the Balearic Islands or Corsica, the preoccupation in California or Andalucía about illegal immigration, unease in New South Wales about the renewal of French nuclear tests, the repercussions for Texas of the fluctuations of crude oil on the world market, or the repercussions for the Canary Islands of the change in the European Community regime of banana importation.

It seems inevitable at this point to refer to the much-discussed *risk* theories. As a starting point, these theories highlight, in one way or another, that in the contemporary conditions of interdependence and technological progress, we are faced with an extraordinary multiplication of *risk*s in world society. This has an objective dimension – ecological disasters, transnational organized crime, industrial delocation, the destruction of the biosphere, the spread of great famines, or the possibility of a nuclear war. It also has a subjective dimension, that is to say, the growing individual and collective perception of this, and our increasing awareness of our political limitations (Beck, 1992; Luhman, 1993). All this imposes the need to create new institutions, and new modes of the attribution of responsibility and co-decision. Although their subsequent development is outside the scope of this article, its heuristic value as an approach to the issues we are touching on seems undeniable. We are faced with a panorama in which the governments, no matter their level, find themselves having to respond to global problems which go beyond the conventional imagination in which domestic as well as foreign policies, until very recently, were formulated.

CONCLUSION

In this chapter we have tried to explore the place of foreign action and paradiplomacy in the redefinition of international security. Although we are dealing with a very complex issue we have tried to develop in a concise manner three different arguments. First, and through the presentation of very different experiences, we have tried to point out the possibilities that the promotion of certain forms of paradiplomacy can offer as an instrument for the reduction of transnational ethnic tensions. After this we considered one of the most important aspects of the subnational dimension, the redefinition of international security. We referred to the recourse to different forms of paradiplomacy, limited but worth considering, for the promotion of confidence and regional concertation. This is a phenomenon which can hardly be said to be new, but has taken on a special interest in recent years. Finally, the chapter concentrated on what constitutes the most complex expression of the subnational dimension of international security, the one which deals with the difficulties of the politically centralized management of some of the most important issues of our time – such as environmental problems and migration issues – as far as it affects the power and competences of regional governments, and which seems to impose the need to rethink the conventional methods of diplomacy as a whole (Hocking, 1993a).

REFERENCES

Alcock, A. (1992) 'The Protection of Regional Cultural Minorities and the Process of European Integration: The Example of South Tyrol', *International Relations,* Vol.XI, No.1, pp.17–36.

Alcock, A. (1994) 'South Tyrol', in H. Miall (ed.): *Minority Rights in Europe: The Scope for a Transnational Regime* (London: RIIA/Pinter), pp.46–55.

Allee, D.J. (1993) 'Subnational Governance and the International Joint Comission: Local Management of United States and Canadian Boundary Waters', *Natural Resources Journal,* Vol.33, No.1.

Anderson, M.S. (1993) *The Rise of Modern Diplomacy* (Longman:New York).

Asiwaju, A.J. (1994) 'Borders and Borderlands as Linnchpins for Regional Integration in Africa: Lessons of the European Experience', in C.H. Scholied (ed.) *World Boundaries/Global Boundaries* (London: Routledge).

Balme, R. (ed.) (1996) *Les politiques du Néo-Régionalisme* (Paris: Economica).

Banuazizi, A. and M. Weiner (eds) (1994) *The New Geopolitics of Central Asia and its Borderlands* (London, Taris).

Barston, R.P. (1988) *Modern Diplomacy* (Longman: New York).

Batt, J. (1998) 'Federalism versus Nationalism in Postcommunist State Building', *Regional & Federal Studies,* Vol.7, No.3, pp.25–48.

Beck, U. (1992) *Risk Society: Towards a New Modernity* (London: Sage).

Bernal Meza, R. (1990) 'Papel de las regiones en la formulación de la política exterior y potencial de articulación con regiones de países limítrofes: antecedentes y perspectivas', *Integración Latinoamericana,* No.156, pp.28–39.

Berridge, G.R. (1995) *Diplomacy: Theory and Practice* (London: Prentice Hall).

Bew, P. and E. Meehan (1994) 'Regions and Borders: Controversies in Northern Ireland about the European Union', *Journal of European Public Policy,* Vol.1, No.1, pp.95–113.

Biucchi, B. and G. Gaudard (ed.) (1981) *Regions Frontalieres et Integration Europenne* (St. Saphorin: Georgi).

Blum, D.W. (1994) 'Desintegration and Russian Foreign Policy', in D.W. Blum (ed.) *Russia's Future: Consolidation or Desintegration?* (Boulder: Westview Press), pp.127–45.

Bokatola, I.O. (1992) *L'Organization des Nations Unies et la Protection des Minorités* (Bruselas: Bruylant).

Bolognessi-Drosdoff, M.C. (1990) 'Iniciativas de integración fronteriza en América Latina', *Integración Latinoamericana*, No.156, pp.28–39.
Bondarevsky, G. and P. Ferdinand (1994) 'Russian Foreign Policy and Central Asia', in P. Ferdinand (ed.) *The New Central Asia and Its Neighbours* (London: RIIA/Pinter), pp.36–54
Broen, M.E. (ed.) (1993) *Ethnic Conflict and International Security* (Princeton: Princeton University Press).
Buchanan, A (1991) *Seccesion: The Morality of Political Divorce from Fort Sumter to Lithuania and Quebec* (Boulder: Westview Press).
Cassese, A. (1994) *Self-Determination of Peoples: A Legal Reappraissal* (Cambridge: Cambridge University Press).
Chaudhuri, Y. (1993) 'Federalism and the Siamese Twins: Diversity and Entropy in India's Domestic and Foreign Policy', *International Journal,* Vol.XLVIII, No.2, pp.448–69.
Christoffersen, G. (1993) 'Xinjiang and the Great Islamic Circle: The Impact of Transnational Economic forces on Chinese Regional Economic Planning', *The China Quarterly*, No.133, pp.130–53.
Cleaver, H. (1994) 'The Chiapas Uprising', *Studies in Political Economy*, No.44, pp.141–57.
Coakley, J. (1992) 'The Resolution of Ethnic Conflict: Towards a Typology', *International Political Science Review*, Vol.13, No.4, pp.343–58.
Cohen, L.J. (1986) 'Federalism and Foreign Policy in Yugoslavia: The Politics of Regional Ethnonationalism', *International Journal,* Vol.XLI, pp.624–54.
Constantin, F. (1994) 'La transnationalité: de l'individu à l'etat. A propos des modes populaires d'action internationales en Afrique orientale', in M. Girard (ed.) *Les individus dans la politique internationale* (Paris: Economica), pp.154–77.
Cornago, N. (1999) 'Diplomacy', in L. Kurtz (ed.) *Encyclopedia of Violence, Peace and Conflict* (San Diego: Academic Press).
Cuthbertson, I.M. and J. Leibowitz (eds) (1993) *Minorities: The New Europe's Old Issue* (Boulder: Westview Press/Institut for East/West Studies).
Dalton, R (1994) 'International and European Standards on Minority Rights', in H. Miall (ed.) *Minority Rights in Europe: The Scope for a Transnational Regime* (London : RIIA/Pinter), p.102.
Dewitt, D., D. Haglund and J. Kirton (eds) (1993) *Building A New Global Order: Emergent Trends in International Security* (Oxford:Oxford University Press).
Diamond, L. and J.W. McDonald (1993) *Multitrack Diplomacy: A Systems Approach to Peace* (Washington, DC: Institut for Multi Track Diplomacy).
Dietz, G. (1995) 'Zapatismo y movimientos étnico-regionales en México', *Nueva Sociedad*, No.140, pp.33–50.
Dreyer, J.T. (1994) 'The Popular Liberation Army and Regionalism in Xinjiang', *Pacific Review*, Vol.7, No.1, pp.41–55.
Dunn.T.J. (1995) *The Militarization of the U.S.–México border, 1978–1992: Low intensity Conflict Doctrine Comes Home* (Austin: University of Texas Press).
Dyment, D.K.M. (1993) 'Substate Paradiplomacy: The Case of Ontario', in B. Hocking (ed.) *Foreign Relations and Federal States* (London: Leicester University Press).
Eide, A. (1993) *New Appoaches to Minority Protection* (London: Minority Rights Groups).
Ercmann, S. (ed.) (1987) *Transatlantic Colloquy on Crossborder Relations: European and North American Perspectives* (Zurich: Schulthess Polygraphischer Verlag).
Ferdinand, P. (1994) 'The New Central Asia and China', in P. Ferdinand (ed.) *The New Central Asia and Its Neighbours* (London: RIIA/Pinter), pp.95–107.
Foucher, M. (1991) *Fronts et Frontières: Un Tour du Monde Géopolitique* (París: Fayard).
Ghebali, V.Y. (1996) 'L'Europe joue des bons offices', *Temps Européens*, No.1, pp.105–8.
Godron, A. (1996) 'Le bassin de l'Amour: une nouvelle zone de co-opération entre la Chine et la Russie', *Le Courrier des Pays de l'Est*, No.406.
Gonzalez-Posse, E. (1990) 'Marco conceptual de la integración fronteriza promovida: las iniciativas de integración fronteriza', *Integración Latinoamericana*, No.156.
Goodman, D.S. and G. Segal (eds) (1995) *China Deconstructs: Politics, Trade and Regionalism* (London: Routledge).
Gurr, T.R. and B. Harff (1994) *Ethnic Conflicts in World Politics* (Boulder: Westview Press).
Halperin, M.H. and D.J. Schaeffer (1992) *Self-Determination in the New World Order*

(Washington: Carnegie Endowment for International Peace).
Hamilton, K. and R. Langhorne (1995) *The Practice of Diplomacy: Its Evolution, Theory and Administration* (London: Routledge).
Hannum, H. (1990) *Autonomy, Sovereignty and Self-Determination: The Accommodation of Conflicting Rights* (Philadelphia: University of Pennsylvania Press).
Hansen, N. (1984) 'Transboundary Co-operation in Centralist States: Conflicts and Responses in France and Mexico', *Publius*, Vol.14, pp.137–52.
Hauslohner, P. (1981) 'Prefects as Senators: Soviet Regional Politicians Look to Foreign Policy', *World Politics*, Vol.33, No.1, pp.197–232.
Heraclides, A. (1991) *The Self-Determination of Minorities in International Politics* (London and Portland OR: Frank Cass).
Herzog, L. (ed.) (1992) *Changing Boundaries in the Americas: New Perspectives on the United States–Mexican, Central American, and South American Borders* (San Diego: Center for United States-Mexican Studies).
Hocking, B. (1993a) *Localizing Foreign Policy: Non-Central Governments and Multilayered Diplomacy* (London: Macmillan).
Hocking, B. (ed.) (1993b) *Foreign Relations and Federal States* (London: Leicester University Press).
Hocking, B. (1995) 'The Woods and the Trees: Catalytic Diplomacy and Canada´s Trials as a Forestry 'Superpower', *Environmental Politics*, Vol.5, No.3, pp.448–75.
Jackson, R.H. (1990) *Quasi-States: Sovereignty, International Relations and the Third World* (Cambridge: Cambridge University Press).
Keating, M. (1996) *Naciones contra el Estado* (Barcelona: Ariel).
Keohane, R.O. and E. Ostrom (ed.) (1994) *Local Commons and Global Interdependence: Heterogeneity and Co-operation in Two Domains* (London: Sage).
Klare, M.T. and D.C. Thomas (eds) (1994) *World Security: Challenges For a New Century* (New York: St. Martin's Press).
Kruszewski, Z.A. (1986) 'Border Problem Solving in the Communist World: A Case Study of Some European Boundaries', in Martinez, O.
Lapidus, G.W. and E.W. Walker (1993) 'Nationalism, Regionalism, and Federalism: Center–Periphery Relations in Post-Communist Russia', in G.W. Lapidus (ed.) *The New Russia: Troubled Transformation* (Boulder: Westview Press), pp.79–113.
Liebich, A. and A. Reszler (eds) (1993) *L´Europe Centrale et ses minorités: vers une solution européenne?* (Paris: P.U.F).
Luben, I. (1991) *Une Structure transfrontaliére en Europe Centrale, des Alpes á l´Adriatique* (Paris: FEDN).
Luhman, N. (1982) 'Territorial Borders as System Boundaries', in R. Strassoldo and G. Delli Ziotti (eds) *Co-operation in Conflict in Border Areas* (Milan: Franco Angelli), pp.235–44.
Luhman, N. (1993) *Risk: A Sociological Theory* (New York: Aldine de Gruyter).
Luke, T.W. (1994) 'Placing Power/Sitting Space: The Politics of Global and Local in the New World Order', *Environment and Planning D: Society and Space*, Vol.12, pp.613–28.
Lund, M.S. (1996) *Preventing Violent Conflicts: A Strategy for Preventive Diplomacy* (Washington, DC: United States Institute of Peace Press)
Lynn Jones, S.M. and S.E. Miller (eds) (1995) *Global Dangers: Changing Dimensions of International Security* (Cambridge:The MIT Press).
Maillot, D. (1990) 'Transborder Relations Between Members of the European Community and Non Member Countries', *Built Environment*, No.16, pp.25–37.
Malik, H.. (ed.) (1994) *Central Asia: Its Strategic Importance and Future Prospects* (New York: St. Martin Press).
Manno, J.P. (1994) 'Advocacy and Diplomacy: NGOs and the Great Lakes Water Qualitiy Agreement', in T. Princen and M. Finger (eds) *Environmental NGOs in World Politics: Linking the Local and the Global* (London: Routledge), pp.69–120.
Martinez, O. (ed.) (1986) *Across Boundaries: Transborder Interaction in Comparative Perspective* (El Paso: Western Press/University of Texas).
Maung, M. (1994) 'On the Road to Mandalay: A Case Study of the Sinonization of Upper Burma', *Asian Survey*, Vol.34, No.5, pp.447–59.
Mawdsley, E. (1997) 'Nonsecessionist Regionalism in India: The Uttarakhand Separate State

Movement', *Environment and Planning A,* Vol.29, pp.2217–35.
McGarry, J. and B.O'Leary (eds) (1993) *The Politics of Ethnic Conflict Regulation* (London: Routledge).
Melvin, N. (1995) *Regional Foreign Policies in the Russian Federation* (London: RIIA).
Miall, H. (ed.) (1994) *Minority Rights in Europe: The Scope for a Transnational Regime* (London: RIIA/Pinter).
Mildarsky, M.I. (ed.) (1993) *The Internationalization of Communal Strife* (London: Routledge).
Moltz, J.C. (1995) 'Regional Tensions in the Russo–Chinese Rapprochement', *Asian Survey,* Vol.35, No.6.
Montville, J.V. (ed.) (1990) *Conflict and Peacemaking in Multiethnic Societies* (Lexington: Lexington Books).
Morrow, D. (1992) ' Regional Policy as Foreign Policy: The Austrian Experience', *Regional Politics & Policy.* Vol.2, No.3, pp.27–44.
Mumme, S.P. (1984) 'Regional Power in National Diplomacy: The Case of the U.S. Section of the International Boundary and Water Comission', *Publius,* Vol.14, No.3.
Muni, S.D. (1989) 'India and Its Neighbours: Persisting Dilemmas and New Opportunities', *International Studies,* Vol.XII, No.1.
Nugent, P. and A.J. Asiwaju (1996) *African Boundaries* (London : Pinter).
Oliveros, R.L. (1995) 'Situación actual y perspectivas de las relaciones fronterizas de los países miembros del Grupo Andino', in CEFIR, *La integración fronteriza y el papel de las regiones en la UE y en el Cono Sur* (Montevideo: CEFIR).
Pelinka, A. (1990) 'Austria', in H.J. Michelmann and P. Soldatos (eds) *Federalism and International Relations: The Role of Subnational Units* (Oxford: Clarendon Press), pp.132–7.
Rochlin, J. (1995) 'Redefining Mexican "National Security" during an Era of Postsovereignty', *Alternatives,* Vol.20, No.3, pp.369–402.
Roeder, P. (1991) 'Soviet Federalism and Ethnic Mobilization', *World Politics,* Vol.43, No.1, pp.204–12.
Rosenau, J.N. (1994) 'New Dimensions of Security: The Interaction of Globalizing and Localizing Dynamics', *Security Dialogue,* Vol.25, No.3, pp.255–81.
Rumley, D. and J.V. Minghi (eds) (1991) *The Geography of Border Landscapes* (London: Routledge).
Safran, W. (1994) 'Non-separatist Policies Regarding Ethnic Minorities: Positive Approaches and Ambiguous Consequences', *International Political Science Review,* Vol.15, No.1, pp.61–80
Schechterman, B.Y. and M. Slamm (eds) (1993) *The Ethnic Dimension in International Relations* (New York: Praeger).
Schumann, K. (1994): 'The Role of the Council of Europe', in H. Miall (ed.) *Minority Rights in Europe: The Scope for a Transnational Regime* (London: RIIA/Pinter), pp.96–7.
Segal, G. (1992) 'Opening and Dividing China', *The World Today,* Vol.48, No.5, pp.77–80.
Silva, K.M. and R.J. May (eds) (1991): *Internationalization of Ethnic Conflict* (London: Pinter).
Silva, K.M. and S.W.R. de A. Samarasinghe (eds) (1993) *Peace Accords and Ethnic Conflict* (London: Pinter).
Smith, P.J. (1993) 'Policy Phases, Subnational Foreign Relations and Constituent Diplomacy in the United States and Canada: City, Provincial, and State Global Activity in British Columbia and Washington', in B. Hocking (ed.) *Foreign Relations and Federal States* (London: Leicester University Press).
Strassoldo, R. and G. Delli Zotti (ed.) (1982) *Co-operation and Conflict in Border Areas* (Milan: Angelli).
Tannam, E. (1995) 'EU Regional Policy and the Irish/Northern Irish Cross-Border Administrative Relationship', *Regional & Federal Studies,* Vol.5, No.1, pp.67–93.
Thayer, C.A. (1995) 'Beyond Indochina', *Adelphi Papers,* No.297.
Thornberry, P. (1991) *International Law and the Rights of Minorities* (Oxford: Clarendon Press).
Thornberry, P. (1994) 'International and European Standards on Minority Rights', in H. Miall (ed.) *Minority Rights in Europe: The Scope for a Transnational Regime* (London: RIIA/Pinter).

Thorup, L. (1993) *Redefining Governance in North America: The Impact of Cross Border Networks and Coalitions on Mexican Immigration into the United States* (Santa Monica: Rand Corporation).

Thual, F. (1994) 'La Chine entre unité et desintegration', *Relations Internationales et Strategiques*, No.15, pp.116–21.

Tokatlian, J.G. and C. Barrera (1991) 'Geografía, desarrollo regional y política exterior: el caso de la frontera tripartita colombo–venezolana–brasileña en la intendencia del Guainia: Una perspectiva desde Colombia', *Estudios Internacionales*, Vol.24, No.93, pp.53–80.

Toledano, E. (1996) 'Le poids des minorités hongroises dans les relations internationales de la Hongrie', *Transitions*, Vol.XXXVII, No.2.

Tomuschat, C. (ed.) (1993) *Modern Law of Self-Determination* (Dordrecht: Martinus Nijhoff).

Trenin, D. (1998) 'Russia and the Emerging Security Environment in Northeast Asia', *Security Dialogue*, Vol.29, No.1, pp.79–88.

Valenciano, E.O. (1995) 'La frontera: un nuevo rol frente a la integración. La experiencia en el Mercosur', in CEFIR, *La integración fronteriza y el papel de las regiones en la UE y en el Cono Sur* (Montevideo: CEFIR).

Watson, A. (1982) *Diplomacy: The Dialogue between States* (London: Methuen).

The European Union and Inter-regional Co-operation

KEPA SODUPE

In the academic literature, it is often claimed that the process of European integration has been accompanied by a reaffirmation of regional identity. Considerations of a cultural or linguistic nature which are generally associated with regionalism are not wholly responsible for this development. New factors, which have emerged in recent decades, must be taken into account (Keating and Jones, 1995; Balme, 1996). To a certain extent, it is possible to say that a new regionalism has appeared which constitutes a response to increasing levels of interdependence. These are a consequence of the elimination of protectionism, the creation of the internal market and the move towards monetary union.

However, the relationship between integration and regionalism is not one-sided. Just as integration gives a new dimension to regionalism, regionalism in turn stimulates integration, since the former contributes to reinforce interdependence. One of the most striking aspects of this new regionalism is inter-regional co-operation. In fact, since the 1970s, organizations which represent regions from different member states have proliferated in Europe. There is no doubt that the activities of these organizations serve to increase interdependence and, as a result, favour the construction of a united Europe.

The purpose of this article is to ascertain whether the European Union is sensitive to this new development in regionalism. More specifically, it will attempt to analyse if community policies, such as the structural policy, provide a suitable framework for the development of inter-regional co-operation. If this is the case, the Community institutions, by bringing the capacity to solve problems nearer to citizens, will be making a greater degree of integration possible. In order to achieve these aims, the article will consider such questions as the definition and classification of the regions, the phenomenon of regional association, and those aspects of structural policy which affect inter-regional co-operation most directly. Finally, certain remarks will be made concerning the relationship between structural policy and inter-regional co-operation.

CONCEPT AND CLASSIFICATION OF REGIONS

Proceeding as outlined above, it would perhaps be useful to study briefly how a region is defined, and also how regions are classified by the European Commission.

Concept of Region

The term 'region' has been interpreted in a variety of ways. Political Science, Economics, Anthropology, Geography, are but a few of the disciplines which have sought to do so, but from very different standpoints (Keating and Loughlin, 1997). Moreover, the concept of a region is liable to change with the passing of time. Events such as European integration, profound economic changes, changing social needs, and the impact of new ideas may transform the concept of the region and its basic functions (Granrut, 1994).

With these observations firmly in mind, it is now pertinent to examine the definition of region given by the Assembly of European Regions (ARE). In a recently published document, this body said that 'a region is a territorial unit immediately below the sovereign state, with a system of self-government'. A region, the document continues, should have its own constitution, statute of autonomy or other law which forms part of the legislation of the state, and which determines how the region is organized and what its powers are (ARE, 1996: 2). This definition has in its favour the fact that it was drafted by the most important organization involved in the defence of the rights of the regions in Europe. However, it may well be a little too restrictive when applied to the European regions. Indeed, many entities which are often described as regions would be excluded. For this reason, it would be more convenient to offer a definition which would cover entities where the existence of self-government was open to debate or totally absent. In this respect the definition suggested by J. Palard is interesting. This author proposes 'to maintain the polysemic notion of region, the concept of mesogovernment, that is, the tier of government between the local level *strictu sensu* and the national level, irrespective of whether the state is a federal one, like Germany, a regional one, like Italy, or a centralised one, like France' (Palard, 1995). According to Palard, a region should not only be understood as an intermediate tier of government within the political structure of the state or in the application of the principle of subsidiarity. It should also be regarded as an entity which manages both economic and financial interests.

It may be convenient to accept such a wide definition, as regional organization within the Community is of a heterogeneous nature. This diversity is due to the fact that the member states have very different political and administrative structures, and that the regional governments themselves are not granted similar powers in all countries. Cultural and linguistic concerns also vary from country to country.

Classification of Regions Produced by the European Commission

The diverse nature of the regional phenomenon is reflected in the European Commission's classification. In accordance with this classification, the territory of the member states has been divided into what are called in Community language NUTS (Nomenclature of Units for Territorial Statistics). The Commission has established different categories of NUTS for two reasons – on the one hand, to provide criteria so that regional statistics can be collected, and on the other hand, to ensure the implementation of regional policy.

The division is based, to a great extent, upon the institutional structure in force in each member country (Labasse, 1991; Puyol y Vinuesa, 1995). Accordingly, each state is divided into NUTS 1 units, which in turn are subdivided into NUTS 2 units; these are then broken down into the smallest units, NUTS 3. On the basis of these divisions a regional map was drafted, which, apart from Community enlargements, has remained unchanged since the third periodic report from the Commission to the Council.

The NUTS 1 consist of the so-called European Community Regions (ECR). They are the largest in size, and usually form the main areas of economic planning. Some of them already existed in some countries. In those where such a division was absent, smaller territorial units which were geographically and economically similar were grouped together. Thus, in Belgium the NUTS 1 are the Regions, in Germany the Länder, and in the United Kingdom they are the Standard Regions. However, in countries like Spain and Italy, the NUTS 1 were created by joining several administrative units. For example, in Spain there are seven NUTS 1 in total, each of which contains more than one Autonomous Community. In Italy there are 11, formed from the union of the Italian Regions. At this level there are 71 units which, in terms of population and area are not homogeneous. Some states have one – this is the case in Denmark, Ireland and Luxemburg – while others, like Germany, Italy and the United Kingdom, have more than ten.

The NUTS 2 are composed of the regional administrative areas in the majority of the member states. Consequently, in France and in Italy this corresponds to the regions, and in Spain to the Autonomous Communities. In the United Kingdom these regions were created for Community purposes only by grouping together smaller administistative units. Nonetheless, in Belgium and in Germany the situation is somewhat different; here the NUTS 2 are lower-tier administrative units –the provinces and regions, respectively. Distribution of the NUTS 2 varies greatly throughout the Community. States such as Denmark, Ireland and Luxemburg have only one, which covers the entire national territory – this was also the case at NUTS 1 level, whereas others, for example, Germany and the United

Kingdom have more than 30. At this level, there are 183 regions in total, which display as striking contrasts in terms of population and area as the NUTS 1.

TABLE 1
NOMENCLATURE OF UNITS FOR TERRITORIAL STATISTICS (NUTS)

	NUTS 1	NUTS 2	NUTS 3
Austria	Gruppen von Bundesländer	Bundesländer	Gruppen von Politischen Bezirken
Belgium	Regions	Provinces	Arrondissements
Denmark	–	–	Amter
Germany	Länder	Regierungsbezirke	Kreise
Greece	NUTS 2 groupings	Development regions	Nomoi
Spain	NUTS 2 groupings	Comunidades Autónomas	Provincias
Finland	Manner-Suomi/ahvenanmaa	Suuralueet	Maakunnat
France	ZEAT + DOM	Régions + DOM	Départements + DOM
Ireland	–	–	Planning regions
Italy	NUTS 2 groupings	Regioni	Provincie
Luxembourg	–	–	–
Netherlands	Landsdelen	Provincies	COROP-Regios
Portugal	NUTS 2 groupings	NUTS 3 groupings	Grouping of concelhos
Sweden	–	Riksomräden	Län
UK	Standard regions	NUTS 3 groupings	Counties, local authority regions

Source: Eurostat, Regions: Statistics Yearbook 1996, Official Journal of the Euopean Communities, Luxembourg, 1997, p.IV

Finally, the NUTS 3 represent the smallest units. They are divisions of the regional administrative areas mentioned above. In Spain and in Italy they correspond to the provinces, and in France to the departments.They are large in number – 1,044 – and again differ greatly, not only in population, area and degree of economic importance, but also in the extent of their administrative powers.

When dividing Community territory into NUTS 2 and NUTS 3, the Commission respected to a greater extent the existing regional organization of the individual member states than it did when forming the NUTS 1. With the notable exceptions of the Belgian regions and the German Länder, the NUTS 1 in the other member states have an artificial character. It must be stressed that the NUTS 2 are the most important, because it is at this level that political decisions are made concerning Community policies such as the structural policy. In general terms, the NUTS 3 have a more limited role except when analysing specific problems, such as high unemployment and the decline of traditional industries in local areas. However, the NUTS 3 are of prime importance in cross-border co-operation, which will be discussed later.

REGIONAL ASSOCIATIONS IN EUROPE

In the 1970s, a new process took place which was marked by the emergence of various regional groupings. These can be defined as associations formed between regional entities of different states whose ultimate purpose is to act as pressure groups in the European institutions, and foster co-operation based upon common interests, needs and aspirations.

Although the formation of regional associations is a wide-ranging and heterogeneous phenomenon, there tend to be two basic categories. On the one hand, there are those whose main function is to be representative, that is, they must articulate to the European institutions the opinions of their members regarding the status and functions of the regions within the Community and the member states. The Assembly of the Regions and the Congress of Local and Regional Authorities are groups of this kind. On the other hand, there are what we could call functional associations. The creation of these groupings responds to altogether more specific criteria. Examples of these bodies are the Association of European Frontier Regions (AEFR) or the Conference of Peripheral and Maritime Regions (CPMR).

Given the main objectives of this article, it will be necessary to concentrate upon functional associations. However, this should not wrest importance from groupings of a representative nature. For instance, the ARE has played a pivotal role, making proposals on the consideration that regions should receive in a united Europe. The creation of the Committee of the Regions, as stipulated by the Treaty of Maastricht, was due in large part to the fact that this organization actively lobbied the Community institutions. Furthermore, there is a clear relationship between the representative and the functional associations. Indeed, the ARE was established by ten functional groupings who saw fit to create a body which would be able to defend the general interests of the regions, something that these organizations, with their highly specific character, were ill-suited to do.

The decision to limit this study to functional associations was taken because it is through these groupings that, in any case, a point of contact between structural policy and inter-regional co-operation can be observed. Associations of this kind, as has already been indicated, are concerned with very specific problems, such as those affecting frontiers, industrial decline and peripheral location. They tend to be of two basic types, the first being those which promote cross-border co-operation, while the second includes regions whose main reason for joining has nothing to do with frontiers. This form of co-operation can be described as transregional.[1] To highlight the vitality of regional associations in recent years, it will now be convenient to examine the activities of some of the principal organizations involved in both cross-border and transregional co-operation.[2]

Associations of a Cross-Border Character

The presence of frontiers offered the clearest opportunity for cross-border co-operation. The frontier regions have been, as a general rule, subjected to the dislocating effects of border divisions. The appearance of nation-states meant that entities which in geographical, historical and cultural terms had a clearly defined regional identity were divided. Wars and other kinds of disputes between states imposed further hardship upon these areas. Their peripheral position within nation-states, far removed from centres of decision making, put them at an economic and political disadvantage (Weyand, 1996). As a result, problems of inadequate development, infrastructure, cultural communication and the environment which stemmed from the political division of the territory were a base for co-operation between these regions.

The Convention on Transfrontier Co-operation which was approved by the Council of Europe in 1980, and the additional Protocol to this Convention, which was passed in 1995, attempted to provide a legal framework for co-operation between regions situated on either side of a frontier (Council of Europe, 1980 and 1995). The Additional Protocol of 1995 was an important step forward. This text, in unequivocal terms, gives these regions the right to conclude agreements on co-operation in areas where their administrative powers allowed them to do so. It also stipulated that any bodies emanating from said accords may be endowed with legal personality, and recognized as public law entities. However, the states, fearful of not being able to control this kind of co-operation, have sought to protect their interests by introducing certain safeguards. Thus, states may make recognition of the legal character of these agreements dependent upon the existence of a prior treaty between them, and may refuse to grant the above-mentioned bodies legal personality, or the right to be a public law entity.

Despite the shortcomings of this legal framework, cross-border regional co-operation has been actively pursued. From the 1970s onwards, the forging of cross-border ties intensified, the reason for this being, perhaps, the increasing difficulties posed by economic recession. The following are examples of this:

Association of European Frontier Regions: This association was created in 1971, and is composed of both regions and cross-border entities.[3] At present, it has almost 40 members. The purpose of the AEFR is to provide a forum for an exchange of ideas. It also organizes conferences and meetings at which frontier problems are discussed, and offers collaboration in the resolution of specific problems. Another of its functions is representative, that is, it defends group interests before public institutions. In 1981, a year after the Convention on Transfrontier Co-operation was approved, the AEFR drew up the European Charter of Border and Cross-border Regions, which would later be revised in 1987. Between 1990 and 1993, with the financial assistance of the Commission, the AEFR completed a pilot project, LACE, which provided technical aid to the frontier regions. The AEFR also has an interesting role as an advisory body to the Council of Europe, the European Parliament and Commission.

The Working Communities of the Alps: There is intense cross-border co-operation in the Alps area. In fact, there are three working communities: The Working Community of the Central Alps, The Working Community of the Eastern Alps, and the Working Community of the Western Alps. Brief mention will be made only of the oldest of these associations, the Working Community of the Central Alps, which was established in 1972. It is comprised of regions from three states: Austria, Switzerland and Italy. Representatives from the German Länder attend this association as observers. The purpose of this community is to solve problems, to achieve consensus on such issues as the environment, culture and the economy, and to promote understanding between the peoples of the region.

The Working Community of the Pyrenees: In November 1983, the agreement which created this association of transborder co-operation was signed in Pau (France). The regions involved are: Catalonia, Aragon, Navarre and the Basque Country in Spain; Aquitaine, Midi-Pyrenees and Languedoc-Rousillon in France; and the Principality of Andorra. The Presidents of the eight Community members adopted a plan of action in 1993. The strategic goals of this plan were to strengthen the role of the CTP, and harmonize the economic and social structure of the territory. This would be achieved by developing communications, and in particular, by extending High-Speed Rail Links to southern Europe, by improving research and training through the network of universities and colleges, and by the development of mountain territory, but in a way which respects the environment. Cultural exchanges which seek to develop shared cultural values are also organized.

Associations of a Transregional Character

A few years after the creation of the Association of European Frontier Regions, a series of organizations was established whose concerns were not dictated by the dislocations associated with political divisions. The existence of a border was no longer relevant. What was of prime importance was the fact that these regions shared similar problems arising from geographical location or economic activity. It must be emphasized that transregional co-operation allows regions belonging to different states to participate in common projects, regardless of the fact that they are not geographically close. Doubtless to say that it is this circumstance which makes transregional co-operation so interesting.

The Convention passed in 1980, and the Additional Protocol refer solely to cross-border co-operation. However, the reason which gave rise to the above texts – that is, the need to facilitate this kind of co-operation by providing a legal framework for it – could also be applied to transregional co-operation. Thus, the Council of Europe produced a Draft Convention on Inter-territorial Co-operation in 1993. But states regarded transregional co-operation with considerable distrust. It is for this reason that the Committee of Ministers of the Council of Europe made no attempt to pass the Draft Treaty on Interterritorial Co-operation in a five-year period. In fact, the states only changed their position in May 1998. At this time, the Committee of Ministers did not approve the old Draft Convention, but a second Protocol, according to which the Convention of 1980 and the Additional Protocol of 1995 also came to regulate transregional co-operation (Council of Europe, 1998).

In spite of the absence of appropiate legislation in the field of transregional co-operation, numerous associations of this kind have appeared. A description of some of these now follows:

The Conference of Peripheral Maritime Regions (CPMR): This Conference was created in June 1973. In the 20-plus years of the Conference's existence, membership has risen to more than 100. The Conference has two goals: to unite the regions on the periphery so as to offset the concentration of economic activity in the centre of Europe, and to promote common initiatives which exploit the maritime and coastal aspects of these regions. It is one of the most important associations owing to the fact that it has a large membership and that it produces work of high quality. This is evident, for instance, in the fact that the European Coastal Charter approved by the Conference in 1990 was later adopted by the European Parliament and conferred official status by the Council of Ministers. In 1997 the CPMR passed a document outlining its position with regard to the direction of structural policy for the period 2000–06. From the organizational point of view, the Conference is divided into four commissions: the Islands Commission, the North Sea Commission, the Inter-Mediterranean Commission and the Atlantic Arc Commission.

The Commission of the Atlantic Arc: In 1989, 21 regions on the Atlantic coastline, which were also members of the CPMR, founded this Commission, with a view to intensifying co-operation and to overcoming the difficulties that their peripheral geographical position posed. At present, there are 32 members. The Atlantic Arc Commission is a coastal area which stretches 3,000 km from Scotland to Andalucia. In 1994 the Atlantic Arc Commission launched a pilot project, called Atlantis, that received 4 million Ecus in financial aid from the European Commission. The programme consisted of a number of projects in areas of particular interest to the Commission of the Atlantic Arc, such as the modernization of the tourist industry, co-operation in the field of technology, maritime and air routes and the environment. In 1995 the Commission approved a document entitled *A Strategy for the Atlantic Arc*, the text of which announced what the Commission's objectives would be for the period 1995–99.

The Working Group of Traditional Industrial Regions: This Commission is yet another example of a regional group united in the pursuit of common interests. It was created in 1984 and included some 20 regions. The goals of this Working Group are to promote an exchange of experiences and to forge links between regions of similar industrial traditions. The achievements of this association throughout the years of its existence have been considerable. For example, when the Reform of the Regional Policy was being discussed in the mid-1980s, it succeeded in making the regions in industrial decline one of the objectives of the new Regional Policy (Objective 2). This association played a role in ensuring that social and economic cohesion became a reality in the Community.

The Four Motors of Europe: This association was established in 1988 and consists of the German Land of Baden-Würtemburg, the Autonomous Community of Catalonia in Spain, the region of Lombardy in Italy, and the region of Rhone-Alpes in France. Other regions, such as Ontario and Wales, have signed protocols of co-operation with the Four Motors. These regions, which are considered to be the most active and innovative within their respective states, are engaged in a highly original process of co-operation. It is not founded upon geographical, historical or linguistic ties but rather, upon a desire to share experiences which may benefit all the regions concerned (Kukawka, 1996). The initial objectives of the Four Motors were to improve transport infrastuctures and telecommunications, to undertake technological co-operation, and promote exchanges in the fields of research and culture. These objectives were later extended to areas such as economic development, professional training, the environment and social policy. In 1995, the Presidents of the these regions agreed upon a European Strategy for the Four Motors, in which they expressed the need to defend their interests before the European institutions and committed themselves to defining a common European strategy.

The associations described, whether they be cross-border or transregional, are clear examples of multilateral co-operation. However, it must be indicated that within these associations there are many bilateral contacts which serve to strengthen a vast network of regional interrelations. These contacts usually give rise to a large number of co-operation agreements.

STRUCTURAL POLICY AND INTER-REGIONAL CO-OPERATION

The regional policy of the European Community changed radically in the mid-1980s. The entry into the Community of less developed states increased regional differences. Moreover, it seemed that plans to introduce the single market would have to be accompanied by further compensatory measures which would mitigate the economic impact of such a move. As a result of both these developments, the Regional Policy was reformed in 1985, 1988 and 1993. Yet another reform, which is still in progress, was undertaken by the Commission in June 1998. The outcome of these reforms, and above all, of that which was executed in 1988, has been to transform the regional policy into a structural action policy.

For the purposes of this article, it will be interesting to consider three major components of the Structural Funds: national initiatives (90 per cent), community initiatives (9 per cent), innovative measures and pilot projects (1 per cent). It can be seen that the greater part of the structural policy is implemented through national initatives. These are based upon the Development Plans which are produced by the Member States to revitalize the regions. Despite the predominant role of the states in these initiatives, the process of fund allocation has led to a vast mobilization in the regions and to the forging of links between them and the Community institutions. However, it must be stressed that national initiatives have no connection whatsoever with inter-regional co-operation. In order to find such a connection between structural policy and inter-regional co-operation, it is necessary to examine Community initiatives, and innovative measures and pilot projects.

Community initiatives, by way of INTERREG, have enabled cross-border co-operation in the European Community to develop. To a far lesser extent, innovative measures and pilot projects, together with recent modifications to INTERREG, have been a basis for transregional co-operation.

The Community Initiative INTERREG II and Cross-Border Co-operation

Community initiatives are instruments created directly and independently by the Commission to carry out regional development projects. The objectives of these initiatives (Structural Funds, 1988) are the following:

- to contribute to the solution of problems directly related to the implementation of other European Union policies;
- to encourage the implementation of community policies; and
- to aid in the solution of problems which are common to peripheral, ultraperipheral and frontier regions.

An analysis of Table 2 shows the extent of aid received by the INTERREG II from the Structural Funds. The promotion of cross-border co-operation is, from the financial point of view, a major activity – it accounts for 22 per cent of funds designated by the Commission to Community initiatives. The AEFR had an undeniable influence on the definition of the INTERREG initiative. Many of its opinions contributed to shape the content of it. Two distinct periods mark the history of this Community initiative: the first, INTERREG I (1989–93), and the second, INTERREG II (1994–99). During the first period, INTERREG prepared the frontier regions in the member states for a Europe without borders. At the end of this period, both the Commission and the member states saw fit to prolong this initiative. Thus, INTERREG II was born. The main contents of this initiative are detailed in a Communication from the Commission to the member states (European Commission, 1994b). The document includes aspects ranging from the definition of objectives to the financial implications of the initiative as a whole.

TABLE 2
COMMUNITY INITIATIVES, 1994–99

Initiatives	Millions of Ecus
1. INTERREG II (Cross-border co-operation)	2,900
2. LEADER II (Rural Development)	1,400
3. NOW, HORIZON, YOUTHSTAR	1,400
4. INDUSTRIAL CHANGE	
ADAPT	1,400
RECHAR II	400
RESIDER II	500
KONVER	500
RETEX	500
Portuguese textile industry	400
SME	1,000
5. PESCA	250
6. URBAN (Urban policy)	600
7. REGIS II (Ultaperiferic regions)	600
Reserve	1,600
TOTAL	**13,450**

Source: Europa-Junta, No.24, February 1994, p.5.

It will be seen presently that the objectives of the INTERREG II are concerned with both the internal and the external frontiers of the European Union. The following are a selection of these objectives:

- to assist both internal and external border areas of the European Union in overcoming the special developments problems arising from their relative isolation within national economies and within the Union as a whole;
- to promote the creation and development of networks of co-operation across internal borders and, where relevant, to link these networks to wider Community networks;
- to contribute to the adjustment of external border areas to their new role as border areas of a single integrated market;
- to respond to new opportunities for co-operation with third countries in external border areas of the European Union; and
- to complete selected energy networks already defined in the initiative REGEN and to link them to wider European networks.

From this list of objectives it is possible to observe that INTERREG II consists of two chapters: that which pertains to cross-border co-operation, and that which refers to the completion of energy networks. Only the former will be analysed here.

Member states wishing to take advantage of this programme have to present to the Commission a single, joint operational programme which describes the co-operation that will take place in the whole cross-border area. For example, the operational programme for co-operation along the frontier between Spain and France is called INTERREG II-Pyrenees. The normative INTERREG II gives the regions the possibility of participating in the elaboration of the projects that will form part of the operational programmes. In fact, the Commission gives priority to those programmes which are produced with the collaboration of regional or local authorities.

Member states and regional and local authorities, in the preparation of operational programmes, are encouraged to present proposals responding to concrete types of action, as for example, the joint planning and implementation of cross-border programmes, the introduction of measures to improve the flow of information among border regions and the setting-up of shared institutional and administrative structures to sustain and promote co-operation. Within the framework of these types of action, the Commission Communication to the member states goes into detail, providing a full list of measures which will be eligible for assistance. These measures range from the realization of studies related to development plans to actions which facilitate the prevention of illicit trade, via the establishment or the development of trade organizations, professional associations, and planning and advisory groups.

In accordance with the INTERREG II normative, NUTS 3 are the basic territorial units involved in cross-border co-operation. Therefore, the aforementioned co-operation occurs in subregional areas which are geographically close to a frontier. Nevertheless, that normative allows a certain degree of flexibility as regards the financing of certain, clearly-defined investments in infrastructures above the level of NUTS 3. This is possible providing that intervention in these areas does not exceed 20 per cent of the overall budget, and does serve to foment real cross-border co-operation.

The INTERREG II operational programmes on cross-border co-operation shall be the subject of joint financing by the member states and the Community. The Commission's decisions on the amount of the Community budget allocated to individual operational programmes will reflect the population and level of development of the border areas concerned, and the quality of the programmes submitted. The 2,900 millon Ecus designated initially to the INTERREG initiative for the period 1994–99, rose to 3,065 millon after the entry of Austria, Finland and Sweden in 1995. From this total, approximately 2,565 million will be allocated to the promotion of cross-border co-operation and 500 million to the completion of energy networks. It must be pointed out that the Commission has imposed a restriction on the application of funds to cross-border co-operation to the extent that 75 per cent of such funds have to be earmarked for Objective 1 regions.

The RECITE Pilot Project and Transregional Co-operation

Innovative measures and pilot projects bring us to the second kind of co-operation previously mentioned: transregional co-operation. The relationship between the structural policy – or more specifically, between innovative measures and pilot projects – and transregional co-operation is far more modest. It can in no way be compared with the more important relationship shared by the Community initiative INTERREG II and cross-border co-operation.

The innovative measures and pilot projects are directed towards finding methods of regional development which enable the regional bodies to assume their responsibilities to the full within an extensive framework of collaboration. As has already been indicated, the European Union earmarks 1 per cent of Structural Funds for this component of structural policy. With these forms of intervention, and more particularly with the pilot projects, the

Community intends (Structural Funds, 1993):
- to foster incentives which favour the creation of infrastructure, investment in enterprises and other specific measures having a marked Community interest, in particular in the border regions within and outside the Community; and
- to encourage the pooling of experience and the development of co-operation between different Community regions and of innovative measures.

It may be said that the first of these points insists once more upon the cross-border phenomenon. It is the second which makes it possible to promote transregional co-operation. The RECITE pilot project is, in the field of innovative measures and pilot projects, the equivalent of INTERREG II in Community initiatives. Like INTERREG, the pilot project RECITE has had two distinct phases. The first, which was experimental in character, and began in 1990, gave rise to 15 transregional co-operation projects, although no formal call for proposals was made. The Commission was aided by representative bodies of European regional associations. Since these activities met with success, the project was extended for a new period, 1994–99, but this time, formal procedures for obtaining funds were established.

In the text which regulates the RECITE pilot project, the European Commission refers to different challenges – such as the globalization of the economy, the trend towards an economy based on services, the speed with which information technology is developing, pressures on the environment and high levels of unemployment – to which regional and local authorities have to respond. The European Commission believes that transregional co-operation offers a forum for an exchange of ideas, methods and practices. Within the financial limits which have been imposed upon it, the RECITE pilot project pursues the following objectives (European Commission, 1996b):

- co-operation between those involved at local level in different areas, intended to facilitate an exchange of experiences either through the transfer of knowledge or through the development of a shared project;
- improved capacity for action and better methods of achieving economic and social development in the less-favoured regions for those involved at local and regional level; and
- achievements in regional or local development which provide examples of how to respond to the challenges of modern society and which can serve as pilot measures for the spread of good practice in the region in question or in neighbouring regions.

Proposals seeking RECITE assistance must be directed towards intervention in specific areas. These could involve, by way of examples, the development of local potential for the creation of permanent jobs, measures to facilitate the access of SMEs to the European market and to technological innovation, and the protection and improvement of the environment.

Organizations with the capacity to be responsible for the whole of the pilot project and for the sound use of Community funds may be regional and local authorities or a body set up under public, semi-public or private law. Therefore, it is the regional and local authorities, and not the state, that play a central role in this type of co-operation. The legal text regulating RECITE confers priority to projects undertaken by regional or local authorities in close co-operation with those engaged in the economic and/or social life of each of the areas concerned. For a project to be evaluated positively, it will have to include partners from at least three and not more than seven areas in at least three member states. A minimum of one third of the areas eligible must be under Objective 1 or 6.

The maximum time limit for the execution of these projects is three years. There are limits upon the amount of funds that the RECITE projects can receive. These amounts range from one to three million Ecus, and the Community will meet up to 75 per cent of costs eligible for subsidy in the regions included in Objectives 1 and 6, and 50 per cent in the rest.

INTERREG II C and Transnational Co-operation

In May 1996, the European Commission decided to develop the initiative concerning cross-border co-operation and energy networks to include a third chapter, called INTERREG II C, concerning transnational co-operation on spatial planning. In terms of its objectives, as well as its programmes, INTERREG II C is entirely distinct from the two previous chapters, both in the extent of the area covered and the types of partnership which it seeks to promote and in the emphasis it places on the development of a strategic vision for the spatial planning of the areas in question.

This new chapter of the INTERREG II initiative, which opens a new option for transregional co-operation, tries to achieve the following goals (European Commission, 1996c):

- to help restore the balance between different areas of the European Union through structuring measures that serve Community interests by contributing to the promotion of economic and social cohesion;
- to foster transnational co-operation in this field by member states and other authorities with responsibilities for spatial planning;
- to improve the impact of Community policies on spatial development; and
- to help member states and their regions to face problems of water resources management posed by floods and drought.

When preparing operational programmes under the INTERREG II C chapter, member states and regional and local authorities will present a joint strategy related to the area concerned and proposals derived from it. For each operational programme, a joint management structure will be competent throughout the territory for the implementation of the joint strategy and will facilitate the carrying out of joint projects between member states. In this respect, the Commission will give priority to proposals made in co-operation with regional and local authorities which include the creation or development of shared institutional or administrative structures for implementing broader and deeper transnational co-operation, supported, where appropiate, not only by public institutions but also by private and voluntary organizations and agencies

The Commission decision on the amount of Community assistance to be allocated to the various operational programmes will be based on the same criteria as INTERREG II, that is to say, the population and level of development of the areas concerned, as well as the quality of the programmes submitted.

On the basis of proposals drawn up jointly by the member states concerned, the Commission will adopt a list of transnational groupings of geographically continuous areas covering in principle at least three states. One member state may participate in several transnational co-operation groupings. The Commission will, in addition, prepare a list of regions eligible for measures concerning the fight against drought. This list will also take into account proposals made by member states. Special rules will be approved by the Commission to promote the participation of European and Mediterranean non-member countries in these transnational co-operation groupings.

As is the case with INTERREG II, the Commission Communication regarding INTERREG II C contains a detailed range of eligible measures. With respect to territorial planning, these include, for example, preparatory studies for the implementation of transnational strategies, actions to improve the territorial management of the marine areas on the periphery of the Union or the development of transnational land administration systems.

The financing of INTERREG II C operational programmes will be jointly attended by member states and the Community. The total contribution of Community Structural Funds to this chapter of INTERREG is estimated at 415 million Ecus. Community expenditure in regions not classified as eligible under Objectives 1, 2, 5b and 6 must represent a minority share of the Community contribution.

SOME REMARKS ON THE RELATIONSHIP BETWEEN STRUCTURAL POLICY AND INTER-REGIONAL CO-OPERATION

A number of remarks can be made about the points raised until now with regard to the relationship that exists between the structural policy and inter-regional co-operation. The contents of these remarks provide an answer to the question asked at the beginning of this study as to whether community institutions, via the structural policy, and particularly the instruments already described therein, do or do not favour inter-regional co-operation, promote more intense levels of interdependence and make the integration process more dynamic.

We should start by making a few general considerations. First, some of the shortcomings found in this relationship arise from the different logic behind, on the one hand, regionalism and co-operation between European regions and, on the other, the structural policy (Loughlin, 1997). Regionalism expresses an aspiration on the part of regions to acquire a greater decision-making capacity, an aspiration which nowadays is largely motivated by the desire to face the challenges of increasing interdependence. The structural policy, however, came into being and was developed for the purpose of reducing economic disparities between Community regions. This different logic explains why it is sometimes difficult to find a meeting point between regionalism and structural policy. Indeed, the essentially technical-economic contents of the structural policy prevail in the aforementioned relationship over the most pressing or innovative aspects implicit in inter-regional co-operation.

Second, the inter-regional co-operation that the structural policy attempts to encourage has little to do with the regional associations described above. These associations have only gained access to Community funds in a few exceptional cases. The inter-regional co-operation encountered in regional associations is in sharp contrast with the inter-regional co-operation under way within the framework of the Community's structural policy. Although we are discussing inter-regional co-operation, it must be borne in mind that such co-operation is subject to close supervision by the state. The involvement of central power bodies is undeniable in initiatives such as INTERREG, both with regard to cross-border and transnational co-operation. The possibilities of the regions participating in the drawing-up of operational programmes vary. In the former, the states may fix the criteria for the participation of the regions, whereas, in the latter, the participation of the regions seems to be compulsory. Inter-regional co-operation is only free from state supervision when innovative measures and pilot projects are involved.

Finally, it can be said that the states, concerned about a development that, in their opinion, could influence their traditional international role, have placed a number of obstacles limiting further progress in the field of inter-regional co-operation. As a consequence, this distrust has resulted in deficiencies or delays in the legal treatment of inter-regional co-operation. The May 1998 Protocol has undoubtedly filled a major gap. Despite the reservations made by member states, however, only modest levels of acceptance of these legal texts have been reported. Although the 1980 Convention was signed by the 26 states and ratified by 19 of them, the same can not be said of the 1995 Additional Protocol that was only signed by 11 states and ratified by three, or the 1998 Protocol which, after remaining open for signature for three months, was only signed by five states and ratified by one. In addition, it is interesting to point out that the legal initiatives regarding inter-regional co-operation have taken place in a framework outside the Community, such as that of the Council of Europe, with no legal approach on the part of the European Union itself. The European Parliament, however, aware of this shortcoming, which contrasts with the co-operation instruments created by the structural policy itself (Diego, 1997), recently passed a resolution requiring member states to engage in further co-operation and take actions to overcome national, bureaucratic and emotional obstacles hindering cross-border and transregional co-operation, by means of a common legal framework (European Parliament, 1997).

To provide greater detail, it is necessary to supplement these general considerations with more specific remarks addressing the relationship between the structural policy and the forms of co-operation that we have been considering, such as cross-border and transregional co-operation. In the case of cross-border co-operation, the structural policy has opened up interesting avenues which favour collaboration between regions, but as far as transregional co-operation is concerned, this is not so. Even in the former case, however, certain deficiencies can be found that attenuate the positive nature of its relationship with the structural policy. The following can be said with regard to cross-border co-operation:

1. The volume of financial resources designated by the Structural Funds to the promotion of the INTERREG II initiative accounts for 22 per cent of the total figure allocated to the 13 initiatives set up by the European Commission. In absolute terms, the part of this percentage which goes to the furthering of cross-border co-operation amounts to 2,565 million Ecus. Not very much has really been said as to the suitability of this figure. The European Parliament, however, in its 1997 Resolution concerning cross-border and inter-regional co-operation, apparently thought it to be insufficient and proposed an increase in financial resources. Moreover, and within the context of this resolution, the European Parliament favoured the simplification of procedures and of financial and economic management practices for INTERREG II programmes.

2. As has already been indicated, member states play an outstanding role in the drawing-up and execution of INTERREG II programmes to the

detriment of the regions. Possibilities of regional participation, moreover, differ substantially depending on the internal organization of each state. Thus, in the case of the Pyrenean border, all projects within the scope of the operational programme on the Spanish side are drawn up by the Autonomous Communities themselves, although it is the central administration that submits said programme to the Commission and that subsequently allocates funds to the regional administrations. On the French side of the border, however, it is not the regions but the central administration that approves the projects that will eventually form part of the operational programme (Balme, 1995). It could also happen that, even if a basic agreement existed between the regional authorities on both sides of the border, cross-border co-operation would not materialize owing to a lack of approval on the part of the French central authorities. The fact that the decision-making capacity does not lie with the agents involved in co-operation cannot be construed as a positive factor for cross-border co-operation.

3. The norms governing INTERREG II give rise to a number of difficulties regarding their geographic scope of application. Indeed, the territorial unit contemplated by INTERREG II for the promotion of cross-border co-operation is NUTS 3. This means that operational programmes do not use the overall region as a point of reference, but rather a specific zone, that is, the area most directly affected by the frontier. An exception to this general rule, which allows 20 per cent of the total budget to be allocated to areas neighbouring frontier territory, does not invalidate this criticism.

A much more serious criticism could be made of that part of the structural policy which, through innovative measures and pilot projects and INTERREG II C, attempts to favour transregional co-operation. The following points can be raised in this respect:

1. Insufficient financial resources possibly become more obvious in this case. Only a part of what is allocated to this type of intervention is earmarked for the promotion of transregional co-operation. Additionally, each project is entitled to receive funding restricted to a figure that ranges between one and three million Ecus. Community aid is controlled by strict economic and social cohesion criteria. It is interesting to point out that the European Parliament, after acknowledging that innovative measures and pilot projects must continue in their support for less developed regions, is of the opinion that Structural Funds must also address a Four Motors kind of co-operation.

2. The RECITE II pilot project defines a number of actors in transregional co-operation. Regional and local authorities and public, semi-public, and private bodies can be held responsible for these projects and all of them seem to deserve the same consideration, although, to a lesser extent, this is also characteristic of INTERREG II. The result is that the region appears diluted in the midst of a pluralism of actors. It might have been suitable, perhaps, to underline the pre-eminence of regional bodies. A more explicit reference to these, although without excluding the participation of local institutions or other types of organization, would have responded better to the aspirations of a truly transregional co-operation.

3. Some requirements of RECITE II could become obstacles to co-operation. In order that a RECITE II pilot project be approved, it is necessary to include from three to seven regions belonging to at least three member states. Furthermore, one third of these regions must be Objective 1 or 6. On the whole, these requirements may well make it difficult for regions which are geographically proximate to address transregional co-operation projects on a joint basis. Moreover, the lack of both economic and infrastructural resources, which many regional and local authorities experience, could give rise to further problems when financing the preliminary and preparatory activities involved in a project.

4. The INTERREG II C chapter refers to co-operation in zones which are much larger than the cross-border ones and encourages direct regional participation. Basic territorial units are currently NUTS 2. Nevertheless, the transnational adjective that is applied to the co-operation developing in accordance with this initiative apparently underlines more the fact of the state than the fact of the region. This becomes clearly manifest in the exclusive ability that states have to make proposals concerning the areas where co-operation will take place. Although, as has already been mentioned, INTERREG II C does allow for greater regional participation, the Committee of the Regions has claimed that the essential part of this initiative must take place at regional and local levels (Committee of Regions, 1997). Finally, mention must be made of the low level of funding available for INTERREG II C. Unfortunately, this prevents many regions from becoming involved.

Apart from these critical observations, it must be emphasized that there are objective factors within the European regional structure which act as obstacles to inter-regional co-operation. One of these concerns the differences in levels of wealth and income between European regions. Although Community norms relating to the structural policy have added complications to inter-regional co-operation, by making said co-operation dependent upon the involvement of a high percentage of underprivileged regions, the disparities in levels of development tend in themselves to restrict co-operation, as there are few points of common interest. Second, the fact that the decision-making powers which are enjoyed by the regions vary from state to state constitutes another obstacle. Even if wealth and income levels were similar, the different distribution of political power among European regions would limit the extent of co-operation or, at best, restrict it to what regions with fewer political powers could do.

CONCLUSIONS

From these remarks, it can be concluded that the structural policy does not make an altogether significant contribution to the development of inter-regional co-operation. This means that Community institutions are missing an excellent opportunity to further advance the integration process. In any case, and as underlined by Weyland (1996), it is in the field of cross-border co-operation, more so than in that of transregional co-operation, where the most notable contributions have been made to the progress of that integration process.

We close with the following final comments on the future of the relationship between the structural policy and inter-regional co-operation and, thus, the possibility of achieving a more united Europe:

1. It seems that the logic of cohesion will continue to be behind European Union policies supporting inter-regional co-operation. Surprisingly, this is also the position adopted by the Committee of the Regions itself. On the occasion of the 1996 Intergovernmental Conference, said Committee made a proposal for the inclusion in the Amsterdam Treaty of a commitment on the part of the Community to foment cross-border and transregional co-operation (Committee of Regions, 1996). The Committee of the Regions suggested that this commitment be formally included under the Heading on Social and Economic Cohesion of the Treaty.

2. Although the proposal submitted by the Committee of the Regions was unsuccessful, efforts to promote inter-regional co-operation will continue to be a goal of the structural policy throughout the new 2000–06 financial period, at least. As stated in Agenda 2000, and also subsequently established in the Commission's proposal for the reform of the Structural Funds put forward to the Council in 1998, the number of Community initiatives will drop from 13 to three. One of these initiatives will deal with the issue of cross-border and transregional co-operation.

3. The volume of resources to be set aside for inter-regional co-operation will depend on two opposing factors. On the one hand, if the number of Community initiatives is reduced, this might well provide more extensive financial means for inter-regional co-operation. On the other hand, the percentage of the total Structural Funds given over to Community initiatives will drop from 9 per cent to 5 per cent. By applying these percentages to the figures estimated for the 1994–99 and 2000–06 budgets, respectively, no significant changes are expected to occur in the amount of available resources.

4. The attitude of the member states is vital for the unfolding of inter-regional co-operation. There are two reasons that explain why a change in the present attitude of the member states is so important: first, to overcome the obstacles that have hindered the coming into being and application of a legal base favouring the spread of this co-operation. It would be positive if a new political mood were capable of encouraging a larger number of states to sign and ratify the 1995 and 1998 Protocols; second, to provide for greater regional participation. Improving the role that the regions play is crucial for the future of inter-regional co-operation. There are likely to be some setbacks, however, in this area. According to the new regulation proposals concerning Structural Funds, it seems that transregional co-operation actions will eventually come under Community initiatives, meaning that the degree of protagonism enjoyed by the regions to date will decline, to the benefit of the states.

5. If changes take place in the logic applied by the Community and the member states to inter-regional co-operation, the above mentioned regional associations could come to play a far more significant role. These associations, by means of a closer involvement in the work of Community institutions, could become active in a strategy aimed at advancing the integration process and achieving a more balanced Community from the economic and social point of view.

Perhaps the most decisive of these comments is that which suggests that the logic behind regionalism and community policies should be brought closer together, as this would serve to influence the evolution of inter-regional co-operation to a much larger extent than other factors. As has already been said, the new regionalism embraces a demand for action capable of meeting the challenges arising from interdependence. In this particular regard, inter-regional co-operation is but a means to cope with the consequences of a world that is becoming more complex. Recognition of this fact, particularly on the part of the member states, is necessary to bring together the logic that lies behind both these phenomena. If this is the case, the importance of inter-regional co-operation for the construction of a united Europe, whose actions are known and understood better by its citizens and where solidarity prevails, as pointed out by the ARE, will then be able to reach its true dimension.

NOTES

1. As can be deduced from the text, the expression 'inter-regional co-operation' refers to any kind of links established by regions belonging to different states. It includes cross-border as well as transregional co-operation. The expression inter-regional co-operation has been used in a general sense, as indicated above, and in a more precise sense to mean co-operation between European regions irrespective of frontier divisions. We have preferred to employ the term transregional in the latter sense.
2. The description of the regional associations has been made, in most cases, drawing on documentation produced by these associations themselves. An interesting account of this kind of associations can be found in Gobierno Vasco (1994).
3. These cross-border entities have been termed Euroregio. A Euroregio is a grouping of municipal units belonging to states on either side of a frontier, which has a common administrative structure.

REFERENCES

Assembly of European Regions (1995), *Proposiciones para la revisión del Tratado de la Unión Europea con ocasión de la Conferencia Intergubernamental de 1996* (Amberes: ARE).

Assembly of European Regions (1996), *Declaration about Regionalism in Europe* (Basilea: ARE).

Balme, R. (1995), 'French Regionalization and European Integration: Territorial Adaptation and Change in a Unitary State', in B. Jones and M. Keating, *The European Union and the Regions* (Oxford: Clarendon Press).

Balme, R. (1996), *Les politiques du néo-régionalisme* (Paris: Economica).

Baños, J. y A. Iglesias (1995), 'La Política Regional Europea y la Cooperación Transfronteriza. Los Programas INTERREG', *Revista de Estudios Regionales,* No 42, pp.181–212.

Borja, A., F. Letamendía y K. Sodupe (1998), *La Construcción del Espacio Vasco-Aquitano. Un Estudio Multidisciplinar* (Leioa: Servicio Editorial de la Universidad del País Vasco).

Cahmis, M. (1993), 'La Cooperación Transfronteriza e Interregional a nivel Europeo', *Europa-Junta,* No 18, pp.5–10.

Committee of the Regions (1996), 'Dictamen sobre la revisión del Tratado de la Unión Europea y del Tratado constitutivo de la Comunidad Europea', *Official Journal of the European Communities,* OJ C100/1 of 2 April.

Committee of the Regions (1997), *Dictamen: La iniciativa comunitaria INTERREG II C y el papel potencial de los entes regionales y locales* (Brussels: Official Publications Office of the European Communities).

Council of Europe (1980), *European Outline Convention on Transfrontier co-operation between territorial communities or authorities* (Madrid).

Council of Europe (1995), *Additional Protocol to the European Outline Convention on Transfrontier Co-operation between Territorial Communities or Authorities* (Strasbourg).

Council of Europe (1998) *Protocol nº 2 to the European Outline Convention on Transfrontier Co-operation between Territorial Communities or Authorities concerning interterritorial co-operation* (Strasbourg).

Diego J. L. (1997), 'La Cooperación Transfronteriza e Interregional de las Comunidades Autónomas', *Seminario sobre la Participación Europea y la Acción Exterior de las Comunidades Autónomas* (Barcelona: Institut d'Estudis Autonomics).

European Commission (1994a), *Guidelines on Community Initiatives (1994–1999)* (Brussels:

Official Publications Office of the European Communities).
European Commission (1994b), 'Commission Notice to the Member States. INTERREG II' *Official Journal of the European Communities*, OJ COM C 180/13 of 15 June.
European Commision (1994c), *Regional Development Innovative Measures (art. 10 of ERDF) 1995–1999* (Luxembourg: Official Publications Office of the European Communities).
European Commision (1996a), *Structural Funds and Cohesión Funds 1994–1999* (Brussels: Official Publications Office of the European Communities).
European Commision (1996b), 'European Programme for the Inter-regional Co-operation and Regional Economic Innovation. RECITE II. Inter-regional Co-operation Projects', *Official Journal of the European Communities,* OJ C326 of 31 October.
European Commission (1996c), 'Commission Communication to the Member States. INTERREG II C', *Official Journal of the European Communities,* OJ COM C 200/07 of 8 May.
European Commision (1997), *Agenda 2000. For a Stronger and Wider Union.* (Brussels: Official Publications Office of the European Communities).
European Commission (1998), 'Proposal for a Council Regulation (EC) Laying down General Provisions of the Structural Funds, *Official Journal of the European Communities,* OJ 98/C 176/01 of 9 June.
European Parliament (1997), 'Resolution about Transfrontier and Inter-regional Co-operation', A4-0161 of 16 May (Strasbourg).
Gobierno Vasco (1994), *Asociaciones de Cooperación Inter-regional* (Vitoria-Gasteiz: Secretaría General de Acción Exterior).
Granrut, C. du (1994), *Europe, les temps des Régions* (Paris: Librairie Générale du Droit et de la Jurisprudence).
Keating, Michael (1995), 'Europeanism and Regionalism' in B. Jones and M. Keating, *The European Union and the Regions* (Oxford: Clarendon Press).
Keating, M. and J. Loughlin (1997), *The Political Economy of Regionalism* (London and Portland, OR: Frank Cass).
Kukawka, P. (1996), 'Le Quadrige européen ou l'Europe par les régions', in R. Balme, *Les politiques du néo-régionalisme* (Paris: Economica).
Labasse, J. (1991), *L'Europe des Régions* (Paris: Flammarion).
Loughlin, John. (1997), 'L'Europe des Régions et la Fedéralisation de l'Europe', in J. Palard (dir.) *L'Europe aux Frontières. La coopération transfrontalière entre régions d'Espagne et de France* (Paris: PUF).
Marks, G. (1992), 'Structural Policy in the European Community', in M. Sbragia, *Euro-Politics* (Washington: The Brookings Institution) pp.190–224.
Palard, J. (1995), 'Les effets institutionells de la Politique Régionale de l'Union Européenne', *Politiques et Management Publique,* Vol. 13, No 3, pp.65–81.
Puyol, R. y J. Vinuesa (1995), *La Unión Europea* (Madrid: Editorial Síntesis).
Structural Funds (1988), 'Coordination Regulation', *Official Journal of the European Communities,* OJ L 2052/88 24 of August.
Structural Funds (1993), 'ERDF Regulation', *Official Journal of the European Communities,* OJ 2083/93 20 of July.
Weyand, Sabine (1996), 'Inter-Regional Associations and the European integration Process' in *Regional and Federal Studies,* Vol. 6, No 2, pp.166–182.

Towards Plurinational Diplomacy in the Deeper and Wider European Union (1985–2005)

FRANCISCO ALDECOA

This article explores new forms of substatal participation in the formulation and implementation of foreign policy in those states which have a complex structure in the context of the European Union, from a political perspective. This does not mean rejecting the formal rules or constitutional legal frameworks for foreign relations. Neither does it imply denying the conditions imposed in international relations by the sovereignty of the state and by international law. Rather, a policy focus allows us to look at the consequences of the various legal frameworks, not merely in juridical terms, but in terms of the practical implications for the evolution of the political systems. While the jurist is interested in the constitutional frameworks and the impact of international law on the state´s foreign relations, the political perspective also has to pay attention to other processes, frequently informal, whose influence on the formulation and the expansion of external politics, whether or not through laws and international obligations, cannot be disregarded (Kincaid, 1993; Hocking, 1993).

We will review the current state of the theoretical debate on the international involvement of the regions, suggesting the need to adopt a new focus for the question in the light of the European Union. However, I would briefly like to refer to a precedent of special interest regarding the complex relationship between the foreign action of the substate bodies and the state´s foreign policy for, while the theme has awakened a special interest in the last decade, the problem is by no means new. In the wake of the Second World War, the Basque government in exile recognized the need to continue the external action which it had begun during the Civil War. As well as the Basque government´s own activities, the Lehendakari Aguirre considered it correct to support foreign relations of the exiled government of the Spanish. Aguirre therefore suggested appointing Basques, as well as Catalans and Gallegos, to the embassies in countries that still recognized the Republic. These officials would have a double role: on the one hand representing the Republic´s own business and, on the other hand, dealing with matters of Basque interest, where they would act as delegates of the Basque government. José Antonio Aguirre called this scheme *federative diplomacy*.[1] In contrast to the formalistic mechanisms usually advocated to handle foreign policy in those states with a complex structure, Aguirre´s proposal is of interest in that it seems to be formulated, not so much as an answer to a problem of sharing competences between different levels of government, but as an international reflection of the plurinational character of the state.

THE INTERNATIONAL SCOPE OF THE REGIONS AND THE EUROPEAN UNION

In the last ten years an important literature has developed the notion of the region as an international actor, stressing the real and growing roles which the regional governments are playing in international relations (Michelmann and Soldatos, 1990; Hocking, 1993a). A new terminology has appeared, still not fully accepted, to describe this controversial phenomenon. Such concepts as *paradiplomacy* or *protodiplomacy* try to reflect, with more or less accuracy, the exterior dimension of the regions but with certain implicit reference to the state (Duchacek, 1986; Duchacek, Latouche and Stevenson, 1988). Although interesting, this approach has, in my opinion, certain echoes of the old political realism which should be reconsidered. In so far as they seem to take as a reference or model the foreign policy of states, such perspectives do not focus on the whole range of the new reality, nor do they take into account the transformation of diplomacy in the contemporary world (Hocking, 1993b). This problem is reinforced by the lack of attention, with a few exceptions (Hamilton and Langhorne, 1995), to the plurinational reality of states, or the specific problems of the external relations of those states with a complex structure, common in the studies on diplomacy (such as Watson, 1982; Barston, 1988; Anderson, 1993; Berridge, 1995).

At the same time, specifically in the context of the European Union, numerous works have appeared in the last few years which stress not so much the external activities of regions as the inter-relationships among regions, states and the institutions of the EU (Jones and Keating, 1995; Rhodes 1995; Balme, 1996; Le Gales and Lequesne, 1997). Such works concentrated at first on the identification of the different kinds of regional participation inside the political system of the European Union, but have more recently extended to the study of the different strategies of substate mobilization within the various international regimes. This approach has revealed the importance of the substate dimension in the transformation, both of the various political systems and of the international regimes themselves (Keating and Loughlin, 1997). This demands that we consider, both in the study of domestic policy and in that of the foreign policy, different levels of action. Such an approach focuses not so much on the singularity of substate foreign action, as on the importance of its vertebration inside a complex political system, which affects not only the regions, but also the very formulation and implementation of the foreign relations of the states (Hocking, 1993b).

This complex reality, which demands a redefining of the forms of foreign relations of the state, is what I call *plurinational diplomacy,* a notion inspired by the literature on *two-level diplomacy*. This approach takes the study of the domestic political arena as a stage upon which different political actors, including regional governments, are able to exert influence on the foreign policy process, through the multiple formal and informal openings that political life offers (Evans, Jacobson and Putnam, 1993). This way, foreign policy can be understood as a double game, one which places its state representatives face to face and another which is developed in the domestic arena in search of ratification, credibility when facing third parties, effective implementation, or political legitimacy (Sidmore and Hudson, 1993; Risse-Kappen, 1995). The image we are describing gets complicated when one considers that those who are responsible for external politics and other governmental and non-governmental actors can use their domestic influence and control of administration with the intention of influencing the final result of the negotiation. From this point of view the concept of *multilayered diplomacy* proposed by Hocking takes on a particular interest (Hocking, 1993b). Such an approach allows us to get closer to the reality of the participation of different levels of government in the formulation and implementation of foreign policy, and to fully understand the changes of course in the world of diplomacy (Hocking, 1993b).

Plurinational diplomacy takes on a special sense in the context of European integration, both in terms of its institutional and formal dimensions and also its sociopolitical repercussions. So the substate forces pressing for more effective participation in the process of European construction are part of a wider phenomenon that includes the transformation of foreign policy, the effects of the process of European construction and, in particular, the matter of shared sovereignty.

Most studies to date have linked the general phenomenon of the regions' foreign action with the wish of some of them, like Quebec or Catalonia, to transform themselves into states (Petschen, 1993). The concept of plurinational diplomacy implies a reinterpretation of the political range of such processes from the recognition of shared sovereignty. In recent years, in both academic and political debate, more and more people are linking the themes of substate action and state transformation, focusing on the articulation of strategies for self government, rather than on the creation of a traditional state (Gottlieb, 1993; Keating, 1996). As Xabier Arzalluz, President of the Basque Nationalist Party (EAJ/PNV), said in a recent interview at the University of the Basque Country: 'We renounce sovereignty but not political power itself.'[2] This political logic is the consequence of a basic common strategy to demand more competences and powers for the region, in both its domestic and external dimensions, but making sure at the same time to get a regional input into decisions prepared, formulated and implemented elsewhere. That is, to develop the ability to influence the political process of the state to which it belongs, and of the European Union.

Although it could turn out to be controversial, under the current conditions, true independence, and the exercise of self-determination, does not depend so much on the exercise and development of competences, or even sovereignty, as on the ability to participate effectively in a political decision-making process which is more and more complex. This logic is visible in the change of strategy of nationalist parties in such contexts as the Basque Country, Catalonia, Scotland or Quebec. In the past, studies on this theme have been rather formalistic, and have generally concentrated on the legal argument (Dehousse, 1991; Charpentier and Engel, 1992, Perez Gonzalez, 1994; Pueyo Losa and Ponte Iglesias, 1997). Even the political debate on the external dimension of the state of the self-governing regions has been over the *right* more than over the *fact*. There exists very little political analysis of the operation of the mechanisms. For this reason I will defend the notion of *plurinational diplomacy* as the most adequate with regard to this new multiform reality. This will allow me to develop a forward-looking analysis, related to the transformation of diplomacy in complex states within the European Union. The basic argument is that alongside developing paradiplomacy, that is, the formalized external action of the regions, there is a process of transformation of the regions, the states and the European Union itself. There are multiple loyalties, to the state and the Union, and these have a complex interrelation in the proceedings of the different public powers.

SHARED SOVEREIGNTY: A COMMON FOUNDATION OF EUROPEAN CONSTRUCTION AND POLITICAL RECOGNITION OF REGIONS

In relation to the connection between European construction and the regional phenomenon there exist two clearly opposed positions. Some see the processes as conflicting, while others see them as complementary, in that they nourish each other. I find myself more and more convinced that the deepening of the integration process is closely linked to the gradual political recognition of the regions (Jones and Keating, 1985; Keating and Jones,

1995; De Castro, 1994). The origin of this deepening integration process lies in the application of the notion of shared sovereignty, which appears for the first time in the Treaty of the European Coal and Steel Community of 1951, paving the way for the process of European construction which transferred sovereignty and, therefore, competences and powers of the states to the common institutions. This same process was produced in reverse form through the decentralization of the state, in the same years although, with very few exceptions, this notion of shared sovereignty was not used in the debate about the decentralization of European states. The very process of the development and consolidation of the European Union has formalized the aspiration of direct participation by the regions in the Community political process, even in the Council, at precisely the same time as the external dimension of regional politics has grown, as a consequence of the expansion of regional competences. In certain cases the formulation and application of European law has produced a competence void in the Spanish autonomous communities and in other European regional governments. Nonetheless, the deepening of the integration process has coincided with that of regionalization. This reality, which will be of even greater relevance with the widening of the European Union, might seem like something quite new, but it does have roots in European federalist thinking. So in 1943, the President of the Basque government in exile, the Lehendakari José Antonio Aguirre, declared:

> It is inconceivable for a Europe that wants peace and its own regulations to be caught up in its networks of oppressed nationalities. The federation is a path of liberties because it is born from a compromise between equals. The idea of the political philosophy which looks to the future, introducing modifications to the idea of the old state sovereignty, is to establish and combine the national liberation of peoples with participation in wider political economic spaces. The guarantee of the peoples, in particular the small ones, lies precisely in these wider supranational structures … Man has managed to raise interest in the universal spirit to the point of limiting and exceeding the closed concept of the state, which considered everything happening within its limits as a domestic affair. The nation without freedom, which is, in the end, a set of men who are deprived of a basic right, should also come out of the domestic framework to enter into the international field and be the object of its attention. International organization will be solidly built on these human and natural bases.[3]

In this way, the Basque prime minister Aguirre brings up the theme in which we are interested, in a radical and pioneering way. He uses a precise terminology which is sometimes ignored today, in order to tackle the question of sovereignty in the relations between nations, states and supranational organization.

THE DEEPENING AND WIDENING OF THE EUROPEAN UNION AND THE EXTERNAL DIMENSION OF THE REGIONAL PHENOMENON (1985–2005)

The European Union arose as a consequence of the transformation of the European Community to address five fundamental problems: democracy, effectiveness, efficiency, presence in the world and solidarity. The appearance of the regional question is tied to these five questions, especially for the issues of democracy, effectiveness and solidarity (Aldecoa, 1993). It is concerned with a process which we are able to analyse, broadly speaking, distinguishing five stages:

- *The definition of the model of the Union* through the resolution of 14 February 1984 of the European Parliament, in which the Project of the Treaty of the European Union was passed. This established, for the first time, the model of the Union. It paid particular attention to the five aforementioned aspects, true structural elements of European construction and preconditions for the definition of what we might call the regional problem.
- *The Single European Act* where the European Union appeared for the first time as an objective, establishing the programme of the single market or a Europe without borders. As a consequence of its application, the region appeared as an economic reality and as a passive subject linked to regional politics and structural funds, that is, to effectiveness and solidarity. This contributed powerfully to reinforcing the dynamics of regionalization in the member states, with the objective of gaining access to the structural funds. The process of creating the European single market, with its strict rules of competition and the difficulties of putting it into action, taught regional governments an important lesson. It soon became evident that the integration of national economies, once the border obstacles were eliminated, demanded the effective co-operation of the different levels of government in the application of European law. This situation favoured regional mobilization, the reconstruction of the problem of substate participation in the Community process and finally, the political recognition of the regions. Such is the context in which arose the argument over substate bodies participating in the process of European construction, through the use of different modes of action like pressure groups or through formal

openings that would have to be set up for the purpose.
- *The Treaty of the European Union of 7 February 1992* which established
  the political nature of the Union. As a consequence of this, the political
  monopoly of the states in the constituent Treaties disappeared. With it, for
  the first time, there appeared, linked to the structural principle of
  democracy, political recognition of the regions. This is made evident in
  such things as the substate dimension of the principle of subsidiarity, the
  creation of the Committee of Regions, the possibility of direct
  participation in the Council meetings and the political administration of
  certain Community funds. Such aspects imply a substantive advance in the
  political recognition of the regional question but, above all, it established
  a new institutional framework for resolving the problem of regional
  participation and for addressing the erosion of substate autonomy. The
  implications of this vary according to developments in each state, with
  their varying institutional frameworks for inter-governmental co-
  operation and substate participation in the Community political process.
  This has brought into being a whole new and complex process of intergovernmental relations within the EU political system (Soldatos and
  Michelman, 1992; Marks Llamazares, 1995; García Segura, 1995).
- *The Treaty of Amsterdam, of 17 June 1997*, which comes into effect on
  1 January 1999 coinciding with the introduction of the euro and with
  Scottish devolution, is intended to bring European political construction
  closer to the citizen through the consolidation of the social dimension.
  This also means a strengthening of the autonomy of the Committee of
  Regions and extension of its consultative role in social affairs.
  Nevertheless, it seems to me that the most important achievement, to
  which we will return later, is the development of themes that interest the
  regions. The preconditions for the reinforcement of the regions' political
  role are established (Aldecoa, 1998). What has become evident as a
  negative aspect of Amsterdam is the lack of agreement on institutional
  reform. However, from a regional point of view, as we shall later see,
  this could prove to be a positive thing, since it allows developments in
  view of enlargement of the Union.[4]
- *The Reform of the Treaty of Amsterdam in 2002.* In the intergovernmental conference a period of five years was given for the reform
  of the Treaty. In my opinion, the regionalization of the member states
  will have a very significant impact on this reform. Nationalist and
  regionalist forces will have to participate effectively in the political
  process of the reform, in a context of negotiation, an experience very
  different from that of Maastricht and Amsterdam. Together with the
  deepening of Italian and Portuguese regionalization, a particularly
  interesting aspect will be the process of British *devolution* and its impact

on the foreign policy of the United Kingdom (Robbins, 1998).

All of these matters require, however, a reconsideration in light of the next enlargement. Of the six founder members, five were unitary states and only one, Germany, was a federal state. With the first enlargement, from six to nine, in 1972, three unitary states were added, Denmark, the United Kingdom and Ireland, but by that time regionalization had begun in Belgium and Italy. The second enlargement, in 1980, with the entry of Greece and the third, in 1986, with Spain and Portugal coincided with more extended regionalizaion in the member states. In 1995, entering along with Finland and Sweden, Austria strengthened its federalism in order to be better prepared for membership. Finally, in the perspective of 2002 there are five candidates; Poland, Hungary, the Czech Republic, Estonia, Slovenia and Cyprus. In these cases, for the first time, the regional question is present in the pre-membership phase, through the setting up of programmes such as the Ouverture, which encourage inter-regional co-operation between the Union and aspirant members. So it seems that although the unitary states still predominate, these end up regionalizing themslves after the process of integration.

PLURINATIONAL DIPLOMACY AS AN ANSWER TO SHARED SOVEREIGNTY IN THE EUROPEAN UNION

The notion of plurinational diplomacy arises as a consequence of the conjunction of three factors which have been developing during recent years: demand for foreign action on the part of the regions; participation of the regions in the formation of state positions in the European Union and in the application of European law; and participation of the regions in the foreign policy of the states. The first two phenomena have been well studied by specialists in European law. However, the third, which will probably be the most interesting in the future, has hardly been studied at all.

The demand for its own foreign activity arises as a consequence of the recognition of the external dimension of substate government. It questions the classic notion of international relations as a domain reserved for states. The second, strictly related to the former, is concerned with not allowing self-government and substate competences to be emptied of content because of the application of European law. The third question is richer and less studied, because it deals with the articulation of interests which do not necessarily reflect the external dimension of regional competences, making them more difficult to define. Nevertheless, it is becoming increasingly clear that there is a need for the regions to participate in the definition of the classic aspects of foreign policy, in what is often called *high politics,* which affects such controversial domains as, among others, the right of active and passive legation. While the first and second aspects are susceptible to a precise legal analysis, the third is much more fluid, and by its very nature often escapes legal definition, generally remaining in the dominion of political negotiation.

Plurinational diplomacy thus refers to the definition, decision and execution of matters of foreign relations which in a plurinational state are the object of formalized political negotiation, whether it is executed at the level of central administration or autonomous substate administration. This, as we pointed out earlier, demands a reciprocal loyalty, so that the action of the central government recognizes the regional dimension and that the paradiplomatic action of the regional government has a state dimension. To understand this, we need to analyse the substantive matters, the instruments and the political process.

The substantive matters of plurinational diplomacy are those derived from the exclusive competences of the regions, and those shared with the state, that is, the external dimension of domestic politics and the domestic implications of external relations. It is clear that the former correspond to the regions and the latter correspond to central government. Usually considered as domestic issues with international relevance are domains such as culture, tourism and education, economic and social policies and environment, among others. Those which are habitually considered exclusively for the state are the ones which refer to international relations in the classic sense.

Plurinational diplomacy arises as a response by the state to the need to rethink the formulation and implementation of external relations in the complex context of the European Union, and from the full recognition of the political consequences of shared sovereignty. Taking into account both the European dimension and the substate dimension, states must pay attention to the following needs:

- The strengthening of substatal participation in the foreign and domestic politics of the state, through establishing openings both at the European Union level and through the member states; openings which are legally formalized modes of consultation and participation in decisions, whenever they affect the exclusive or shared competence of the substate bodies. We refer to the substate co-participation before the adoption of international treaties on shared competences, and the recognition of the treaty-making capacity of the regions in matters of their exclusive competence. This situation arises in states with a complex structure, when international negotiation could lead to the imposition of legal obligations in matters exclusive to the substate authority or shared with the state. In such cases and in spite of the prerogatives which the state normally reserves for the central government in international relations, various constitutional systems provide for participation of the substate governments in the formation of state positions, because of their competence in certain functions. This participation can be as little as an obligation for the central government to provide timely information to the substate authority on the course of the negotiations, or simply to consult regional governments at appropriate moments on the position to adopt. Sometimes, however, they also require formal approval by the regions or even the recognition of a treaty-making capacity for the substate authority itself.

• There are reasons of efficiency for establishing channels for consultation with regional governments, when decisions the state is thinking of adopting, even in matters of its own exclusive competence, could require the collaboration of substate authorities in implementation, or when a regional input can make for better policy. This applies in the negotiation of agreements, foreign representation, the international responsibility of the state, and the management of foreign affairs. At a time when international negotiations increasingly deal with matters that affect substate self-government, this explains the emergence of various innovations in inter-governmental relations. These are usually intended to link the regional governments in some way to the foreign policy process. Sometimes national governments are looking for backing or at least wish to neutralize opposition before decisions are taken that affect the regions. Concessions and reciprocal forms of compensation are widely used here. It is often important for states to achieve a domestic agreement before entering international negotiations since, without it, states may lack credibility before third parties.

• The need to develop a growing sensitivity to the regional question and the extension of a multicultural and plurinational citizenship. This sensitivity can strengthen the internal legitimacy of the decisions of the central government in matters of foreign and European politics and help gain parliamentary and electoral backing for the action of the central government. This demands the development of a new political culture, plurinational, conscious of both its internal dimensions inside the state and also its international scope. Even when it is not formally necessary, the central government might consider it politically necessary or useful to have domestic backing before making a decision. This arises in those decisions which have great social impact and which provoke unease among social movements, trade unions, employers' asociations and sometimes regional governments themselves. However, it may also arise as a strategic option, a way of building consensus behind government policy. This requires the government to mobilize resources and support in order to obtain sufficient consensus before a decision, because it seems necessary or simply because it provides it with greater political legitimacy.

• True plurinational diplomacy will also involve substate collaboration in the redefinition of some aspects of its foreign action and the development of a double loyalty. On the one hand, the foreign agenda of the state must pay attention to the international needs of the regional governments. On the other hand, regional governments must respect the state's position when forging their own external policies. We can illustrate this with some examples: During a recent visit to Morocco, the President of the Generalitat of Catalonia, Jordi Pujol, besides his own task of the foreign promotion of Catalonia, dedicated part of his agenda to personally explain the *Estado de la Autonomías* to King Hassan, to allay Hassan's suspicions about the Autonomy Statute of Ceuta and Melilla. During a recent visit to Cuba, the President of the Basque government, Prime Minister Ardanza, besides his own agenda which was concerned with the promotion of Euskadi, could have contributed to improving relations between Cuba and Spain – at the time somewhat tense – during his interview with foreign minister Robaina.

CONCLUSION

The point of view that identifies the unitary state with the strong state and the plurinational state with the weak state – and its corollary, that unity in external relations precludes plurinational diplomacy – reminds me of the sophism that identifies single-party government with strong and lasting foreign policy. Policy analysis has shown us that non-majority or coalition governments can keep longer lasting positions in the international arena. This is because they do not rely on an assured parliamentary backing. Something similar occurs with plurinational diplomacy. It not only better represents the different sensitivities of a plurinational or multicultural state, but it can also have more effectiveness in foreign policy. We have presented the concept of *plurinational diplomacy*, as a necessary reformulation of the ways of diplomacy which have to be developed by member states from the recognition of the legal and political reality of shared sovereignty within the European Union. *Plurinational diplomacy* will mean the development of a double loyalty: on the one hand, the incorporation in the exterior agenda of the state of specific attention to the necessity of the international projection of regional governments and, on the other hand, attention to state policies in the paradiplomatic foreign action of the regional governments. To conclude, the process of European integration and the transformations of the state which are associated with it, have important implications for the conventional concept of nation and nationality (Brubaker, 1996) and their corresponding loyalties. This will become noticeable in the coming years, not only in the domestic political organization of the member states but also in their external relations.

NOTES

1. My gratitude to Alexander Ugalde who pointed out this extreme into which he has gone into depth in the framework of his unpublished research, *La actuación del Gobierno Vasco en el exilio 1940/1960: Un caso singular de acción exterior*, financed by the Basque government.
2. Interview with Xabier Arzalluz in *Eurokon*, , No.2 (1996), p.1.
3. Taken from the 1943 text by Jose antonio Aguirre, entitled, 'Coordinación de nacionalidades Europeas', quoted in Aguirre Zabala, 1987, pp.94–5.
4. It is interesting to point out the 1996 document of the Basque government/Eusko Jaurlaritza, *Euskadi ante la reforma de la Unión Europea: La participación de los pueblos y los ciudadanos de Europa en un proyecto político común*, in which are made explicit their aspirations regarding the general model of the European Union and in particular, the European social model, and not so much those aspects of immediate political demand.

REFERENCES

Aguirre Zabala, I. (1987) 'Nacionalismo vasco y relaciones transnacionales en el contexto de la frontera hispano-francesa: cuatro modelos históricos', in C. del Arenal (coord.): *Las relaciones de vecindad* (Bilbao: UPV/EHU).

Aldecoa, F. (1993) 'Eficiencia, eficacia, y democracia: condiciones estructurales para la trasnformación de la Comunidad Europea en Unión Europea', *Sistema*, No.114–15, pp.55–82.

Aldecoa, F. (1998) 'El Tratado de Amsterdam: un pequeño gran paso en la consolidiación del modelo de la Unión', *Cuadernos Europeos de Deusto*, No.18, pp.11–48.

Anderson, M.S. (1993) *The Rise of Modern Diplomacy* (New York: Longman).

Balme, R. (ed.)(1996) *Les politiques du néo-regionalisme* (París: Economica).

Barston, R.P. (1988) *Modern Diplomacy* (New York: Longman).

Berridge, G.R. (1995) *Diplomacy: Theory and Practice* (London: Prentice Hall).

Borras-Alomar, S. T. Christiansen and A. Rodriguez Pose (1994) 'Towards a 'Europe of the Regions'? Visions and Reality fron a Critical Perspective', *Regional Politics & Policy*, Vol.4, No.2, pp.1–27.

Brubaker, R. (1996) *Nationalism Reframed: Nationhood and the National Question in the New Europe* (Cambridge: Cambridge University Press).

Charpentier, J. and Ch. Engel (dir.)(1992) *Les regions de l´espace communautaire* (Nancy: Presses Universitaires de Nancy).

Dehousse, R. (1991) *Fédéralisme et relations internationales* (Bruselas: Bruylant).

Duchacek, I.D. (1986) *The Territorial Dimension of Politics: Within, Among, and Across Nations* (Boulder: Westview Press).

Duchacek, I.D., D. Latouche and G. Stevenson (eds)(1988) *Perforated Sovereignties and International Relations: Trans-Sovereign Contacts of Subnational Governments* (New York: Greenwood Press).

Evans, P.B., H.K. Jacobson and R.D. Putnam (eds)(1993) *Double Edged Diplomacy: International Bargaining and Domestic Politics* (Berkeley: University of California Press).

García Segura, C. (1995) 'La actividad exterior de las Comunidades Autónomas y la integración europea', *Meridiano Ceri*, No.5, pp.19–22.

Gobierno Vasco/Eusko Jaurlaritza (1996) *Euskadi ante la reforma de la Unión Europea: La participación de los pueblos y los ciudadanos de Europa en un proyecto político común* (Vitoria-Gasteiz: Gobierno Vasco/Eusko Jaurlaritza).

Gottlieb, G. (1993) *Nation against State: A New Approach to Ethnic Conflicts and the Decline of Sovereignty* (New York: Council on Foreign Relations).

Hamilton, K. and R. Langhorne (1995) *The Practice of Diplomacy: Its Evolution, Theory and Administration,* (London: Routledge).

Hocking, B. (ed.)(1993a) *Foreign Relations and Federal States* (London: Leicester University Press).

Hocking, B. (1993b) *Localizing Foreign Policy: Non Central Governments and Multilayered Diplomacy* (London: Macmillan).

Hocking, B. (1993c) 'Managing Foreign Relations in Federal States: Linking Central and Non-Central International Interests', in B. Hocking (ed.): *Foreign Relations and Federal States* (London: Leicester University Press) pp.68–89.

Jones, B. and M. Keating (eds)(1995) *The European Union and the Regions* (Oxford, Oxford University Press).

Keating, M. (1996) *Naciones contra el Estado* (Barcelona: Ariel).

Keating, M. and B. Jones (eds). (1985) *Regions in the European Community* (Oxford: Clarendon Press).

Keating, M. and J. Loughlin (eds) (1997) *The Political Economy of Regionalism* (London and Portland, OR: Frank Cass).

Kincaid, J. (1993) 'Constituent Diplomacy and the Nation-State: Conflict and Co-operation', in H.J. Michelmann and P. Soldatos (eds): *Federalism and International Relations: The Role of Subnational Units* (Oxford: Clarendon Press) pp.54–75.

Le Gales, P. and P. Lequesne (ed.)(1997) *Les paradoxes des régions en Europe* (Paris: La Decouverte).

Marks, G. and I. Llamazares (1995) 'La transformación de la movilización regional en la Unión Europea', *Revista de Instituciones Europeas*, Vol.22, No.1, pp.149–70.

Michelmann, H.J. and P. Soldatos (eds)(1990) *Federalism and International Relations. The Role of Subnational Units* (Oxford: Clarendon Press).

Perez Gonzalez, M., F. Aldecoa and F. Mariño (coord.)(1994) *La acción exterior y comunitaria de los Länder, Regiones, Cantones y Comunidades Autónomas* (Oñate: IVAP/HAEE).

Petschen, S. (1993) *La Europa de las Regiones.* (Barcelona: Generalitat de Catalunya).

Pueyo, J. and M.T. Ponte (eds)(1997) *La actividad exterior y comunitaria de Galicia. La experiencia de otras Comunidades Autónomas* (Santiago de Compostela: Fundación Brañas).

Rhodes, M. (ed.)(1995) *The Regions in the New Europe: Patterns in Core and Periphery Development* (Manchester: Manchester University Press).

Risse Kappen, T. (ed.)(1995) *Bringing Transnational Relations Back: Non State Actors, Domestic Structures and International Institutions* (Cambridge: Cambridge University Press).

Robbins, K. (1998) 'Britain and Europe: Devolution and Foreign Policy', *International Affairs*, Vol.78, No.1, pp.105–17.

Skidmore, D. and V.M. Hudson (ed.)(1993) *The Limits of State Autonomy: Societal Groups and Foreign Policy Formulation* (Boulder: Westview Press).

Soldatos, P. and H.J. Michelmann (1992) 'Subnational Units' Paradiplomacy in the Context of European Integration', *Journal of European Integration*, No.15, pp.129–34.

Ugalde Zubiri, A. (1996) *La actuación internacional del Gobierno Vasco en el exilio 1940/1960: un caso singular de acción exterior*, unpublished research.

Watson, A. (1982) *Diplomacy: The Dialogue Between States* (London: Methuen).

The Other Dimension of Third-Level Politics in Europe: The Congress of Local and Regional Powers of the Council of Europe

JOSE LUIS DE CASTRO

The intention of this essay is to examine one aspect of the international projection of regional governments, to which this volume is dedicated. It is special not only because we are concentrating on the European case, which offers the most defined and characterized profiles, but also because we are looking at one of the least studied aspects of the regional phenomenon in Europe.

In recent years the emergence of substate powers in general, and the regions in particular, has been studied in various aspects, including its 'vertical' dimension – regional participation in the formulation of state policies, as well its 'horizontal' dimension – different strategies of interregional and cross-border co-operation, and the creation of institutionalized structures and frameworks of political and functional co-operation – such as the Assembly of European Regions, Conference of Peripheral and Maritime Regions, European Regions of Industrial Tradition, Association of European Frontier Regions, among others.

Recently, and with the positive effect the Treaty of the European Union had on the regional question, the Committee of Regions has occupied researchers. All of this is a logical and reasonable consequence of the relevance of the European Union and of the importance derived from its policies. However, in the *other* Europe, in the *Great Europe* which is represented by the Council of Europe, there have also been important advances and interesting innovations regarding the regional phenomenon. We will concentrate on these in the following pages, as a different aspect of growing international relevance, with different profiles and objectives but which are not less important, or with less potential, than other developments of the regional phenomenon in the European continent.

CONCEPT OF THIRD LEVEL POLITICS

The assertion that the state has ceased to be, if it ever really was, the exclusive player of international relations, is ever more unquestionable. Economic globalization and the resulting internationalization of political life, as well as the interdependence and transnationalization of social life in general, converts the state into one more among the different actors who perform in the international arena. A wide range of varied mesogovernments, both territorial and functional, public and private intervene in this arena.

International relations now represents a field where different bodies with their own degrees of self-government coexist and interpenetrate (Krämer, 1995). In the new political order of globalization, authority and power are becoming more and more dispersed, sovereignty is redefined, being increasingly shared (Camilleri and Falk, 1992; Jauregui, 1997). In this way, the very sense of public activity is being transformed. It is more and more necessary to work in different networks or frameworks of co-operation in different fields such as security, economy or culture, among others. A new kind of politics has been born, in which institutions and competences overlap (Bullmann, 1996; Ferguson and Mansbach, 1992; Rosenau and Durke, 1995).

The distinction between internal competence and international competence is becoming less clear. New kinds of representation have emerged which emphasize the role of subnational spheres or non-central governments and reinforce their status (Hocking, 1996). Politics is changing in scale as is shown by the multiple phenomena of regionalization which have emerged in recent years (Balme, 1996: 20).[1] I refer to the so-called *phenomenon of multiple voices* with which we characterize the plurality of actors who go directly from the interior of the states to the international sphere. Apart from its North American antecedents, it is in Europe where the phenomenon of regionalization has emerged most strongly during the last decade (Garcia Segura, 1996). International regimes, depending on their structure, offer substatal bodies various possibilities, ranging from the independence, as with the Scottish National Party's policy of independence in Europe, or the Quebec nationalist vision of sovereignty in NAFTA, to the possibility of regional affirmation not to mention independence, a more possible option for the Catalans of *Convergencia i Unió* in the Europe of the Regions formula, among other possible forms (Keating, 1997). It is in this context that we affirm that Europe offers the most complete framework of regional participation. The process of European integration is legitimating numerous and varied types of regional mobilization, so varied that they do not permit, for now, the establishment of a true comprehensive theory of regional mobilization (Castro Ruano, 1994). This phenomenon of regional participation in the Community decision-making process takes us to the ever more accepted concept of multilevel government, in order to consider the emergence of varied channels of intervention in the European political process, at times direct, at others intrastatal (Keating, 1997). Perhaps the latter are the most effective, as practical experience shows that those regions which are best integrated in the state circuits enjoy a greater influence in Brussels (Keating, 1997).

The concept of third-level politics in Europe has two different meanings (Jeffery, 1996). In a strong sense, it expresses the political aspiration to build a 'Europe of the Regions' outside the state system, and on equal footing with these and other European institutions. In a weak sense, it refers to the multiple and varied forms and channels of expression of substatal demands, not exclusively regional, to the Community authorities. Taking a similar line, Loughlin (1996; 1997) states that the concept Europe of the Regions can also be understood in the sense of a federal Europe, where the regions replace the states, and as a Europe in which the regions of a varied nature, through various openings, play different roles with a different grade of participation in the decision-making process (Loughlin, 1996). Although the Europe of the Regions has been leading the way in recent years (Jeffery, 1996), a complementary expression of this, understood in a wider sense, and generally underrated, is the Congress of Local and Regional Powers of the Council of Europe.

THE SUBSTATAL QUESTION IN THE COUNCIL OF EUROPE'S PERSPECTIVE

The process of unification and European integration does not stop at the European Union, although this is perhaps its most relevant expression. In recent decades the Council of Europe has also played a role in reconciliation, dialogue and co-operation.

The Council of Europe, the first post-war European political organization, has had as its main objective the establishment of links between the democracies which form it, helping to strengthen European union through various initiatives of co-operation. The Council of Europe believes that true European union has to do with the will, the understanding and reconciliation between the men and women who inhabit the European territory. The fundamental interest which has on the Council of Europe since its creation, has been to reinforce democracy and human rights through, among other things, the promotion of local democracy, that is, a way of organizing the state that gives self-government to bodies at a lower level (Albanese, 1994).

It is with this interest in strengthening democracy and reinforcing those levels of government with which the citizens identify most that the Council of Europe was the first international organization to integrate substate representatives in their work and organizational structure, giving birth to the Conference of Local and Regional Powers of Europe (Castro Ruano, 1996). The promotion of these levels of government is considered by the Council of Europe, as a further dimension of the Europe of Democracy and Human Rights which it promotes.

The Council of Europe is an international organization of co-operation, set up in 1949 as a consequence of the activity of federal political movements for European unification in the period immediately after the Second World War. Although during the Cold War it was composed only of western European states, with the fall of the Berlin Wall it acquired a new dimension as a pan European organization. At the moment it is made up of 40 European states and is a forum for East–West co-operation, a meeting point between the two Europes which were separated for more than four decades.

The achievements of the Council of Europe in matters of regional and local development have been many and varied; but of particular relevance are the following treaties: the European Framework Convention for Transborder Cooperation of 1980 (Fernández de Casadevante, 1990; 1994; Levrat, 1994) with its two Additional Protocols (Perez González, 1995),[2] the European Charter of Local Self-Government of 1985 (Clotet i Miró, 1992),[3] the Charter of Regional and Minority Languages of 1992,[4] the Project of Convention on Interterritorial Cooperation of 1993 (Casals, 1994; Jauregui, 1996),[5] the Framework Convention for the Protection of National Minorities of 1994,[6] and the Convention on the Participation of Foreigners in Public Affairs at a Local Level, which shows the beginning of the progressive concession of civil and political rights to resident foreigners.

THE CONGRESS OF LOCAL AND REGIONAL POWERS:
ORGANIZATION AND COMPOSITION

In 1994, the Conference of Local and Regional Powers experienced a significant reform inspired by the Secretary of the Council of Europe himself. The objective was, first, to reinforce the Conference, transforming it into a true political organism at the same level as the Parliamentary Assembly and the Committee of Ministers; and second, to achieve a stronger regional representation, in accordance with the political development of the regional level. Initially the Conference included only local representatives and only later was it extended to include the regional level. An imbalance in favour of local representation persisted until recent changes.

With the explicit desire to reinforce and develop the role of local and regional organizations within the institutional frame of the Council of Europe, in its session of 4 January 1994, the Committee of Ministers passed the Statutory Resolution setting up the Congress of Local and Regional Powers of Europe, as well as its Charter.[7] The Vienna Summit of the then 32

Heads of State and/or the Government of the Council of Europe, in October of the same year, gave the go-ahead to the transformation of the Conference of Local and Regional powers in the Congress of Local and Regional Authorities (referred to from now on in the text as CLRAE). The profile of the institution was to be changed from that of a mere consultative committee of experts – created within the framework of article 17 of the Council of Europe Statute – to a true organ of consultation, at the same level as the Parliamentary Assembly.[8] The idea of this transformation was to adapt to a new European political reality characterized by the generalized progress of the local and regional administrative self-government in many member states of the Council of Europe. It was also intended to play a new role in the promotion of local and regional democracy in Central and Eastern European countries which have recently joined the organization.

This last point was one of the main motives for reform in the structure of local and regional co-operation which had existed until then. What was needed was an organ with a more elevated political profile, able to satisfy and channel a good part of the substate expressions which existed in Central and Eastern Europe. The improvement of local and regional democracy in these countries was also going to constitute, from the beginning, one of the principal tasks facing the new CLRAE of the Council of Europe, which was given more power compared to the old Conference.

The objectives of the CLRAE which are laid out in article 2 of the Statutory Resolution, are the following: (a) to ensure the participation of local and regional collectives in achieving the ideals of European union, as well as its representation and implication in the work of the Council of Europe; (b) to submit proposals to the Committee of Ministers with the aim of promoting local and regional self-government; (c) to promote co-operation between local and regional collectives; (d) to maintain contact with other international organizations, European organizations representing local and regional authorities of member states and associations of local and regional authorities.

The Committee of Ministers and the Parliamentary Assembly of the Council of Europe has agreed to consult the Congress over those questions which are likely to affect the competences and essential interests of local and regional authorities.[9] The CLRAE also has a clause of general competence and the right of initiative in matters of local and regional self-government, which allows proposals to be submitted to the Committee of Ministers of the Council of Europe. Each member state has the same number of seats in the CLRAE as they do in the Parliamentary Assembly and, in order to affirm the political and representative profile of the organ, every member must be an elected member of a local or regional authority.[10] In this way the political legitimacy of the Congress is guaranteed, as it is composed of members who have stood for election, chosen by the voters to represent them. The composition of each state's delegation in the Congress, designated by a procedure established by each member state,[11] should ensure a balanced geographical distribution of delegates in the member state territory, an equitable representation of the different categories of the local and regional authorities in the Member State as well as the different political groups represented in them.[12]

Within the CLRAE political groups may be formed. Each group should include members of at least three different nationalities and should have at least 15 members.[13] The CLRAE has a Permanent Commission made up of two representatives from each national delegation, with the task of ensuring the work of the organisation between the Plenary Sessions, and to work in its name. In particular this Commission follows the different areas of activity of the Council of Europe. In short, the CLRAE is the voice of the regions and constituencies of Europe, a privileged place of dialogue which offers the chance to debate common problems, confront experience and express their points of view to state governments. It works in close collaboration with the national and international organizations which represent local and regional powers.

THE CHAMBER OF REGIONS

The bicameral structure of the new CLRAE is one of the most important features. Since the opening up of Permanent Conference of Local Powers to the Regions, there has been a more or less conflicting cohabitation between local and regional authorities. The former exercised a *de facto* monopoly in the institution, and many people wanted a clearly differentiated representation between the two political levels. Above all, the regionalist movement had clearly reiterated the necessity of structures of representation independent of the local authorities, which would answer to their own needs and singular characteristics. Article 4 of the Statutory Resolution establishes that the CLRAE will exercise its attributions through two chambers: one representative of the local authorities, the *Chamber of Local Powers*, and the other representative of the regional authorities, the *Chamber of Regions*. In this way, the nature and the different roles of regional local powers is recognized, satisfying a longstanding claim of the regional movement.

Each Chamber has the same number of seats as the Congress itself. This number amounts to 286 regular members and another 286 reserves.[14] Each Chamber chooses its own *Bureau*, composed of a President along with six other members.[15] The two *Bureaux* are constituted in the *Bureau* of the CLRAE, which is responsible for co-ordinating the jobs of the two Chambers and for distributing material between them.[16] It is presided over by the President of the CLRAE. The President of Congress and the Presidents of each of the two Chambers are elected for two years.

Each of the two Chambers has the capacity to hold its own sessions according to the specific themes with which they deal.[17] They also have the capacity and autonomy to create their own working groups, as well as their own Permanent Commission – a reflection of, and with functions similar to, those of the Permanent Commission of the CLRAE. Each Chamber also adopts its internal regulations independently.[18] It should also be noted that when considering its composition, that the Assembly of European Regions participates in a permanent manner, as an observer with the right to a voice in the work of the Chamber of Regions as well as in the Permanent Commission.[19]

In this way, the regional movement has achieved, within the Council of Europe, one of its greatest aspirations: that of obtaining institutionalized and independently official representation, separate from the local representatives, as well as a political and administrative level of a different nature. Once again the Council of Europe has become the vanguard of regional representation at the European level, adopting a singular and innovative initiative in symphony with regional claims, and a possible precedent for similar solutions in other forums, such as the Committee of Regions of the European Union which, against the reiterated will of the regional majority and of the Assembly of European Regions, mixes local and regional representation, with all the dysfunctions which this produces, from a regional perspective.

In its eagerness to experiment with innovative proposals, the Council of Europe has dealt with the principal problem posed by a chamber of exclusively regional representation: the fact that there are states which do not have this political level. Consequently they could find themselves without representation in an organ of such characteristics. It was for this the reason that until now, the emergence of European institutions of exclusively regional representation had been blocked, whether in the old Conference of Local and Regional Authorities of the Council of Europe, in the Consultative Council of Local and Regional Authorities of the European Commission, or currently, in the Committee of Regions of the European Union.

In this sense, the CLRAE establishes that, as a transitional measure, which will last approximately until the year 2000, when it will be revised,[20] those states which do not have regions are allowed to designate representatives of local bodies or regional associations made up of local bodies. Although the strength and will of the Council of Europe in confronting such a difficult question is admirable, the solution adopted is not without its faults. This composition of the Chamber of Regions is not going to stop representatives of true regions from continuing to sit side by side, albeit temporarily, with representatives of another kind of body. And so the solution reproduces the problem which the creation of the bicameral system had tried to avoid. There are different possible solutions to this situation (Levrat, 1996):

• The most radical would consist of not allowing the possible extension which is contemplated in the Transitory Disposition when it officially expires – that is, the year 2000 – so that those representatives of bodies which do not strictly adhere to the predetermined concept of the region would be excluded from the Chamber of Regions. This solution would further reduce the size of the Chamber of Regions – already smaller than the Chamber of Local Powers because of small states which do not wish to be represented in the former – which would make the work of the CLRAE more difficult, as, in theory, it contemplates a formal parity between the two Chambers both in their decision-making processes, and the election of their Presidents.[21] Furthermore, to exclude from the Chamber of Regions some representatives of states whose structures lack any kind of real regional level but who favour decentralization, would deprive them of important support and legitimization for the regionalist cause.
• The least radical option would be to extend the transitional period during which non-regional representation is allowed. In this way the Chambers' position within the CLRAE would not be weakened, but its ability to prioritize regional affairs would be negatively affected by the inclusion in the Chamber of representatives with little sensitivity to the regional question. The role of the Chamber would also be weakened as it would no longer be exclusively composed of regionally elected representatives with their own competences. In spite of its drawbacks, it seems probable that this solution will be adopted, alongside the continuing process of regionalization throughout Europe and especially in the countries of Central and Eastern Europe.

APPRAISAL OF FOUR YEARS OF ACTIVITY

Given that the CLRAE meets once a year, since its foundation it has only held four Plenary Sessions, so it is perhaps too soon to make definitive conclusions about its activity. The CLRAE has three different instruments of activity. *Opinions* are directed to the Parliamentary Assembly and to the Committee of Ministers of the Council of Europe in reply to consultations formulated by these bodies and are for the internal use of the Council of Europe in its day-to-day business. *Resolutions* directed at the local and regional bodies are the main instrument of the organization and the official and direct path of communication with the people it represents. *Recommendations* are non-binding proposals of action submitted to the Committee of Ministers or to the Parliamentary Assembly with the aim of promoting local self-government and regionalism in its various facets.

As for the concrete activity developed in these four years, the CLRAE has made 58 Resolutions, 37 Recommendations and five Opinions, the analysis of which allows us to start to undertake an approximate evaluation of its activity. In its First Session, celebrated in June 1994, the CLRAE emitted nine Resolutions and seven Recommendations, dedicated basically to the establishment of the organization, to regionalization in the countries of Central and Eastern Europe, and to the execution of the European Charter of local self-government, the oversight of which has become one of its main activities.[22] In this First Session, the CLRAE also issued a Resolution and Recommendation inviting its two Chambers to draw up a *European Charter of Regional Self-Government*.[23]

In the Second Session, held in June 1995, it issued 16 Resolutions, eight Recommendations and three Opinions.

In the Third Session, held in July 1996, seventeen Resolutions were made, along with twelve Recommendations, and two Opinions. From among them we extract Resolution 35,[24] in which the CLRAE decided to examine the possibility of joining forces with other international organizations to draw up a *World Charter on Local Self-Government*, in order to study the possibility of applying the principles of the Local Self-Government Charter to other parts of the world. Resolution 37 is also of singular importance.[25] It has an annex which contains the articles of the Initial Project of the European Charter on Regional Self-Government, as well as recommendation 22, which invites the Parliamentary Assembly of the Council of Europe to examine and be aware of its opinion, in order to prepare a final project for the Committee of Ministers in its Fourth Session.[26]

It is also important to stress the interest of the CLRAE in favouring those processes which deal with the prevention of conflicts. This is carried out through the reinforcement of local democracy, as well as through cross-border activity by local bodies. According to the CLRAE, the reinforcement of a pluralist civil society and of solidarity between territorial authorities could become an important factor in the mutual comprehension and reconciliation between societies with a high potential of conflict. As a consequence of this feeling, the CLRAE created the Embassies of Local Democracy.[27]

In its Fourth Session, held in June 1997, the CLRAE made 16 Resolutions, ten Recommendations and two Opinions, and gave its full and definitive support to the Charter of Regional Self-Government, which is dealt with in detail in the next section. The Resolutions and Recommendations issued by the CLRAE in these four years of activity cover the following thematic areas:

Territorial administration: Regionalization and regional self-government, local self-government, specific reports on the situation of local and regional autonomy in some countries such as Romania, Albania, Turkey, Russia, or Italy; local and regional finances, subsidiarity, participation of citizens and users and consumer rights.

Inter-territorial Relations: Specifically, cross-border co-operation, twinnings and reports on geographical zones or types of regions such as mountain[28] or Mediterranean regions, East/West economic border regions or Danube Regions. This is the second area in terms of the number of interventions by the CLRAE.

Social questions and those of citizenship: In particular, health, social exclusion and unemployment, specific problems facing different social categories and citizenship itself. It occupies third place in the number of interventions.

Other thematic areas which have been the object of the CLRAE's attention in these four years are: territorial management and regional development; inner city development; urban planning and policies; environmental issues; minorities; youth; culture and sport; education and training; North/South co-operation; and East/West relations. Apart from this we should also consider the internal documents of the organization, those of its component Chambers[29] and the relations with other organisms of the Council of Europe and other international institutions.

It is important to mention the wholehearted and constant support shown by the CLRAE for the creation of structures of local and regional democracy in the countries of Central and Eastern Europe, as an inevitable component of the democratic consolidation of these countries. It acts as a watchdog in the implementation of the European Charter of Local Self-Government. Finally, the main objective of the CLRAE since its creation, and for the future, is the Project for a European Charter of Regional Self-Government.

The European Charter of Regional Self-Government

The European Charter of Local Self-Government, according to the CLRAE,[30] constitutes the only international instrument for the defence and development of local self-government, representing, together with the

European Convention of the Human Rights, one of the pillars of democratic conscience and of the values affirmed in the Statute of the Council of Europe. Similarly the proposed European Charter of Regional Self-Government would define the democratic principles of regionalization, as well as the role which the regions should play. The success of the Charter of Local Self-Government, which, after more than ten years, has become one of the most prominent legal instruments of the Council of Europe, spurred on the desire for a similar instrument for regional self-government.

In 1994,[31] in its Fourth Plenary Session, the CLRAE issued a Recommendation to the Committee of Ministers for the elaboration of a project of international convention on the European Charter of Regional Self-Government,[32] following the same process as the European Charter of Local Self-Government, with the intention of leaving the Convention project open to the signature of the member states on the occasion of the fiftieth anniversary of the Council of Europe, in its session of 5 May 1999.

The objective of this document is to guarantee regional self-government at an international level and to secure its major principles. The Charter deals with the regulation of the following matters: legal foundation and definition of regional self-government, as well as its legal protection; types and areas of competences in the regions; institutional organization and financing of the regions; relations between regional and local authorities; inter-regional relations; participation of the regions in affairs of the state, as well as in European and international institutions.

Without wishing to make a detailed study of its content, we can look at some of these aspects. The Charter does not give a precise definition of the term 'region'. Such an attempt would have been complicated and controversial, given the institutional diversity of the various member states. The definition would necessarily have been reductionist given the variety of the regional phenomenon. This would have made a consensus virtually impossible.[33] With a much more moderate sense and following the example of the European Charter of Local Self-Government, the regional charter establishes a framework definition with the title 'The Principle of Regional Self-Government',[34] which allows it to adapt to the evolutionary and varied character of the regional reality.

In this pragmatic perspective and following a formula already tried in the European Charter of Local Self-Government, and in order to help the evolution of the processes of regionalization and to adapt to the diversity of institutional situations in the member states, the project established that the states which cannot adhere to it in its entirety, due to their weak regionalization, can restrict themselves to certain articles and reserve others.[35]

The document does not contain an abstract description of the ideal region, as this is not its objective. Rather, it is concerned with the adoption of a legal instrument, valid in at least the 40 states which today compose the Council of Europe. The Charter therefore has a reasonable chance of adapting to European institutional realities (Levrat, 1996).

It must be pointed out, once again, that the European Charter of Regional Self-Government still has a long way to go until it becomes an International Convention open to the signature and ratification by the member states of the Council of Europe. But the model of the European Charter of Local Self-Government from which it has come, and the extremely positive role which this has played, makes us think that there will not be any insuperable obstacles for the project to reach its final destination, becoming an international treaty in its own right.

CONCLUSIONS

Once again it is the *Great Europe* of the Council of Europe which is in the vanguard of regional representation. This organization was the first to introduce substate representatives into its structures, and was therefore the precedent for what is today becoming a Europe of the Regions, and now it is attempting to respond to the principal demand of the European regionalist movement, that is, singularized and differentiated representation between regional and local bodies.

This ambition has today become a question which the European institutions have to face in a political framework in which the territorial powers are playing an ever more important role in various policy areas. Although the variations among the regional institutions are important, there are much wider differences between the regional and the local levels, due to their different political nature and functions.

It is the Council of Europe, in its territorial structure – the Congress of Local and Regional Powers – which has pioneered this differentiated representation. It can be said that this is the principal achievement of the CLRAE since its creation in 1994. Certainly, the European Charter of Regional Self-Government is an important project. When the project becomes a reality, Europe will have a framework of reference for European regional reality, above all in those states of central and eastern Europe for which the regions should become instruments for the promotion of democracy. The European Charter of Regional Self-Government does not offer a fixed definition of the term "region', but rather lays down general criteria. This is understood in a dynamic form which is at the same time evolutionary and pragmatic. The reference which this offers, as well as the fruits of its labour, serves as a catalyst and helps to give a little more substance to the third level in the European politics.

NOTES

1. The idea of scale, suggested by Balme, shows that the government works on the basis of a territorial representation of the exercising of political activity. This territorial paradigm could evolve and be modified and as a consequence, change its scale. The notions of global village or Europe of Regions are significant images of such a change in territorial representation as a result of political or economic decisions. This way politics is converted into a modulable institution, where a kind of variable geometry of political action exists.

2. Experience showed that the Framework Convention was an important text from a political point of view because of its symbolic value, for instance as a source of inspiration for later agreements, but quite a bit more limited in terms of its practical legal content, as it has not yet established any precise legal obligation whereby states can recognize the power of the territorial authorities to pass agreements of co-operation or to create transborder institutions, as more relevant limitations. In order to complement its content, the Council of Europe has formed two Additional Protocols, the first passed by the Council of Ministers on 9 November 1995, explicitly establishes that the agreements of cross-border co-operation which the territorial authorities form will have the same effects as the accords who perform in their respective legal state orders; the second, passed by the Council of Ministers on 17 March 1998, recognizes the right to sign twinning agreements and fix the legal framework for them. This second Protocol has been open to the signature of member states since 5 May 1998, to come into effect three months after its ratification by four member states.

3. In May 1998, it came into effect in Austria, Bulgaria, Croatia, Cyprus, Denmark, Estonia, Finland, Germany, Greece, Hungary, Iceland, Italy, Latvia, Liechtenstein, Luxembourg, Malta, Moldavia, The Netherlands, Norway, Poland, Portugal, Slovenia, Spain, Sweden, Former Yugoslavian Republic of Macedonia, Turkey, Ukraine and Romania. It was also signed by Belgium, France, Ireland, Lithuania, Russia and the United Kingdom.

4. In effect since 1 March 1998 for Croatia, Finland, Hungary, Liechtenstein, The Netherlands, Norway, and Sweden from 1 April 1998. This Charter is destined to impede the decline of regional or minority language, an essential aspect of European cultural heredity, and contribute to developing them and promoting their use. On its objectives, principles, execution, etc. (Fenet, 1995)

5. This Convention would extend to all the European Regions, whatever their geographic location, the controlling rule of the relations between the Regions that the Agreement of 1980 had exclusively limited to the border territories. The project confirms the explicit recognition of the right of the territorial collectives to maintain relations of inter-territorial co-operation and, especially, to form agreements of co-operation in the area of their competition. The Project is currently being examined by the Council of Ministers.

6. In effect since 1 February 1998, it was ratified on 31 January 1998: Croatia, Cyprus, Denmark, Estonia, Finland, Germany, Hungary, Moldavia, Rumania, San Marino, Slovakia, Spain, Former Yugoslavian Republic of Macedonia, Italy, Liechtenstein, Czech Republic, Ukraine and the United Kingdom. With this Agreement the Contracting Parts basically promise to fight against discrimination, promote full and effective equality between national minorities and majorities, to promote, conserve and develop the culture of national minorities, such as preserving their identity, language, religion and tradition (Benoît Rohmer, 1996: 39).

7. Resolution Statutaire (94)3 relative a l'instiution du Congres des Pouvoirs Locaux et Regionaux de l'Europe (adoptée par le Comité des Ministres le 14 janvier 1994 lors de la 506e réunion des Délégués des Ministres). Through a Statutory Resolution, the Committee of Ministers of the Council of Europe makes decisions which affect the Statute of the Organization, without altering its articles, until a formal revision is produced.

8. In any case, the nature of the new CLRAE is not clear. However, it is evident that its range within Organization has noticeably grown, the Congress is not included in the closed lists of organs of the Council of Europe (Article 10 of the Statute of Organization, establishes that 'the organs of the Council of Europe are: 1. the Committee of Ministers; 2. the Parliamentary Assembly). An amendment would be required to modify the Statute of the Council of Europe, with the resulting signature and ratification by all the member states for article 10 to

include the CLRAE as an organ of the Council of Europe. Such an act has not occurred, so that, strictly speaking, we cannot affirm that the CLRAE is an organ of the Council of Europe, but it is not a mere consultative committee (Grau Tanner, 1997).

9. See Article 2.2 of the Statutory Resolution.
10. See Article 3 of the Statutory Resolution and article 2.1 of the Charter. Consequently, they would have to abandon the CLRAE if they lost such a local or regional electoral mandate (article 2.5 of the Charter).
11. See Article 3.1 of the Charter.
12. See Article 2.2 of the Charter
13. See Article 5 of the Interior Regulations of the CLRAE, currently there are three Political Groups constituted: Socialist, European Popular Party and the Liberal Democratic Independent Group.
14. Distributed through the states in the following way: Albania (4); Germany (18); Andorra (2); Austria (6); Belgium (7); Bulgaria (6); Croatia (5); Czech Republic (7); Cyprus (3); Denmark (5); Slovakia (5); Slovenia (3); Spain (12); Estonia (3); Finland (5); France (18); Greece (7); Holland (7); Hungary (7); Ireland (4); Iceland (3); Italy (18); Latvia (3); Liechtenstein (2); Lithuania (4); Luxembourg (3); Malta (3); Ex Yugoslavian Republic of Macedonia (3), Moldavia (5); Norway (5); Poland (12); Portugal (7); Rumania (10); United Kingdom (18); Russia (18); San Marino (2); Sweden (6); Switzerland (6); Turkey (12); Ukraine (12).
15. See Article 6 of the Charter.
16. See Article 8.1 of the Charter.
17. See Article 5.1 of the Charter. It should also be pointed out that the CLRAE has an ordinary session each year, the same as each of the two component Chambers.
18. See Article 12.1 of the Charter.
19. The Assembly of European Regions is the principle forum of regional representation in Europe. It currently includes almost 300 Regions from 25 European states (Castro Ruano, 1994; Beltran García and Pinol Rull, 1997)
20. The Charter of the CLRAE was adopted by the Council of Europe Committee of Ministers, 4 January 1994, and the established transitory period will be finalized six years later.
21. This option has been discussed in the Parliamentary Assembly. Indeed the Assembly has suggested the reduction of the transitory period from six to three years, and the temporary overrepresentation of some states in order to maintain the number of components in both the regional and the local powers chambers. See Council of Europe, Rapport sur les régions au Conseil de l'europe et la mise en place du CPLRE, 13 January 1995, Doc.7220.
22. See Resolution 1 (1994) on the regulation of the CLRAE.
23. See Resolution 8 (1994) on the Conference on 'Regionalisation in Europe: Evaluation and Perspectives' (Geneva, 3–5 June 1993): ...The Congress...invites the Chamber of Regions and the Chamber of Local Authorities to draw up a "European Charter of Regional Self-Government" along the lines of the European Charter of Local Self-Government in co-operation with the Parliamentary Assembly, as stipulated in paragraph 23 of the Geneva Declaration...'. See Recommendation 6 (1994).
24. Resolution 35 (1996) on North/South Local Democracy: The European Charter of Local Self-Government in Action.
25. Resolution 37 (1996) on the European Charter of Regional Self-Government, passed by the Chamber of Regions, 3 July 1996, and adopted by the Standing Commission of the Congress 5 July 1996.
26. Recommendation 22 (1996) on the European Charter of Regional Self-Government.
27. Resolution 39 (1996) on Local Democracy Embassies. A Contribution to Democratic Security. Local embassies will be established by an agreement between, on the one hand, a host local authority in selected European countries approved the Congress Bureau – Bosnia and Herzegovina, Croatia, 'The Former Yugoslav Republic of Macedonia', the Federal Republic of Yugoslavia and Slovenia – and a number of European local authorities who are prepared to keep a permanent staff on the spot for the purpose of encouraging or preserving the democratic process via confidence-building measures. The aims of local embassies are the following: to foster peaceful co-existence and the development of civil society, to strengthen the democratic process where it exists and to establish confidence building

measures, to combat racism, intolerance and xenophobia and to promote dialogue and mediation, as well as socio-economic co-operation.
28. See Recommendation 14 (1995) on the European Charter of Mountain Regions.
29. Resolutions 13 and 14 (1995).
30. Resolution 34 (1996) on Monitoring the implementation of the European Charter of Local Self-Government.
31. The Resolution 8 (1994) announces the intention to elaborate a Project of European Charter of Regional Self-Government, in co-operation with the Parliamentary Assembly.
32. Recommendation 34 (1997) which includes the final draft of the European Charter of Regional Self-Government.
33. In other contexts it interesting to remind that this difficulty to achieve consensus in such a topic was clearly showed during the debate on the European Charter of Regionalization in the European Parliament, which finally was incorporated as an annex to the Resolution on the Regional Policy and the Role of the Regions –OJEC No.C326, 19 December 1988 (Castro, 1994: 322)
34. See Article 3 of the European Charter of Regional Self-Government, which defines regional self-government in the following terms: 'Regional government denotes the right and the ability of the largest territorial authorities within each state, having elected bodies, being administratively placed between central government and local authorities and enjoying prerogatives either of self-organisation or of a type normally associated with the central authority, to manage, on their own responsibility and in the interests of their populations, a substantial share of public affairs in accordance with the principle of subsidiarity'.
35. See Point 2 of Article 20 on Undertakings and Reservations: 'In order to take account of the diversity and developing nature of regional situations in European States, States shall be authorized to enter reservations.'

REFERENCES

Albanese, F. (1994), 'El proceso de descentralización del Consejo de Europa' in *Revista Vasca de Administración Pública*, No.40 (II).

Balme, R (1996), 'Pourquoi le gouvernement change-t-il d'échelle?' in R. Balme (Dir.), *Les Politiques du néo-régionalisme* (Paris: Economica).

Beltran Garcia, S. and J.L. Piñol i Rull (1997), 'La contribución de la Asamblea de las Regiones de Europa (ARE) al desarrollo de las acciones internacionales de las Comunidades Autónomas', in *Informe Pi i Sunyer sobre Comunidades Autónomas 1995–1996* (Barcelona: Fundació Carles Pi i Sunyer d'Estudis Autonómics i Locals).

Benôit-Rohmer, F. (1996), *La question minoritaire en Europe. Vers un systéme cohérent de protection des minorités nationales* (Strasbourg: Editions du Conseil de l'Europe).

Bullman, U. (1996), 'The Politics of the Third Level', *Regional and Federal Studies*, Vol.6, No.2.

Camilleri, J.A. and J. Falk (1992), *The End of Sovereignty: The Politics of a Shrinking and Fragmenting World* (Aldershot: Edward Elgar).

Castro Ruano, J.L. de (1994), *La emergente participación politicade las Regiones en el proceso de construcción europea* (Oñati: Instituto Vasco de Administración).

Castro Ruano, J.L. de, A. Borja, *et al.* (eds) (1994), *Cooperación transfronteriza Euskadi-Aquitania: Aspectos políticos, económicos, y de Relaciones Internacionales* (Leioa: Servicio Editorial de la Universidad del País Vasco).

Clotet i Miro, M.A. (1992), *La cooperación internacional de los municipios en el marco del Consejo de Europa. La obra de la Conferencia Permanente de Poderes Locales y Regionales de Europa* (Madrid: Cìvitas).

Diego Casals, J.L. (1994), 'El proyecto de convención sobre la Cooperación Interterritorial' in *Cursos de Derecho International de Vitoria-Gasteiz,* 1993 (Madrid: Tecnos/ Servicio Editorial de la Universidad del País Vasco).

Fenet. A. (Dteur.) (1995), *Le droit et les minorités* (Bruxelles: Etablissements Emile Bruylant).

Ferguson, Y.H. and R.W. Mansbach (1992), 'The Subject is Politics', *Paneuropean Conference on International Relations*, Heidelberg.

Fernandez de Casadevante, C. (1985), *La frontera hispano-francesa y las relaciones de vecindad* (Leioa: Servicio Editorial de la Universidad del País Vasco).

Fernandez de Casadevante, C. (1990), *La cooperación Transfronteriza en el Pirineo: su gestión por las Comunidades Autónomas* (Oñati: Instituto Vasco de Administración Pública).

Garcia Segura, C. (1996), 'La actividad exterior de las entidades políticas subestatales', *Revista de Estudios Políticos*, No.91.

Grau Tanner, C. (1997), La representacion institutional de los entes locales ante los organismos europeos', in *La posición institucional de la Administración Local en el S.XXI*, a course directed by Demetrio Loperena in Summer Courses in Donostia-San Sebastian (paper provided by the author).

Hocking, B. (1996), 'Bridging Boundaries: Creating Linkages. Non-central Governments and Multilayered Policy Environments', *Welt Trends*, No.11.

Jauregui, G. (1997), *Los nacionalismos minoritarios y la Unión Europea* (Barcelona: Ariel).

Jeffery C. (1996), 'Sub-National Authorities and "European Domestic Policy" in *Regional & Federal Studies*, Vol.6, No.2 (special issue C. Jeffery, ed., *The Regional Dimension of the European Union: Towards a Third Level in Europe?)*

Keating, M. (1997) 'Les régions constituent-elles un niveau de gouvernement en Europe?' in P. Le Gales and C. Lequesne, *Les paradoxes des régions en Europe* (Paris: Editions La Découverte).

Kramer, R. (1995) 'Catching Up or Setting Up a New Agenda? East German Länder International Involvement: The Case of Brandenburg', in *Second Pan-European Conference on International Relations*, Paris.

Levrat, N. (1994) *Le droit applicable aux accords de coopération transfrontière entre collectivités infraétatiques* (Paris: Presses Universitaires de France).

Levrat, N. (1997) 'Assessment and perspectives of regionalism and regionalisation in Europe' in Assembly Of European Regions, *The Regions in the construction of Europe*. Proceedings of the Seminar organized by the ARE aln Alsace Regional Council. 22nd may 1996.

Loughlin, J. (1996) 'Representing Regions in Europe : The Committee of The Regions' in *Regional and Federal Studies*, Vol. 6, no. 2,

Palard, J. (Dteur) (1997) *L'Europe aux frontières* (Paris: Presses Universitaires de France).

Perez Gonzalez, M. (1995) 'La coopération interrérgional et sa possible couverture conventionnelle' in AA:VV; *Le droit appliqué a la coopération interrégionale en Europe* (Paris: Librairie Générale de Droit et de Jurisprudence).

Roseanu, J,N. and Durke, M.(1995) *Thinking Theory Thoroughly, Coherent Approaches to an Incoherent World* (Boulder: Westview Press).

The International Competence of US States and Their Local Governments

JOHN KINCAID

The 50 states of the United States of America possess limited international competence derived from their (1) constitutional authority to engage the international arena in limited ways as states but not as nation-states, (2) political freedom to pursue state–local interests internationally, and (3) governmental capacity to act independently in the international arena. Such competencies were exercised in varying degrees by a number of states during the late eighteenth and early nineteenth centuries. The exercise of such competencies fell largely dormant during the late nineteenth century and much of the twentieth century as the United States emerged as a superpower and as the US economy generated sufficient capital, consumption, and exports to satisfy the needs of most states.

International competencies began to be resurrected during the late 1950s, however, as southern states – embattled by economic stagnation and by federal pressure to abolish racial segregation and to modernize their polities – sought to promote exports and attract foreign investment. As the US economy entered a decade-long period of stagflation in 1973, as the so-called Rustbelt (northern urban-industrial) states experienced huge losses of manufacturing jobs, and as global economic competition became increasingly evident, states outside the South also began to look abroad (Kincaid, 1984). Today, therefore, among other activities, the US states have approximately 183 offices in foreign countries (whereas only three states had foreign offices in 1970); all states have at least one 'sister-state' relationship abroad; and more than 1,100 municipalities have some 1,775 'sister cities' in 123 nations.

CONSTITUTIONAL COMPETENCE

Although many of the framers of the US Constitution of 1787, especially James Madison and Alexander Hamilton, advocated the creation of a strong union government, the prevailing political ideas and practices of their era required extensive concessions to the 13 states. Consequently, while the US Constitution delegates clear powers of international competence to the federal government, it does not delegate all such powers to the federal government, nor does it deny states all international competence. Yet, it is difficult to specify precisely either the outer limits on federal powers or the full extent of state powers because the US Constitution is vague about most of these matters and because it contains no concurrent list of federal and state powers. Furthermore, the Tenth Amendment (1791) to the US Constitution reserves 'to the States respectively, or to the People', all 'powers not delegated to the United States by the Constitution, nor prohibited by it to the States.' Hence, authority for state and local international activity has rested largely on constitutional interpretation, political practice, historical tradition, and intergovernmental comity.

The US Constitution prohibits certain state actions. Principally, Article I, Section 10 announces unequivocally that: 'No State shall enter into any Treaty, Alliance, or Confederation; [or] grant Letters of Marque and Reprisal.' These are, however, the only absolute prohibitions of state action in foreign affairs. Other prohibitions are implied in specific powers delegated to the federal government, such as congressional authority to declare war and presidential authority to receive ambassadors from foreign governments.

Additional limits on the states are politically conditional. These are as follows:

> No State shall, without the consent of the Congress, lay any Imposts or Duties on Imports or Exports, except what may be absolutely necessary for executing its inspection Laws; and the net Produce of all Duties and Imposts, laid by any State on Imports or Exports, shall be for the Use of the Treasury of the United States, and all such Laws shall be subject to the Revision and Controul of the Congress.

> No State shall, without the Consent of the Congress, lay any duty of tonnage, keep Troops, or Ships of War in time of Peace, enter into any Agreement or Compact with another State, or with a foreign Power, or engage in War, unless actually invaded, or in such imminent Danger as will not admit of delay (Article I, Section 10).

In short, the US Constitution envisions limited state international action subject to the consent of the Congress as the superintending authority acting on behalf of all the states. Given that the Congress consists of representatives from the states and that the US Senate was originally composed of two senators from each state selected by the legislature of each state (until 1913), the framers of the federal Constitution apparently expected the Congress to approve, as well as to deny, various state international activities.

The states also possess implicit international competencies in fields not occupied by the federal government under its constitutional authority. For example, even though plenary power 'to regulate Commerce with foreign Nations' is delegated to the US Congress, the states can regulate, tax, and otherwise act in this field so long as (1) the Congress does not enact legislation to preempt specific state action, and (2) the US Supreme Court does not strike down a specific state law as a violation of the Court's 'dormant commerce clause' doctrine. State taxation of foreign and multinational corporations, for instance, has long been a matter of some domestic and international controversy.

An expectation of state international competence is also suggested in the federal Constitution's judicial article (Article III, Section 2), which states that: 'The judicial Power of the United States shall extend to all Cases...[or] Controversies between a State, or the Citizens thereof, and foreign States, Citizens or Subjects.' This provision does not prohibit state international activity; it simply assures that conflicts arising between US states and foreign states can be contained and adjudicated by the federal courts before such conflict inflames relations between the United States and a foreign nation or results in an injustice because of the absence of an impartial judicial forum in the effected US states.

The federal Constitution's strict and narrowly drawn treason provision in Article III, Section 3 also suggests that the Constitution's framers contemplated international activity on the part of both private citizens and state and local government officials. This provision is so strict that it is extremely difficult to convict a US citizen of treason. Although the Congress weakened this provision in 1799 by passing the Logan Act to prevent private citizens, including state officials, from contacting foreign governments and attempting to influence their behaviour 'in relation to any disputes or controversies with the United States', no one was ever successfully prosecuted for violating the law. Hence, private citizens and representatives of state and local governments possess substantial freedom to engage the international arena, even in ways strongly critical of US policies. When some cities, for example, established sister-city relations with cities in Nicaragua and provided aid to those cities during the Sandinista era in defiance of US foreign policy, the administration of President Ronald Reagan (1981–89) was unable to abrogate those relationships or to punish local government officials.

Put differently, in the federal Constitution, the international competencies of the US states are more implicit than explicit. As with many other policy matters, the framers of the US Constitution did not attempt to resolve all such matters definitively and explicitly in 1787; instead, many matters were left to the political process and to the vagaries of history.

The states, which are mentioned 50 times in 42 sections of the US Constitution (Lutz, 1988), also have institutionalized voices in foreign policy making as well as formal mechanisms for endeavouring to protect their interests against adverse foreign policies or foreign actions through 'the political safeguards' of federalism (Wechsler, 1954; Palumbo, 1969). These 'safeguards' pertain mainly to the composition of the federal government, in which the states are equally represented in the US Senate and are represented on the basis of population size in the US House of Representatives. The electoral college system of electing presidents also gives large states and small states enhanced voices in the selection of presidents. In addition, the US Senate (the states' house) has important exclusive powers relevant to state interests in foreign policy. These are the requirements that treaties be ratified by two-thirds of the senators present (though this is a lower threshold than two-thirds of the Senate membership) and that presidential nominations of, for example, new members of the US Supreme Court and lower federal courts, Cabinet secretaries (including the Secretary of State), ambassadors, other public ministers and consuls, and many other federal officers be approved by the US Senate. Consequently, foreign policy making on matters of great significance to the states and their local governments often involves intergovernmental bargaining (federal–state–local) (Kline, 1983).

Finally, the federal Constitution affords the states a partnership role in national defence. From 1789 to the Second World War, the United States Army remained small, as did the Navy too, because of public fear of a standing army during peacetime and the generally isolationist sentiments of most Americans. With the outbreak of war, therefore, the US Army swelled with state militia units called into federal service by the president. Since the Second World War, these state units (called the National Guard – army and air force) have been largely absorbed into the 'total force structure' of the US military for deployment purposes, and they must stand ready (with federal aid) to be called up quickly for service in time of war, such as the Persian Gulf War, or international police actions. In 1995, moreover, the US Supreme Court interpreted broadly the president's power to deploy Guard units abroad, even over governors' objections (*Perpich*, 1990; Beckman, 1991).

National Guard units also perform domestic defence tasks. For example, more than 90 per cent of the interceptor missions flown daily to protect the continental air space of the United States are carried out by state Air Guard units. Otherwise, however, as has always been true since 1789, each state governor commands and deploys their National Guard forces for local police and rescue missions. Although Guard units are, as provided by the US Constitution, trained according to US military rules prescribed by Congress, National Guard officers are appointed by the states, and Guard units perform most of their duties for their states, not the federal government (US Advisory Commission on Intergovernmental Relations, 1993).

Local governments derive their authority to act internationally from the same sources, though indirectly so because they are legal creatures of their state, and they are additionally subject to state constitutional and statutory rules. However, given the tradition of local self-government in the United States, the states have enacted few rules targeted at local international activities. Local governments are generally free to pursue their international interests within the state rules that govern them generally.

In summary, while the US Constitution establishes the international personality of the United States and grants the federal government sufficient powers to conduct the nation's foreign affairs, to allow the United States to speak with one voice internationally, and to engage in war, the Constitution does not deprive the states or, indirectly, local governments of all international competence or deny them access to foreign policy making.

GOVERNMENTAL COMPETENCE

State exercises of international competencies since 1789 have been aimed overwhelmingly at commerce and economic development. State and local officials, tied closely to their voters, tend to be pragmatic, home-grown, and service-oriented. States have not, therefore, sought to assert distinctive international personalities or to claim diplomatic rights, nor has the federal government had need to suppress or police state actions. Early in the nineteenth century, the states accepted the international personality of the United States and, with few exceptions, did little to disrupt or interfere with the diplomacy of the nation. Since the War of 1812, when some states threatened to secede because of the war, there have been few state challenges to the pre-eminence of federal authority in foreign affairs and national defence, although states have often made use of the political safeguards of federalism to protect their interests in foreign policy making and defence spending. Consequently, there has been little fundamental federal–state conflict over these matters, and the federal government's attitudes towards state exercises of international competence have ordinarily ranged from forbearing toleration to supportive co-operation.

Early History

Why the states readily accepted federal pre-eminence and limited their exercises of international competence cannot be definitively explained, but a combination of factors appears to have been important. For most of the nineteenth century, the federal government was slow to exercise its commerce powers. Regulation and taxation of domestic and foreign commerce rested mostly with the states, some of which acted vigorously in these fields. At the same time, most of the diplomatic activities of the United States posed little threat to state interests. Americans were also primarily inward-looking and frontier-focused, especially after British, French, Russian and Spanish military forces were driven out of what is now the continental United States during the first half of the nineteenth century, and after the War of 1812 reduced foreign naval threats to US shipping on the high seas. President George Washington's 1797 admonition to avoid 'permanent entangling alliances' with foreign powers had also reinforced a powerful isolationist sentiment, still evident among many Americans.

No region, with the partial exception of the South, has had enduring interests fundamentally antithetical to the foreign policy interests of the United States. Furthermore, unlike Canada with Quebec in its federation, or Spain with the Basque Country and Catalonia, the United States has never had a strong, territorially concentrated national, ethnic, religious, or linguistic group desirous of asymmetric domestic autonomy or a distinct international personality. American Indian tribes were the only partial exceptions, but their subjugated condition, scattered locations, small sizes, and legal status as 'domestic dependent nations' (*Cherokee Nation*, 1831) have all muffled their international voice. Otherwise, as a nation of immigrants, Americans placed a strong emphasis on assimilation and on a conviction that 'politics stops at the water's edge'. Although a number of states sent agents to Europe to recruit immigrants, especially from regions of the same or similar ethnic stock as the states' residents, they did not seek to foment ethnic conflict, nor could they, in any event, build ethnically homogeneous states. Such recruitment became unnecessary during the latter half of the nineteenth century when more than 60 million Europeans emigrated to the United States on their own accord.

During the union's early decades, there were occasional federal–state conflicts over international obligations. In 1796, for instance, the US Supreme Court voided a Virginia statute that would have cancelled a debt to a British subject owed by a Virginia citizen because the state law violated the Treaty of Paris. Three decades later, however, the federal government was unable to enforce a US-British commercial convention against South Carolina, which had imprisoned black British seamen under an 1823 state law. After other southern states took similar action, Great Britain opened consulates in the South and negotiated with state officials to gain the release of their seamen and obtain changes in the laws.

The principal internationally relevant intergovernmental conflicts during the nineteenth century centred on federal tariff policies that usually benefited the industrial North and disadvantaged the agricultural South. In 1832, for example, South Carolina threatened to mobilize its militia to prevent federal enforcement of the 1828 'Tariff of Abominations', but President Andrew Jackson's counterthreat to send US forces into South Carolina caused the state to retreat; then, the following year, Congress began reducing the tariff from an average duty of 92 per cent to 20 per cent. Consequently, while the federal government rarely failed to assert its powers against direct state challenges to its authority, the federal government rarely threatened state interests, the states rarely challenged federal authority (except for the southern states that seceded from the union and precipitated the Civil War in 1861), and the federal government found numerous ways to satisfy state concerns.

By the time the United States asserted its international personality more forcefully and even imperialistically during the late nineteenth century, the states had little reason or incentive to interfere with federal prerogatives. The Civil War (1861–65) had settled the question of secession and, indirectly, repudiated any notions of state international personalities or diplomatic status. (The federal government still regards the states as 'non-governmental' actors in international affairs.) The United States had also achieved economic independence by the mid-1890s insofar as its economy created most of its own capital, produced most of the goods and services needed to meet domestic demand, and generated a growing volume of exports. At the same time, concerns about assimilating and securing the loyalty of millions of immigrants led state and local officials to avoid assertions of international competencies and foreign policy interests that could trigger ethnic resentments. The Senate's refusal to ratify the League of Nations Treaty after the First World War, moreover, while not directly a result of state-government opposition, nevertheless tarnished even the states' intergovernmental role in foreign policy making.

During the first half of the twentieth century, therefore, the federal government acquired a thickening patina of virtually exclusive and plenary competence over foreign affairs and foreign policy, which was accepted by state and local officials, regarded as legitimate by the general citizenry, and supported by the US Supreme Court. As the Court's majority opined in 1936: 'In respect of our foreign relations generally, state lines disappear...As to such purposes, the State of New York does not exist' (*United States*, 1936).

Nevertheless, in 1947 the US Supreme Court upheld a California statute that affected international affairs but did not contradict federal statutes. In making its ruling, the Court rejected as 'farfetched' the US solicitor general's argument that the federal government possesses a reservoir of inherent, unwritten foreign policy powers that override state powers (*Clark*, 1947). In 1968, though, the Court asserted its authority to void state laws or local ordinances that have 'a direct impact upon foreign relations [which] may well adversely affect the power of the central government to deal with problems' of foreign affairs (*Zschernig*, 1968), even though the US Department of State had no objection to state–local action in this case. This ruling, however, has not provided clear guidance for the federal government or functioned as a severe limit on state and local action. The ruling was also soon criticized by a prominent constitutional scholar: 'What the Constitution says about foreign affairs provides little basis for the Court's doctrine...Nor is there support for *Zschernig* in the history of the Constitution in practice' (Henkin, 1972: 476).

The final result is that state and local actions in the international arena are governed more by custom, political practice, and intergovernmental comity than by enforcement of constitutional and statutory rules. The federal government does not unduly interfere with state and local international activities, and state and local governments do not unduly interfere with federal prerogatives or sensitive foreign policy issues. For the most part, state and local governments exercise economic, social, cultural and educational competencies internationally. The states also accord their local governments substantial freedom to engage in international activities and to lobby the federal government on behalf of their own foreign-affairs interests.

Contemporary History

States, and then local governments, began to reassert international competencies during the late 1950s. Such actions were initiated primarily by southern states which, having long recruited aggressively and often successfully in the northern states for manufacturing plants and investment capital, turned their attention abroad as well, for manufacturing facilities and investment capital. The northern states began to follow the same path during the 1970s when it became apparent that their economies were declining, because of the closing of the urban-industrial era and the rise of a service economy, the increase of international economic competition, and the long-term stagflation and then slower growth of the US economy. The Vietnam War also played a role because the rise of vigorous and culturally divisive dissent over the war fractured the previously elite 'foreign policy establishment' in Washington, DC, and democratized foreign policy making by admitting many more voices into the process, including the voices of members of Congress (who had often previously deferred to presidential judgements), diverse interest groups, ethnic groups, environmentalists, state and local governments, and others. Some state and local officials criticized US involvement in the Vietnam War, and anti-war protesters often sought resolutions from state legislatures and city councils condemning the war (Kincaid, 1989). Hence, the notion that 'politics stops at the water's edge' was eroded by the unpopularity of the war and by the increasing interrelationship between domestic policy making and foreign policy making, giving rise to what one observer has called 'intermestic affairs' (Manning, 1977).

Since the 1970s, there has been a steady, though slow, institutionalization of international capacities in state governments and big-city governments. Virtually every governor's office and state executive bureaucracy now has offices and personnel devoted wholly or partially to international affairs, primarily economic affairs, and to foreign policy making (mostly trade policy) in Washington, DC. Many state legislatures have at least one international affairs committee in one legislative chamber (49 states have a bicameral legislature). On average, the states also have more than three foreign offices each – mostly in Western Europe, Japan, South Korea and Mexico – devoted mainly to export promotion, investment attraction and tourism. Indeed, states have more offices in Tokyo than in Washington, DC. Similar institutional developments have been occurring in big-city governments, although cities have very few offices or contract representatives in foreign countries.

International capacities and activities have also been institutionalized within the 'Big 7' national associations of state and local governments: the National Governors' Association, Council of State Governments, National Conference of State Legislatures, National Association of Counties, US Conference of Mayors, National League of Cities, and International City/County Management Association. Many regional organizations that include state and local governments as well as private-sector interests, such as the Southern Growth Policies Board, also have international components. These national and regional organizations facilitate interstate co-operation where possible and disseminate information to state and local governments.

These institutions are new, and their number surpasses previous levels of state and local international activity; however, 'international affairs' still constitutes a very small portion of state and local budgets and only a tiny sector of state and local bureaucracies. At best, state and local governments expend only about $250 million directly on international programmes (excluding investment incentives), which is less than .03 per cent of their total $1 trillion budgets. These institutions represent primarily a recognition that 'international affairs', especially economic affairs, is an increasingly important, often interesting, and permanent dimension of state and local governance requiring institutionalized competence, but not a dimension compelling sizeable expenditures or expansive bureaucratic effort. These institutions are likely to grow, therefore, but only slowly.

There appear to be several reasons for the small size of this dimension:

* The United States has a huge $8.2 trillion economy (the output of which constitutes nearly one-quarter of total world production); imports and exports together accounted for only about one-quarter of US Gross Domestic Product (GDP) in 1997 (compared to 10.9 per cent in 1970).

At the same time, though, global economic turbulence can severely affect particular regions and locales. In Minnesota's Twin Cities (Minneapolis and St. Paul), for example, St. Paul was affected in 1998 by 3M's plans to release some 4,000 employees because of plummeting sales in Asia. The company, which makes Scotch tape and Post-It Notes, had earned 23 cents out of every dollar of profits from Asian sales in 1997. Meanwhile, on the Minneapolis side of the Mississippi River, the 4.2 million-square-foot Mall of America was anticipating a record $800 million in sales from domestic consumption (Chandler, 1998).

- Voters have little understanding of the need for state and local international competence. In 1998, for example, 62 per cent of Americans confessed to having no knowledge 'about the issue of trade' (Conway, 1998). Many Americans also fear the effects of global economic competition. Polls have found 51 per cent of Americans believing that 'America's integration in global markets...mainly benefits multinational corporations at the expense of average working families,' while 64 per cent believe that 'trade agreements between the US and other nations cost more jobs than they create' (Public Citizen, 1998). Nevertheless, 59 per cent approve of trade agreements (Sarpolus, 1998). Question wording obviously affects public responses, indicating that public opinion in this field is ill-informed, fluid, and vulnerable to demagoguery, as was evident in the appeal of Pat Buchanan's economic protectionist message during the 1996 presidential primary elections when, among other things, he campaigned in Louisiana against 'communist crawfish' being illegally dumped on the US market by China (see also Buchanan, 1998).
- The strong emphasis on economic development in state and local international activities does not require large expenditures on bureaucratic and programmatic activities of an exclusively international nature. Moreover, the tax-resistant mood of the electorate since 1978 constrains state and local spending on programmes peripheral to key voter concerns.
- The United States is an attractive target for foreign investors in any event, thus alleviating any need for most states to desperately pursue foreign investment. During most of the 1980s and 1990s total foreign direct investment in the United States, which exceeds $750 billion, increased substantially.
- State and local governments rely greatly on private-sector business, non-profit institutions and civic organizations to help promote and protect state and local interests in the international arena. Many international social, cultural and educational activities, such as sister-city programmes, world affairs councils and world trade associations, are

conducted wholly or largely by non-governmental groups with state or local government participation but little or no direct tax support.

- State and local officials still regard domestic economic competition as being more significant than global economic competition. Although data on the attitudes of state officials are not available, a recent survey of US mayors (Kincaid with Handelsman, 1997) found that domestic economic competition far outweighs global economic competition as a municipal policy concern (see Table 1). State officials, especially governors, would probably give more weight than mayors to international competition, though not overwhelming weight.

TABLE 1

PERCEPTIONS OF US CITIES' MAJOR US COMPETITORS, RANK ORDERED, 1996

		Degree of Competition*	Per cent Very High/High
1.	Immediate metropolitan area	1785	65.3%
2.	Rest of your state	1591	46.3
3.	Next-door states	1559	45.1
4.	Southern states	1337	34.9
5.	Southwestern states	1235	24.8
6.	Western states	1200	23.6
7.	Midwestern states	1197	21.4
8.	Japan	1166	22.1
9.	Mexico	1136	18.5
10.	Asia (e.g. China, India, Thailand)	1117	17.2
11.	Northeastern states	1062	11.3
12.	Canada	1016	9.5
13.	Western Europe (European Union)	989	8.4
14.	Central and South America	935	7.4
15.	Middle East	842	3.4
16.	Eastern Europe	814	1.7
17.	Former Soviet Union	750	1.2
18.	Africa	734	1.0

Source: John Kincaid with Joshua L. Handelsman (1997), *American Cities in the Global Economy: A Survey of Municipalities on Activities and Attitudes* (Washington, DC: National League of Cities).

*The numbers in this column are weighted additions of the scale responses, as follows: 5N + 4N + 3N + 2N + 1N.

In summary, all the US states and all large cities possess considerable governmental capacity to exercise international competencies, and all have used such capacity to engage the international arena, but neither state governments nor local governments have plunged deeply into international affairs. Instead, they skim the surface of international affairs in search of specific benefits for their jurisdictions.

STATE ROLES

Given this background and context, one can delineate ten roles that have emerged for state governments, and often local governments too, in international affairs. Not all state or local governments fulfil all ten roles; emphasis on the various roles also varies with circumstances.

Partners in Foreign Policy Development

The political safeguards of federalism ensure state representation or influence in the legislative, executive and judicial branches of the federal government. Through the US Senate, especially, the states can assert their international interests as states of the union. On matters of foreign trade in particular, senators have become more attentive to the economic interests of their states. Local governments more often find allies in the US House of Representatives because House members are elected from smaller districts within each state, although House members are frequently more attuned to the concerns of interest groups within their districts than to the concerns of local government officials. In light of the growing interdependence of domestic and foreign affairs, state and local officials have increased their efforts to inform their congressional delegations of the potential impacts of foreign and foreign-trade policies on state and local economies.

The electoral college system magnifies the impact of large and small states on the presidency, thus requiring presidents to pay some extra attention to the interests of those states. This is one reason why California, which has the single largest impact on the electoral fortunes of presidents, has been able to shield some controversial tax policies affecting international business from federal assault. Neither Republican Ronald Reagan nor Democrat Bill Clinton wished to risk the wrath of California voters by openly and vigorously opposing the state's internationally relevant tax policies.

Beginning with the administration of Dwight D. Eisenhower (1953–61), presidents have often encouraged state international activity. The long-standing Pearson Fellowship Program, for example, allows about 14 foreign-service officers to spend a year working with a state or local government. Under John F. Kennedy's administration (1961–63), the US Department of Commerce encouraged states to become involved in international economic affairs. Commerce was then headed by Luther Hodges, former governor of North Carolina, who had led one of the states' first trade missions to Europe in 1959. Presidents Lyndon Johnson, Richard Nixon and Jimmy Carter also encouraged states to seek out foreign investment and promote exports. At the request of President Carter, the National Governors' Association formed a new standing committee in 1978 on International Trade and Foreign Relations.

New institutions have also been developed within the federal government to facilitate state and local representation in certain aspects of foreign policy making and also to promote intergovernmental co-operation. For example, the US Department of State has an intergovernmental affairs office that endeavours to channel state and local government concerns to appropriate officials and to respond to state and local needs for information, advice and technical support. An Intergovernmental Policy Advisory Committee to the Office of the US Trade Representative (USTR) was established in 1988 to advise the president on state and local government concerns in international trade and trade agreements. The US Department of Commerce has also improved its ability to provide state and local governments with data and other information relevant to their international economic concerns. Some states that operate export-financing programmes co-operate closely with the US Export-Import Bank and the US Small Business Administration. Relevant federal agencies, such as the USTR, have also encouraged governors to establish 'single points of contact' in their states in order to facilitate rapid communication and consultation. Thus, there have been new and co-operative institutionalized responses by the federal government to the institutionalization of international affairs in the states and big cities.

Paralleling the internationalization of state and local governments has been a growing internationalization of federal domestic agencies, some of whose activities intersect with those of state and local governments. A recent report by the US General Accounting Office (GAO) showed that spending on international affairs outside the federal government's 150 account, which funds US embassies and most foreign aid, equalled $7.6 billion for 70 different programmes in 1998. Interestingly, moreover, while 'the total number of US personnel posted in US diplomatic missions abroad has changed little over the past 10 years, the portion from domestic agencies has increased by 25 per cent, from about 8,000 positions in 1988 to over 10,000 in 1998' (GAO, 1998: 7). Thus, while the State Department has reduced staffing since 1988, domestic agencies have increased international staffing.

Pressure Points in Foreign Policy Making

State and local officials also lobby in Washington, DC on foreign policy issues that affect their jurisdiction's interests. They lobby as individual governments; they lobby together through regional organizations (for example, the Western Governors' Association); and they lobby through national organizations, such as the National Governors' Association (NGA) and the US Conference of Mayors (USCM). There is no constitutional barrier to this type of activity.

Governors, for example, were especially active in supporting President Clinton's efforts to obtain congressional approval of the North American Free Trade Agreement (NAFTA) in 1993 and the Uruguay Round of the General Agreement on Tariffs and Trade (GATT) in 1994. Forty governors publicly supported NAFTA and about an equal number supported GATT. During the GATT debate, there was also intense lobbying from the National Association of Attorneys General, the Multistate Tax Commission and other state organizations about state representation in dispute-resolution processes under the World Trade Organization (WTO) and in US compliance with WTO rulings that might require federal pre-emption (that is, displacement) of state law. State officials did not achieve their full agenda, but they achieved many concessions and compromises, including regular federal consultation with state officials and continuing attention to state and local government concerns.

Since presidential fast-track authority – which allows the president to bring trade agreements to Congress for a simple 'yes' or 'no' vote – expired in 1994, the National Governors' Association has urged renewal of fast-track authority. Most governors also support bringing Chile into NAFTA and creating a larger Free Trade Area of the Americas. Other currently prominent issues of concern to governors include more US funding for the International Monetary Fund, and congressional suspension of the implementation of Section 110 of the Illegal Immigration and Immigrant Responsibility Act of 1996 along the Canadian and Mexican borders. This act provides for an automated control system to document the entry and exit of every alien arriving and leaving the United States. Governors believe that implementation of the untested system will hamper cross-border trade and tourism.

State sovereignty is also an issue for the United States in the Multilateral Agreement on Investment (MAI) being negotiated in Paris under the auspices of the Organization for Economic Cooperation and Development. State and local officials argue that proposed provisions would severely limit state and local economic, land-use and environmental regulation; performance standards used to hold companies accountable when they receive government assistance; and state–local policies favouring local businesses.

Although state and local officials achieve some successes through lobbying, they are, nevertheless, consigned to what Robert Putnam has called Level II of 'two-level bargaining games', namely, domestic constituencies that are courted by, and seek to influence, the Level I bargainers in the White House and Congress who actually make foreign policy and conclude trade agreements (Putnam, 1988). As such, state and local officials must compete with all the other interest groups (such as business, labour, agriculture and environmental) in the federal arena where their interests also become conflated with those of these other groups. The votes and campaign contributions that can be delivered to members of Congress by private-sector interests often outweigh the democratically authoritative but largely voteless and penniless voices of state and local government officials. Thus, a recent analysis of bargaining over NAFTA did not even mention state and local officials as viable actors (Avery, 1998).

Self-Governing Political Communities

States and localities are self-governing political communities in their own right, having a full range of constitutional powers for domestic governance, including authority to promote public health, safety and welfare in ways that significantly affect interstate and foreign commerce. Through their powers of taxation, regulation, service provision and law enforcement, state and local governments also create climates in their jurisdictions that encourage or discourage a wide range of internationally relevant activity – especially trade, tourism and investment. Furthermore, states enforce and implement many provisions of US law, including treaties and trade agreements.

Domestic state regulatory powers can sometimes be projected into the international arena. Recently, for example, state insurance commissioners in California, New York, and Washington state helped spearhead an influential campaign, independent of the federal government but in co-operation with domestic Jewish constituencies, to pressure European insurance companies and Swiss banks to respond to claims made by Holocaust victims and their heirs. State officials are also helping potential beneficiaries to file, process and litigate claims, and pressure has developed in several states to place economic sanctions on recalcitrant banks and insurers.

State and local governments can wield financial muscle in the international arena. Two states – California and New York – rank among the top ten nation-states in terms of GDP; and even the GDPs of the poorest US states, such as Mississippi, outrank the GDPs of about 120 nation-states. The California economy alone is about the seventh largest in the world (ahead of China and slightly behind Italy); the Los Angeles metropolitan economy is about the twelfth largest (larger than Belgium, Sweden, Switzerland and Taiwan, respectively); and the budget of the government of California is larger than the budgets of most national governments. Consequently, for example, the political situation in South Africa during the apartheid era was considerably affected by US state and local policies requiring divestiture of state and local idle cash and pension funds, as well as refusals to purchase goods and services, from corporations that conducted business there. President Reagan attempted to overturn these state and local disinvestment policies as contrary to the foreign-policy interests of the United States, but he was unsuccessful.

Under WTO, however, it may become necessary and legally possible for the federal government to overturn state economic sanctions against foreign nations. Sanctions imposed on Cuba, Indonesia, Myanmar, Northern Ireland, Nigeria and Tibet by states – especially large states such as California, Massachusetts and New York – and many cities have drawn strong protests from the European Community and Japan, which have threatened to file complaints with the WTO. When Massachusetts enacted sanctions against Myanmar in 1996, the Office of the US Trade Representative sought, unsuccessfully, to persuade Governor William F. Weld to withdraw the sanctions. In 1997, the EU did file a WTO complaint, still pending, over Massachusetts' sanctions on Myanmar, and in 1998 a US business group, the National Foreign Trade Council, filed suit in court against Massachusetts, arguing that the sanctions are an unconstitutional intrusion into federal foreign-affairs powers. In November 1998, a federal district court struck down the Massachusetts sanctions. The state has appealed the ruling.

The principal challenges facing the self-governing autonomy of states and localities will be the long-term implementation of free-trade rules under NAFTA and WTO. These agreements potentially threaten to override a wide range of state and local powers of self-government (Weiler, 1994). For example, California's voter-initiated law (Proposition 65), which imposes a strict standard for labelling products containing chemicals known to cause cancer or birth defects, has drawn protests from many nations. State and local governments have achieved some protections and extended periods of compliance under NAFTA and WTO, but in the long run, the logic of free trade requires the obliteration of tariff and non-tariff trade barriers. In the United States, it is state and local policies that can most often be attacked as non-tariff trade barriers. The EU already has a sizeable list of US state laws it wishes to challenge under WTO, and many foreign enterprises wish to compete in the $250 billion state and local government procurement market.

Promoters of Area Interests

Perhaps the international role for which state and local governments are best known is that of promoters of their own interests in foreign markets. Through advertising, trade missions and foreign offices, state and local governments are seeking to promote exports of their products and to attract foreign investment and tourists. There has been a significant increase in these activities since the 1970s, and they are likely to continue increasing for the foreseeable future. Tourism is attractive, for example, because the US Department of Commerce estimates that 50 million international visitors to the United States in 1997 spent $75 billion during their stays. Although foreign visitors account for less than 15 per cent of US tourist business, it is a growing sector of the tourism industry and an important sector for Florida, California, New York and Hawaii which, together, captured 53 per cent of all foreign pleasure visitors in 1996.

States have undertaken many programmes of assistance to small and medium-size businesses having export potential (Nothdurft and Grossman, 1996). According to one estimate, '49 states currently offer export outreach or counselling to local businesses, 42 participate in "trade lead" matching programmes, 41 are involved in joint-venture agreements which assist businesses to become involved in international commerce, 38 sponsor trade development seminars and conferences, 21 publish international newsletters, and an equal number provide export financing, mainly in the form of loan guarantees' (Fry, 1998). States have also become more creative about identifying products for export, as reflected in Oklahoma's 1998 decision to treat foreign student education as an export. The state is advertising its universities through its overseas offices, the major selling point being that Oklahoma's universities have the lowest out-of-state tuitions in the United States.

Governors and mayors, of course, have long been active in leading trade missions abroad (Kincaid, 1984). 'In 1993, governors from 27 states and territories directed 81 trips abroad for economic development purposes' (Fry, 1998). Members of Congress also assist in promoting their states and districts, not only when travelling abroad but also by arranging for diplomats and other dignitaries to visit their state or district to explore trade opportunities, exchange ideas, and sometimes stay overnight in constituents' homes.

Again, systematic data on the range of state activities are not available, but a recent survey of mayors provides some evidence of the scope and frequency of various internationally relevant municipal activities (see Table 2).

Controversies in this field less often involve federal–state issues than interstate and intrastate issues. Although states and localities frequently co-operate on such matters as export promotion and tourism, the attraction of foreign investment frequently sparks keen competition between states and between local communities. The public, moreover, is divided over the wisdom of attracting foreign investment ('the selling of America'), certain methods of attracting investment ('tax giveaways'), and state and local trade missions and foreign offices ('junkets and boondoggles'). In addition, there are few competent evaluations of the effectiveness of state and local promotional activities.

Proxies for the Nation

Although state and local officials cannot officially represent the United

States abroad, elected state and local officials do, in effect, often represent,

TABLE 2

LEVELS OF INTERNATIONALLY RELEVANT ACTIVITY BY CITY SIZE

	Very Active/ Active Responses		
	Small	Medium	Large
Attracting foreign investment	27.5%	50.6%	94.5%
Promoting exports of local products	42.8	60.5	88.9
Sister-city relations	41.4	68.2	83.4
Working with state officials	31.3	29.7	55.5
Cultural exchanges	27.2	51.7	77.8
Working with business partners	28.0	48.4	100.0
Idea and technical exchanges	22.7	49.5	77.7
Improving international education	22.4	35.2	44.4
Enhancing foreign language education	22.1	34.1	44.4
Working with civic groups	22.1	29.7	72.2
Attracting foreign tourists	18.8	37.4	61.1
Working with neighbour cities	16.4	28.6	55.6
Working with federal officials	16.4	25.3	61.1
Advertising city abroad	14.9	29.7	44.4
Recruiting protocol person	11.4	24.2	72.2
Conducting trade missions abroad	10.9	29.7	61.1
Attracting foreign immigrants	4.6	11.0	5.6
Foreign office or representative abroad	3.8	13.2	22.3

Source: John Kincaid with Joshua L. Handelsman (1997), *American Cities in the Global Economy: A Survey of Municipalities on Activities and Attitudes* (Washington, DC: National League of Cities).

in the minds of others, what is best or worst about the United States. Sometimes state and local officials can also open doors in unofficial ways that would be awkward or impossible for the US government to do officially. In addition, state and local officials and their counterparts abroad can initiate discussions on issues of mutual concern, and then carry constructive proposals back to their respective national governments – a common practice along the US–Mexico border, for example, where Mexican states have less autonomy than US states to act unilaterally. At times, state and local officials also provide aid to equivalent governments in another country where it is awkward for the United States to do so, or for the other national government to accept direct US aid.

A dramatic and controversial example occurred in 1983, when Governor Mario Cuomo of New York, a Democrat, and Governor Tom Kean of New Jersey, a Republican, ordered the Port Authority of New York and New Jersey to deny landing rights to Soviet aircraft, including any carrying Soviet Foreign Minister Andrei Gromyko to a United Nations General Assembly meeting. The governors were protesting against the Soviet destruction of a South Korean airliner three weeks earlier. The Reagan administration did not attempt to overrule the governors; instead, it offered landing rights at a nearby US (military) air base. Gromyko protested and then cancelled his planned address to the General Assembly. The outcome accorded with administration sentiments even while the administration could claim that the United States had not violated any UN agreements or treaty obligations.

This role of state and local governments is not well developed, nor is it likely to be developed with much vigour – with two exceptions. First, if the democratization of authoritarian regimes continues to spread throughout the world, the federal government, as well as private foundations and international organizations, will call on state and local officials to lend their expertise to government reform in those countries. Second, as laboratories for experimentation, state and local governments are likely to serve as sources of ideas for national responses to globalization, whether those responses be embodied in federal law or in state laws and policies across the country.

Parties to Agreements with Foreign Governments

There are thousands of formal and informal agreements and accords between state and local governments and foreign governments. Most of these agreements, however, are with equivalent regional or local governments abroad, not with national governments. Along the Canada–US border, for example, many state–province agreements involve housekeeping matters, such as roads and bridges, traffic, fire protection, animal control, environmental protection and civil defence.

There has been little federal–state conflict over such agreement-making activity. Although, constitutionally, these agreements require congressional consent, Congress does not wish to be inundated with time-consuming approval requests. State and local governments, therefore, are substantially free to enter into agreements, with Congress reserving the authority to abrogate any agreements that contravene US foreign policy or suborn US sovereignty. State and local governments, however, have largely confined their activities to matters appropriate to their jurisdictional concerns, and when they are in doubt about the appropriate scope of their contemplated action, they will ordinarily consult with the US Department of State. Hence, few agreements have ever been abrogated by the federal government.

Public Education and Opinion Forums

A major key to a successful economy today is a well-educated workforce attuned to world events. Local and state governments have primary responsibility for education, and global competition has increased awareness by state and local officials of needs to reform and improve public education. Consequently, education reform has been one of the highest state and local priorities since the governors met with President George Bush in 1988 for an 'education summit'.

At the same time, states and localities have emerged as public-opinion forums on foreign policy. City councils and state legislatures occasionally pass resolutions on foreign policy; mayors, county commissioners, and governors speak out on foreign affairs; and foreign-policy propositions sometimes appear on state and local ballots. Although many of these legislative resolutions and ballot propositions criticize US foreign policies, and although many citizens regard these resolutions as improper, there is no constitutional barrier to such expressions of opinion. Other expressions of local opinion, such as 'nuclear free zone' propositions or ordinances occupy an uncertain legal status. They can be set aside by the federal government under its interstate commerce power; however, the political impact of these declarations makes federal officials reluctant to arouse unnecessary conflict with local citizens and governments.

Problem Solvers on the World Scene

'Think globally, act locally' has become an attractive slogan in this era of interdependence and rising concern about the global effects of local behaviour, such as environmental pollution. Here, state and local governments can demonstrate one of the virtues of federalism, namely, the ability to experiment with different solutions to public problems and, at the same time, actually do something constructive and share information with others around the world while also learning from others.

State and local governments can also make direct contributions to easing cross-border tensions and resolving cross-border problems. In so doing, they can help prevent manageable problems from becoming less manageable international controversies. State–province co-operation helps to maintain cordial relations along the unfortified US–Canada border and to resolve emerging problems locally. Now that Mexico is attempting to implement a New Federalism and Mexican states enjoy slightly more freedom of action than in the past, more state–state co-operation is springing up along the US–Mexico border, an area fraught with many serious and contentious problems. The governors of the contiguous Mexican and US border states meet annually to address cross-border issues.

States have also been active in technical assistance programmes, usually with federal assistance. The Council of State Governments (CSG), for instance, operates a State Environmental Initiative funded by the US Agency for International Development to provide environmental technologies and services to five countries in Southeast Asia. Since the programme began in 1994, CSG has awarded $2.4 million in competitive grants to 18 state agencies, each of which has matched its grant with cash and in-kind service contributions.

Patrons of Democracy

If state and local governments wish to open more markets for their constituents' products, and if the Sunbelt states are to resolve their concerns about illegal immigration and drug smuggling from Latin America, they will have to be attentive to the economic and democratic development needs of many countries around the world. State and local government officials are uniquely qualified to help because they possess hands-on expertise, and because economic development and democratization require competent local and regional institutions of government that can provide essential services, unleash entrepreneurial energy, and stimulate citizen participation.

Many state and local government officials, usually in co-operation with US agencies and private and non-profit organizations, are providing technical assistance, equipment and other aid to many regional and local governments abroad. Exchange programmes also have taken on more importance, and there has been a quantum leap in information-sharing among state and local governments worldwide. Furthermore, state university systems are excellent vehicles for contributing to economic and democratic development abroad. For example, the federal government has funded state universities in California and Minnesota to conduct democratization and privatization projects in Eastern Europe and former Soviet republics. Of course, the Fulbright programme, established 50 years ago, has long involved state as well as private universities in exchange programmes, and recent recommendations by the National Humanities Center call for the Fulbright programme to establish new partnerships with 'internationalizing' communities in the US and to broaden participation to two-year community colleges (ordinarily funded by county taxes and state aid) and minority (for example, African-American) institutions.

An underdeveloped dimension of this role, however, is gubernatorial and mayoral participation in international organizations seeking to preserve and strengthen regional and local democratic self-government generally, not only against intranational obstacles but also international threats to autonomy posed by free trade, globalization and supranational rule-making. Prominent mayors of major US cities, for example, have not ordinarily been prominent participants in such organizations as the International Union of Local Authorities and World Associations of Cities and Local Authorities Coordination, or outspoken proponents of the proposed worldwide Charter of Local Self-Government. Perhaps being situated in a superpower nation and having a long, secure tradition of local self-government, state and local officials in the United States see little need to seek international support or legitimacy.

Practitioners of Goodwill

Finally, state and local governments play useful roles in attempting to promote goodwill abroad and to improve cultural understanding between Americans and other peoples. State and local governments are well suited for this role. Such activities are often best carried out on small-scale, person-to-person bases so that participants can see how other people really live and think about issues. State and local governments can also work closely with their private and non-profit counterparts to build different kinds of bridges between peoples and to assemble rich cultural and educational programmes. In addition, state and local programmes are less freighted with the ideological baggage and policy antagonisms that separate national governments, thus enabling state and local initiatives to break through barriers that otherwise divide peoples.

CONCLUSION

The emergence of state and local governments as actors on the world scene can be characterized, thus far, as co-operative dual federalism. That is, state and local governments have, by and large, been carving out international niches for themselves, and by themselves, in the fashion of nineteenth-century dual federalism where the federal government and the states were regarded as occupying separate spheres of authority. At the same time, in the fashion of twentieth-century co-operative federalism, the federal government has been mostly tolerant and benignly co-operative, neither interfering in overt ways with state and local initiatives nor going out of its way to lend a helping hand. There are some direct points of co-operation as well as friction, but there has been relatively little federal–state conflict over these matters. The principal challenge is to continue carving out appropriate roles for the federal sector and for the state–local sector so that each can do what it is best equipped to do, and the two sectors can co-ordinate and co-operate as necessary and appropriate.

REFERENCES

Avery, William P. (1998), 'Domestic Interests in NAFTA Bargaining', *Political Science Quarterly*, Vol.113, No.2, pp.281–305.
Beckman, Norman (1991), 'The Governors and the National Guard in *Perpich* v. *Defense*', *Publius: The Journal of Federalism*, Vol.21, No.3, pp.109–24.

Buchanan, Patrick J. (1998), *The Great Betrayal: How American Sovereignty and Social Justice Are Being Sacrificed to the Gods of the Global Economy*, Boston: Little, Brown.

Chandler, Clay (1998), 'The Best of Times, the Worst of Times', *The Washington Post National Weekly Edition*, 24 August, p.20.

Cherokee Nation v. *Georgia* (1831), 30 US 1.

Clark v. *Allen* (1947), 331 US 503.

Conway, Carol (1998), 'Southerners Need More Trade Information', *Southern Growth Update*, Vol.23, No.4, p.7.

Fry, Earl H. (1998), 'The Expanding Role of State and Local Governments in US Foreign Relations'. Paper presented at Annual Meeting of American Political Science Association, Boston, Massachusetts, 3 September.

Henkin, Louis (1972), *Foreign Affairs and the Constitution* (Mineola, NY: Foundation Press, 1972).

Kincaid, John (1984), 'The American Governors in International Affairs', *Publius: The Journal of Federalism*, Vol.14, No.4, pp.95–114.

Kincaid, John (1989), 'Rain Clouds Over Municipal Diplomacy: Dimensions and Possible Sources of Negative Public Opinion', in Earl H. Fry, Lee H. Radebaugh and Panayotis Soldatos (eds), *The New International Cities Era: The Global Activities of North American Municipal Governments* (Provo, UT: David M. Kennedy Center for International Affairs, Brigham Young University), pp.223–49.

Kincaid, John with Joshua L. Handelsman (1997), *American Cities in the Global Economy: A Survey of Municipalities on Activities and Attitudes* (Washington, DC: National League of Cities).

Kline, John M. (1983), *State Government Influence in US International Economic Policy* (Lexington, MA: Lexington Books).

Lutz, Donald S. (1988), 'The United States Constitution as an Incomplete Text', *Annals of the American Academy of Political and Social Science*, Vol.496, pp.23–32.

Manning, Bayless (1977), 'The Congress, the Executive and Intermestic Affairs: Three Proposals', *Foreign Affairs*, Vol.55, No.1, pp.306–24.

Nothdurft, William E. and Ilene K. Grossman (1996), *Small Firm Export Assistance in Europe: Lessons for States* (Lombard, IL: Council of State Governments, Midwestern Office).

Palumbo, Dennis J. (1969), 'The States and the Conduct of Foreign Relations', in Daniel J. Elazar (ed.), *Cooperation and Conflict: Readings in American Federalism* (Itasca, IL: FE Peacock).

Perpich v. *Department of Defense* (1990), 496 US 334.

Public Citizen (1998), Web Site: www.citizen.org/pctrade/FastTrack/poll.html.

Putnam, Robert D. (1988), 'Diplomacy and Domestic Politics: The Logic of Two-Level Games', *International Organization*, Vol.42, No.2, pp.427–60.

Sarpolus, Ed (1998), 'The WIIT/EPIC-MRA Survey of Public Opinion on International Trade', *Clearinghouse on State International Policies*, Vol.8, No.6, p.5.

United States v. *Curtiss-Wright Export Corporation* (1936), 299 US 304.

US Advisory Commission on Intergovernmental Relations (1993), *The National Guard: Defending the Nation and the States* (Washington, DC: ACIR).

US General Accounting Office (1998), *International Affairs Activities of Domestic Agencies*, Washington, DC.

Wechsler, Herbert (1954), 'The Political Safeguards of Federalism: The Role of the States in the Composition and Selection of the National Government', *Columbia Law Review*, Vol.54, No.2, pp.543–67.

Weiler, Conrad (1994), 'Foreign-Trade Agreements: A New Federal Partner?' *Publius: The Journal of Federalism* Vol.24, No.3, pp.113–33.

Zschernig v. *Miller* (1968), 389 US 429, 441.

Federal–State Relations in Australian External Affairs: A New Co-operative Era?

JOHN RAVENHILL

Federalism inevitably complicates the making and execution of foreign policy. The growth of interdependence, with the accompanying blurring of boundaries between the domestic and the international, has increased the potential for conflict between federal governments and their state counterparts. International treaties, less formal international agreements and the activities of foreign actors all impinge on issue areas such as the environment, resource development and various dimensions of human rights that in Australia lie within the constitutional competence of the states. Moreover, the states have their own legitimate interests to pursue in international affairs – the attraction of investment, the promotion of tourism, and so forth – which they have regarded as best promoted through the establishment of their own representation overseas.

External affairs have intruded on relations between the states and the Commonwealth (federal) government in Australia in the last three decades, principally through two sets of issues. The first has been the international diplomatic activities conducted by the states. The second has been the impact that the Commonwealth government's negotiation and entry into international treaties has had on the division of powers established by the constitution. Both dimensions have caused considerable tension between the states and the Commonwealth. This article reviews how, in the 1990s, collaborative relations on both sets of issues have emerged as the states and the Commonwealth reached a new *modus vivendi*.

AUSTRALIAN EXCEPTIONALISM?

Like other subnational governments, Australian states have responded to the challenges of an increasingly interdependent global economy by engaging in paradiplomacy. However, the international diplomatic activities of Australian states have been conditioned by factors that distinguish the Australian experience from that of subnational governments elsewhere.

Unlike in many federal states, cultural heterogeneity in Australia is not regionally defined. Federalism in Australia has always been more a matter of geography and history than of culture. The states' existence as separate British colonies before Federation in 1901, coupled with the vast distances between major centres of population in Australia, made federalism the logical choice for the new country's system of government. And since Federation, it has been the distance factor – the sense that Canberra is remote from their interests – that has sustained state governments and their population's identity with the state rather than the national capital.

Although states have been perennial critics of the Commonwealth government's policies, both domestic and foreign, on only one occasion (in the 1930s) has a state, Western Australia, given serious consideration to seceding from the Federation. Australia's population became increasingly multicultural after the Second World War, first with the large-scale migration from Southern and, to a lesser extent, Eastern Europe, and then with an influx of migrants from Asia and the Middle East following the termination of the 'White Australia' policy in the 1960s. The new multiculturalism introduced cross-cutting cleavages that weakened rather than strengthened popular identification with individual states.

Australia's island geography has also affected the paradiplomacy of Australian states. Unlike most other federations, Australia shares no land boundaries with other countries. Consequently, states are generally not involved in the management of day-to-day cross-boundary issues, which so significantly increases the international activities of states such as Texas or British Columbia. Queensland and the Northern Territory have maritime boundaries with foreign countries – Papua New Guinea and Indonesia – which generate international involvement for these subnational governments. The Northern Territory has also fostered close relations with the adjacent Brunei, Indonesia, Malaysia, Philippines–East Asian Growth Area (BIMP–EAGA). For the most part, however, the territorial interests of Australian states are confined to their jurisdiction over the three miles of territorial seas around their coasts.

The regional schemes to which Australia is a party do not encourage separate representation from subnational units. The two most significant regional arrangements involving Australia are the Australia–New Zealand Closer Economic Relations Trade Agreement (ANZCERTA), and the Asia-Pacific Economic Co-operation (APEC) grouping. ANZCERTA is very much a market-oriented arrangement. Rather than attempting to construct an elaborate institutional superstructure, Australian and New Zealand governments have sought as far as possible to promote further economic integration through the harmonization of legislation and practices, and through mutual recognition of one another's commercial regulations.[1] New Zealand ministers participate in many of the state–Commonwealth councils (of which over 20 currently exist) that deal with various dimensions of trade, industrial and environmental issues, (Harris, 1993: 100). But these are essentially Australian arrangements rather than new international bodies.

APEC is the second regional arrangement in which Australia in recent years has played a particularly active part. APEC again eschews the construction of supranational arrangements. Indeed, from its founding, Asian states, particularly ASEAN member countries, have strongly signalled that their participation was conditional on APEC's not following the European path towards institution-building at the regional level. East Asian governments view regionalism in the Asia-Pacific and more specifically in East Asia, as a means of strengthening rather than undermining their sovereignty. There is no official role for subnational units in APEC committees. Australian states are represented on some of the Australian working parties on APEC but not in their own right on any APEC bodies.

Of the three reasons that Keating lists (in this volume) for subnational units engaging in paradiplomacy – economic, cultural and political – the cultural factor has never been important for Australian states. Political reasons, on the other hand, have been significant: state leaders have coveted the publicity that can be gained by making pronouncements on foreign policy, and by strutting the international stage. Such antics have tended to be greeted with increasing cynicism by the electorate in a period when economic concerns have been uppermost in their minds.

It is the third of Keating's categories – economic concerns – that have dominated the international activities of Australian states. Most important among these has been the promotion of inward investment, technology transfer, tourism and exports. States have also given foreign aid, often as a means of providing a subsidy to their own manufacturing and service industries. In recent years, in response to changes in Australia's trade relations, substantial geographical diversification has occurred in the international representation of the states. Cost pressures have also had a significant influence on states' paradiplomatic activities. In response to budgetary problems, the states in the 1990s retreated from some of their international activities and increasingly entered collaborative arrangements with one another and with the Commonwealth government.

CHANGES IN THE OVERSEAS ACTIVITIES OF THE STATES

The states' overseas representation was originally in London, established both to maintain the link with the Imperial government and to promote the states' commercial interests. As the Imperial connection became less important, particularly in the commercial field, the Agents-General, as the states' overseas offices were known, came to represent states' interests in other European countries as well as the United Kingdom. States also began to establish representation outside Europe: the first, the New South Wales

TABLE 1

OVERSEAS REPRESENTATION OF THE STATES AND TERRITORIES, 1997

State/Territory	Office	Australian-based Staff	Locally-based Staff	Total Staff
ACT	Tokyo	–	1	1*
New South Wales	London	–	2	2
	Tokyo	1	2	3
Northern Territory	Beijing	–	1	1*
	Hong Kong	–	1	1*
	Jakarta	–	1	1*
	Macao	–	1	1*
Queensland	Hong Kong	–	6	6
	Jakarta	1	1	2
	London	–	8	8‡
	Los Angeles	–	3	3
	Semarang	–	2	2
	Shanghai	1	3	4
	Taipei	–	6.5	6.5
	Tokyo	2	4	6
South Australia	Hong Kong	–	5	5
	Jakarta	–	5	5
	Jinan	–	5	5
	London	2	5	7
	Shanghai	–	5	5
	Singapore	–	6	6
	Tokyo	2	3	5
Tasmania		–		0±
Victoria	Dubai	–	3	3
	Frankfurt	–	4	4
	Hong Kong	–	5	5
	Jakarta	1	3	4
	London	–		8
	Seoul	–	2	2
	Tokyo	1	4	5
Western Australia	Bangkok	–	1	1§
	Beijing	–	1	1*
	Hangzhou	–	1	1
	Hong Kong	–	2	2
	Kobe	–	1.6	1.6
	Kuala Lumpur	–	2	2
	London	1	8	9
	Madras	–	1	1*
	Mumbai	1	4	5
	Seoul	–	2	2
	Shanghai	1	2	3
	Singapore	–	2	2
	Surabaya	1	3	4
	Tokyo	–	–	1*

Key
* Part-time representatives engaged on an 'as needed' basis.
‡ to be reduced to 6.5 in September 1997
± Tasmania has a representative based in Macao employed on a consultancy basis who is not regarded as a formal representative.
§ Western Australia pays 100 per cent of the salary of a locally-based AUSTRADE staff member.

Source: Data provided by the state governments and by the Department of Foreign Affairs and Trade.

Centre in New York, was opened in 1958. The growing importance of Japan to the Australian economy was reflected in the opening of state offices in Tokyo: New South Wales and Western Australia led the way by establishing representation in 1968.

Table 1 lists the international offices of the states in 1997. Particularly striking about this table is the greatly increased geographical spread of these offices, particularly within Asia, compared with a decade before when I previously conducted a survey of their representation (Ravenhill, 1990, Table 4). Although the total number of employees has increased only marginally since 1988–89 (up from 119 to 136), the number of offices has grown disproportionately while the distribution of personnel has changed dramatically.

A decade ago, 60 per cent of the employees in states' overseas offices were based in London. All states except Western Australia had representation in the United States. The only Asian location where the states had offices was Tokyo. By 1997, the share of employees in London had fallen to one quarter of the total. Only Queensland maintained its representation in the United States (the absence of other states is surprising in that the US remains a significant market for Australia's manufactured exports and a major source of tourists). But, apart from New South Wales, which has substantially cut its overseas representation (down from 31 a decade ago to the current total of five) and Tasmania, which as in 1988–89 has no permanent foreign representatives, the other states have greatly diversified their representation in Asia. China, Hong Kong, Indonesia, Korea, Macao, Malaysia, Taiwan and Thailand now all host one or more state offices. In addition, the Western Australian government, keen to promote its Indian Ocean links, has established offices in Madras and Mumbai, and the Victoria government has opened an office in the United Arab Emirates.

The new pattern of state representation mirrors changes in Australia's export markets. By 1995, East Asian markets together accounted for more than 60 per cent of Australian exports, up from 50 per cent at the start of the decade. The most rapidly growing market until the onset of the East Asian financial crises was the ASEAN countries whose share of Australian exports increased by more than 50 per cent in the first half of the 1990s. East Asia's increasing share of Australian exports came primarily at the expense of Western Europe and North America. Although the European Union, if considered as a single market, was the second most important destination of exports after Japan, its share continued to decline, reaching 11 per cent at the end of the period. To some extent the new diversification in state representation also reflects the changing composition of Australian exports. With tourism now among the major export earners for several states, a major function of their overseas offices is the promotion of their state's attractions for foreign visitors.

What explains the differences in foreign representation of the states? Western Australia has by far the most offices overseas, standing in marked contrast to New South Wales, the most heavily populated of all Australian states, which has significantly curtailed its representation in the last fifteen years. Again, geographical location provides much of the explanation. Western Australia is geographically distant from the Sydney–Melbourne corridor where most of Australia's population resides, and from these two cities that, together with the federal capital, Canberra, that lies between them, are most often on the itineraries of foreign business visitors to Australia. The Western Australian capital, Perth, is not significantly further from Singapore than from Sydney; not surprisingly, the Western Australian government has been more active in establishing links with the Southeast Asian countries than have the other Australian states. Western Australia's interest in the Indian Ocean has already been noted. As a significant exporter of minerals, Western Australia has particular interests in the major Asian markets for these products – Korea, as well as China and Japan. In contrast, New South Wales depends much more heavily on service industries. New South Wales has Australia's premier international airport in its state capital, Sydney. Moreover, the Commonwealth's capital, Canberra, is located in a small territorial enclave (the Australian Capital Territory) surrounded by New South Wales. New South Wales thus is more likely to be on the itinerary for foreign business visitors (and tourists) than any other in Australia, perhaps a factor in its relatively small presence internationally.

The states have argued that the functions carried out by their offices are simply too important to leave to the Commonwealth, which they do not trust to pursue their particular interests with the same vigour. Traditionally states have also been concerned that in seeking foreign markets and sources of investment they are competing not only with foreign countries but also with other states. After interviewing representatives of the states based in Tokyo, the Japan Secretariat (a Commonwealth government research and administrative unit attached to the Department of Foreign Affairs and Trade) noted:

> Some of the state offices were unapologetic about their need to overlap some areas of Embassy work and to compete with other states. They saw this as a valid and important function (Commonwealth of Australia, 1981:20).

State rivalry was captured in the exhortation of the former Queensland Premier, Sir John Bjelke-Petersen, on the opening of the state office in Tokyo: 'Come to Queensland, not to Australia' (quoted in Hocking, 1984 2290: 137). Commonwealth governments over the years have complained about what they perceived as an unnecessary duplication of activities in the states' overseas offices, and about the rivalry among the states that potentially allows foreign business partners to play them off against one another. In the 1990s, however, a more co-operative relationship developed among the states themselves, and between them and the Commonwealth government.

This improved collaboration has been driven both by a shared perception of the necessity of representing Australian economic interests abroad more effectively, and by a desire to economize at a time when Commonwealth and state budgets alike are being cut. The Commonwealth's concern with a more effective overseas promotion of Australian economic interests is reflected in the decision, in 1987, to merge the Department of Foreign Affairs with the Department of Trade. Much of Australian diplomacy in the last fifteen years, such as the founding of the Cairns Group of agricultural-exporting countries, and the APEC initiative, has been devoted to the protection and promotion of Australian economic interests. In 1991, as part of the Labor Government's Economic Statement, *Building a Competitive Australia*, a National Trade Strategy Consultative Process (NTSCP) was established. The process was intended as a vehicle for improving consultation and co-operation between Commonwealth and state/territory governments, the business community and trade unions. In particular, the Commonwealth government wanted to promote better co-ordination between its departments and those of the states in their foreign trade-related activities and promotional visits.

The NTSCP is the vehicle used by the Commonwealth to advance its 'Team Australia' approach to trade and investment priorities. Commonwealth, state and territory ministers responsible for international trade and business development meet annually under its auspices. In addition, government officials, industry, and trade unions hold meetings on a more regular basis. Team Australia is intended to ensure that the strategies and activities of various levels of government are effectively co-ordinated and reflect the priorities of the business community, that appropriate assistance is provided to Australian firms, and that domestic impediments to international competitiveness are addressed. The annual NTSCP ministerial forum is supposed to reach a consensus on where governments should be concentrating their trade and investment promotion in the following year. Team Australia publishes an annual Trade and Investment Priorities Report, for which the Commonwealth Department of Foreign Affairs and Trade has primary responsibility but with inputs from state governments, and the NTSCP business and union participants. It features trade and investment promotion strategies for 30 priority markets, and strategies for 45 industrial sectors. In addition, Team Australia is responsible for the National Trade and Investment Outlook Conference.

Another indication of the Commonwealth's determination to improve co-ordination of activities with the states is the enhanced status given to the offices of the Department of Foreign Affairs and Trade in the individual states. The state offices used to be regarded as a dumping ground for personnel viewed by the Department as 'awkward'. In recent years, however, the offices have been headed by staff of the highest calibre who, in some cases, have subsequently moved on to senior ambassadorial appointments.

The Commonwealth and states alike face financial pressures that have fostered a more collaborative relationship. At both levels, governments have been under pressure to reduce or eliminate budget deficits. This pressure has led to substantial cuts in public expenditure, to a 'downsizing' of government departments, and to the elimination of a significant range of government services. At the Commonwealth level, Australia's overseas representation, both in the regular diplomatic service and its trade promotion arm, AUSTRADE, has been substantially pruned. In 1997 alone, 225 staff were offered voluntary redundancy packages.

Despite the concurrent cutbacks in Commonwealth representation abroad and increase in the number of state employees, the total number of Commonwealth representatives continues to overshadow state representation. In 1997, whereas the states and territories had slightly fewer than 100 employees in their offices in Asia, some of whom were part-time, the Department of Foreign Affairs and Trade employed 245 Australian-based staff and more than 600 locally-based staff in its Asian offices. In addition, AUSTRADE, the Commonwealth government's trade promotion agency, employed 50 Australian-based staff and more than 230 locally-based staff in its Asian offices. Although the states have significantly increased the number of their overseas offices in the last decade, the numbers of staff in many of the offices are small; most are locally based rather than Australian expatriates. It is clearly in the states' interest to take advantage whenever possible of the expertise in Commonwealth agencies abroad.

Economies have been generated through the sharing of offices. New creative arrangements have been devised to facilitate co-operation and cost-effectiveness. The Western Australian government, for instance, pays the full salary of an AUSTRADE employee in its Bangkok office. Even the traditional rivalries of the states in their foreign activities are being transcended in unprecedented collaboration. In London and Tokyo, for instance, the states have established offices in the same buildings to economize on rents and to provide a 'one-stop shop' for potential business partners and to promote tourism.

NEW COLLABORATION BETWEEN THE COMMONWEALTH AND THE STATES IN EXTERNAL AFFAIRS

The new collaboration between the Commonwealth and the states in international representation has built on improved relations between the parties in other dimensions of Australia's international relations. Two issues historically have been particularly contentious: the Commonwealth's use of its constitutional powers on external relations to override the states on issues that would otherwise fall within their jurisdiction; and the Commonwealth's failure to involve the states in the negotiation and implementation of international treaties.

In Australia, the power to enter into a treaty is an executive function, derived from the Crown's prerogative. At the time of Australian Federation in 1901, the power was exercised by the English monarch on the advice of the Imperial government. As Australia gradually achieved sovereignty – in the foreign affairs sphere this is generally regarded as having been finalized in 1942 with the passage of the Statute of Westminster Adoption Act – the power to enter into treaties was transferred to the Australian Commonwealth government as part of its general executive powers (section 61 of the Constitution).

Although the Constitution nowhere provides that the Commonwealth has exclusive competency in external affairs, the High Court has consistently asserted that only the Commonwealth can speak for Australia in international affairs. A series of court cases in the years between Federation and the Second World War determined that the states had no legal international personality and thus no right to enter into Treaties. Before Federation, the colonies had negotiated no bilateral agreements other than postal conventions. These limited arrangements came to be viewed as *sui generis* and not evidence of any grant to the colonies of the executive's treaty-making powers. The states can, and do, enter into international agreements with other governments (more often with their statutory authorities). Such agreements often take the form of memoranda of understanding, and lack the status of international treaty (indeed, some legal authorities deny that these agreements are governed by international law). Although in principle the Commonwealth could delegate its treaty-making powers to the states, it has chosen not to do so.

While the power to enter into a treaty is an executive function, derived from the Crown prerogative, the power to implement a treaty is a legislative power. This is contained in s. 51 (xxix) of the Constitution, which gives the Commonwealth Parliament the power to enact laws in relation to external affairs. It is the interpretation of this provision that has been the most controversial aspect of relations between the Commonwealth and the states in recent years, and which has occupied a good deal of the High Court's time. In part this controversy has arisen because of the vastly increased number and scope of international treaties in recent years. At Federation, the treaties power was generally uncontroversial because of the limited scope of such arrangements (primarily relating to commerce, diplomatic representation, extradition and defence). The extension of treaties (Australia is currently a party to over 950) in the post-war era to issues such as the environment and human rights has greatly enhanced the potential for conflict between the Commonwealth and the states.

In prescient remarks in 1936, Chief Justice Latham declared:

> No criterion has been suggested which can result in designating certain matters as *in se* concerning external relations and excluding all other matters from such a class. It is very difficult to say that any matter is incapable of affecting international relations so as properly to become the subject matter of an international agreement. It appears to me that no absolute rule can be laid down upon this subject.

And, indeed, much to the annoyance of the states, this has proved to be the case. In successive judgements, the High Court has ruled that the Commonwealth may use its legislative powers to implement its obligations under treaties that it has entered on a *bona fide* basis. The principal restrictions on the Commonwealth's use of this power are that the legislation must be directed specifically at implementing the obligations contained in the treaty, and that the treaty itself has objectives defined with sufficient specificity to place obligations for action on its signatories.[2]

In the 1970s and 1980s, Commonwealth governments increasingly used obligations they had assumed through entering international treaties as a legal basis for encroaching on areas that otherwise would have been reserved by the constitution for the states. Particularly prominent in this context was the use of obligations under World Heritage treaties to override states' approval for development projects in areas regarded as of significant environmental value. In addition, the Commonwealth used its obligations under the Convention on the Elimination of All Forms of Racial Discrimination to override state legislation relating to the rights of indigenous peoples.

In principle, the Commonwealth government thus has the constitutional power to extend its competence and to override the states on many issues that would normally be considered to be within their jurisdiction. Over the last 25 years, since the election of the Whitlam Labor government at the federal level in Canberra ended more than two decades of conservative rule, the policies of Commonwealth governments have fluctuated between attempting to override the states and seeking to reach accommodation with them. Shifts in the Commonwealth's approach have coincided to some degree – certainly not perfectly – with changes in the party in government in Canberra. Conservative governments (comprising a coalition of the Liberal Party and the National [formerly Country] Party) have generally been more willing to seek accommodation with the states.[3] The Labor Party, in contrast, has traditionally been more centralist in its orientation, and more willing to resort to constitutional powers to overturn state legislation and decisions.

Recently, however, Commonwealth governments of both political persuasions have adopted a new, more co-operative approach in their interactions with the states on external affairs. The Labor government began the new collaborative approach in the late 1980s. The Coalition government that came to power at the March 1996 election has accelerated and deepened it. The move towards more co-operative relations after a period of considerable conflict largely resulted from two factors. The Commonwealth government wished to avoid the political costs of conflict with the states. Second, co-operation between the Commonwealth and the states was necessary if effective legislative solutions to increasingly complex problems were to be introduced. Undoubtedly, the election of a Liberal–National Party coalition government at the 1996 federal election has facilitated the consolidation of the collaborative relationship between the Commonwealth and the states. At the time of writing, in mid-1997, all except one of the eight state and territory governments (New South Wales) were also controlled by one or both of the coalition parties.

Commonwealth governments have increasingly recognized the political necessity of cohabitation with the states on matters of external affairs. The political cost to the Commonwealth of reliance on its external affairs powers to override the states was obvious. Not only was the Commonwealth likely to alienate state governments in using these powers, but it also risked making the passage of its legislation through the Senate more difficult. No recent Commonwealth government has enjoyed a majority in the Senate, traditionally regarded as the 'states' house'.[4] Moreover, for Canberra to be seen as continually overriding the wishes of state governments was to risk losing support at the next federal election (although on some issues where the Commonwealth used its external affairs powers to overturn state policies, particularly on environmental matters, such a risk was offset by possible electoral benefits from gaining the support of groups favouring the policy objectives pursued).

The necessity of collaborating with the states on some issues if effective legislative remedies for problems were to be introduced also drove the desire for cohabitation. The need for concurrent state legislation to implement policy change on some issues had long been recognized. For instance, although the Whitlam Labor government won a famous Constitutional victory when the High Court upheld the validity of the *Seas and Submerged Lands Act 1973*, which established Commonwealth control over offshore minerals, its Coalition successor found that it was more practical to negotiate a co-operative agreement for an offshore minerals regime rather than legislating to override the states. Commonwealth sovereignty over the territorial sea did not exclude state legislative power over some activities, for example, fishing. The regime, taking advantage of s. 51 (xxxviii) of the Constitution which permitted the Commonwealth with the agreement of the states to exercise any power that could otherwise be exercised only by the UK Parliament, vested in the states the title to the seabed within territorial waters, and created 18 offshore areas to be governed by newly-created joint authorities comprised of the relevant federal and state ministers.

With the boundaries between the external and the domestic increasingly blurred, effective solutions to new issues on the political agenda often required such collaboration between the Commonwealth and state authorities.

Treaties and Commonwealth–State Relations

State governments have long complained of a 'democratic deficit' in treaty making and ratification and, in particular, of the failure of the Commonwealth to engage in appropriate consultation with them.

In the post-war period, the Commonwealth government has used two principal mechanisms to consult states in the negotiation of treaties and to give states a role in their implementation. The first was to table treaties in both Houses of Parliament before the government ratified or acceded to them. The second was to include, wherever possible, a 'federal clause' in the treaties to which Australia became a party (in which the Commonwealth government would only accept responsibility for those matters within its traditional constitutional authority). Both of these means fell into disuse.

In 1961, the Coalition government of Prime Minister Menzies announced that the Commonwealth government would, 'as a general rule', table treaties in both Houses of Parliament for at least 12 sitting days before Australia ratified or acceded to them. As Taylor (1996) records, gradually this commitment lapsed, with treaties often being tabled only after they had been ratified. Of the treaties tabled in 1994, Australia was already obliged by international law to comply with two-thirds of them before they were tabled, denying any meaningful kind of Parliamentary scrutiny.

Similarly, the Commonwealth's commitment to include 'federal clauses' in its international treaties was abandoned in the 1980s, in part because of the criticism of non-federal countries (and the EC) of the use of such clauses. The Commonwealth's willingness to use federal clauses and to allow states to decide whether or not to legislate to implement obligations arising from international conventions had constrained Australia's participation in a number of international conventions, particularly those pertaining to labour issues. By 1982, Australia had ratified only 43 of 158 International Labour Organization treaties because states had failed to enact the necessary legislation.

Both domestically and internationally, there was a belief that Commonwealth governments under control of the Coalition parties had used the states as a convenient excuse for failing to ratify conventions for which they had little enthusiasm. Despite foreign criticism, the Coalition government of Malcolm Fraser reaffirmed its commitment to federal clauses at the Premiers' Conference in October 1977. The government stated that 'The Commonwealth will not become a party to a treaty containing a federal clause until the laws of all states conform with the mandatory provisions of the treaty.' Territorial units clauses, such as those utilized by Canada, that enable treaties to be implemented only in specified territorial units of a federal state, were regarded at the time as insufficient to provide protection of the position of the Australian states.

When Australia ratified the International Covenant on Civil and Political Rights three years later, it included a reservation that explained the federal system of government in Australia, and stated:

> the implementation of those provisions of the Covenant over whose subject matter the federal authorities exercise legislative, executive and judicial jurisdiction will be a matter for those authorities; and the implementation of those provisions of the Covenant over whose subject matter the authorities of the constituent states exercise legislative, executive and judicial jurisdiction will be a matter for those authorities; and where a provision has both federal and state aspects, its implementation will accordingly be a matter for the respective constitutionally appropriate authorities (quoted in Parliament of Australia, 1995, chapter 3).

Australia's reservation attracted widespread international criticism. Nonetheless, the government reaffirmed its commitment to federal clauses in treaties that refer to subjects traditionally subject to state law in its 1982 'Principles and Procedures for Commonwealth–State Consultation on Treaties'.

The election of a Labor government in the following year led to a reversal of policy. The government in November 1983 reaffirmed most of the 'Principles and Procedures' but stated that it did not favour the inclusion of federal clauses in treaties and that, in the future, Australian delegations would not seek such clauses when participating in treaty negotiations. Henceforth, the Commonwealth government would be prepared to make a 'Federal Statement', noting that treaty implementation would be effected by the federal, state and territory government with regard to their respective constitutional powers, but not to suggest that such a division of powers would interfere with its capacity to implement a treaty. Indeed, the High Court's liberal interpretation of the powers that the Commonwealth enjoys under s.51 (xxix) of the Constitution to legislate for its treaty obligations, largely undermines the credibility of a claim by any Australian Commonwealth government that it lacks the legislative powers to implement an international treaty that it has entered in good faith.

With the demise of federal clauses, the protection of the interests and traditional prerogatives of the states in treaty making rested primarily on the provisions within the 'Principles and Procedures' for consultation between the Commonwealth and the states. These provide for consultation on matters of particular sensitivity or importance to the states and territories in relation to both the negotiation and implementation of treaties provided that they do not lead to 'unreasonable delays' in the negotiation, joining or implementing of treaties by Australia. The states do not, however, enjoy a veto power: their agreement is not required before the Commonwealth ratifies a treaty. The 'Principles and Procedures' provide that a state or territory representative should be included, where appropriate, in the Australian delegation to treaty negotiations. Representatives of the states have participated, for example, in Australian delegations on the Law of the Sea, on the Framework Convention on Climate Change, as well as on bilateral negotiations with Indonesia on the demarcation of maritime boundaries (Parliament of Australia, 1995, para 13.21).

In addition, in a move towards a more co-operative relationship on treaty negotiation and implementation, the meeting of the leaders of the state and territory governments and the Commonwealth Prime Minister (formerly called the Premiers' Conference, now the Council of Australian Governments) in July 1991 agreed to the establishment of a Standing Committee on Treaties. Its functions are:

- to identify treaty and other international negotiations of particular sensitivity or importance to states, and propose an appropriate mechanism for state involvement in the negotiation process;
- to monitor and report on the implementation of particular treaties where the implementation of the treaty has strategic implications, including significant cross-portfolio interests, for states; and
- to co-ordinate as required the process for nominating state representation on delegations where such representation is appropriate.

Other Commonwealth/state consultative bodies, such as those dealing with the environment, transport, forestry and labour matters, review treaties that include provisions on matters within their sphere of responsibility.

The Senate's Legal and Constitutional References Committee's 1995 inquiry into the negotiation and implementation of treaties found, however, that the states were still unhappy about the extent to which they were consulted and represented. In particular, the states complained that:

- The level of information provided by the Commonwealth to states and territories varied immensely from treaty to treaty.
- State and territory views were sometimes sought too late in the negotiation process.
- Complex multilateral treaties affect many departments in different ways. The Department of Foreign Affairs and Trade was sometimes not aware of all the state departments which deal with matters affected by a treaty.
- The system of consultation did not allow states and territories to track the progress of consultation on treaties through different departments; they could not ensure therefore that all of their knowledge was passed on to the Commonwealth.
- The consultation process was not transparent, and the public remained unaware of state and territory concerns and of Commonwealth responses to them.
- The Commonwealth had the power to override state and territory objections to a treaty even in circumstances where it may be unreasonable to do so (Parliament of Australia, 1995, para. 13.32).

Moreover, since the Standing Committee on Treaties met only twice per year it had not fulfilled its intended purpose. The states complained that the Commonwealth had refused to discuss the substance of individual treaties at the Committee. And because the Standing Committee was composed solely of officials, it was not politically accountable.

In contrast, the Commonwealth government, through its Attorney-General's Department, concluded that the methods for consultation with the states and territories were satisfactory, and that any problems lay primarily in the failure of the states to avail themselves of the opportunities open to them. The Commonwealth blamed the state governments for problems in the consultative process, arguing that the states frequently failed to give sufficient resources to the consideration of treaties, failed to co-ordinate the process of treaty evaluation between the various departments in their administrations that had an interest in implementation, and that states had seldom sent senior officials to represent them at the Standing Committee on Treaties. The federal election in March 1996, however, produced a government more sympathetic to the states' concerns.

A New Co-operative Approach to Treaty Ratification and Accession

The report from the Senate Committee's 1995 inquiry reflected not only the concerns of the state and territory governments about lack of appropriate consultation in the treaty making and implementation process but also a wider public concern about the 'democratic deficit' in such activities. The Coalition parties supported many of the Committee's recommendations in their statement on foreign affairs and defence for the March 1996 election and implemented them two months after they were returned to government. To a considerable extent, these revised procedures on consultation should meet the concerns of the state and territory governments. The principal changes in procedure adopted by the Coalition government were:

- Treaties would be tabled in Parliament at least 15 sitting days before the government took binding action on them (except where urgent action was required).
- The treaties tabled would be accompanied by a National Interest Analysis. This would list the reasons why Australia should become a party to the treaty. Where relevant, the statement was to include a discussion of the economic, environmental, social and cultural effects of the treaty; the obligations imposed by the treaty; its direct financial costs to Australia; how the treaty will be implemented domestically; what consultation has occurred in relation to the treaty and whether the treaty provides for withdrawal or denunciation.
- The government would set up a Parliamentary Joint Standing Committee on Treaties whose role would be to make recommendations on the treaties tabled.
- The Commonwealth would support the creation of a Treaties Council as an adjunct to the Council of Australian Governments.
- The Commonwealth would establish an electronic database of treaty information.

At its meeting in June 1996, the Council of Australian Governments adopted a new set of 'Principles and Procedures for Commonwealth–State Consultation on Treaties'. These provided for new procedures for forwarding information on treaty discussions to the states, and a commitment that states would be consulted at an early stage in the preparation of the National Interest Analyses for Parliament. The Council agreed to the creation of a Treaties Council, consisting of the Prime Minister, Premiers and Chief Ministers – thereby overcoming the complaint that the Standing Committee on Treaties (which would continue in its existing form) lacked democratic accountability. The Commonwealth, however, reiterated its opposition to the inclusion of federal clauses in treaties but did allow that where a suitable 'territorial units' clause is included in a treaty, it would consider the possibility on a case by case basis that only those states and territories that wished to adopt the treaty would be bound by it.

The changes introduced in 1996 mark a new step forward in co-operation between the Commonwealth and the states in consultative procedures on international treaties. It is too early to judge at this stage how successful the new consultative procedures will be. The Parliamentary Joint Standing Committee on Treaties noted, however, in its fourth report that:

> The committee believes that the revised processes for treaty-making are working well, with one exception: consultation with the states and territories. Although no specific action was taken, in both the first and second reports we had concerns about the quantity and quality of some of the consultation which seemed to have taken place with the states and territories in the processes which led to the tabling of treaties and the accompanying National Interest Analyses (NIAs)... The process of parliamentary scrutiny of treaties was established, in part, to ensure that the views of the states and territories were registered because of their legal responsibilities for some matters about which the Commonwealth Government enters into binding international obligations for Australia... NIAs should in future include information on the actual responses received from the States and Territories about the texts of the treaties proposed for accession (Parliament of Australia, 4th Report of the Joint Standing Committee on Treaties, 2 December 1996).

Whether these are just teething problems for the new system remains to be seen.

CONCLUSION

To suggest that a new co-operative era has dawned in Commonwealth–state relations on external affairs is probably premature. Certainly, relations between the parties as we approach the new millennium are better than they have been for many years. Budgetary pressures combined with a new commitment to a more effective international promotion of Australia's economic interests have produced both a rationalization of state and Commonwealth representation abroad, and new collaborative relationships among states and between them and the Commonwealth. Yet while states are able to collaborate in pursuit of some of their economic interests, such as the promotion of tourism, others still constitute much more of a competitive relationship, such as the attraction of investment.

If the states can be satisfied that they have finally received a response to their longstanding complaints about the need for appropriate consultation on treaty ratification, they can draw little comfort from the constitutional situation in respect of the Commonwealth's use of its external affairs power. The Commonwealth may now be obliged to consult the states in its adherence to international treaties but the states do not have a veto over the process (at best they can attempt to embarrass the government through questions raised by opposition parties in the Commonwealth Parliament). And the new consultative procedures do not address the issue of the use that the Commonwealth may make of treaties to override state legislation. Indeed, it is unlikely that all the potential ramifications of treaties (insofar as they may affect the Commonwealth's capacity to override state legislation) will be foreseen in the National Interest Analyses. And the states themselves lack the necessary resources to play a timely and effective role in the consultation process.

The High Court's opinions have indicated few limitations on the scope of the external affairs power. It is highly unlikely that any change in this imbalance in constitutional powers will eventuate. To achieve limitations on the Commonwealth's powers would require an amendment to the Constitution, an act that has proved extraordinarily difficult in Australian history.[5] The states will have to rely on the Commonwealth government's commitment to 'co-operative federalism', on its unwillingness to risk electoral unpopularity by appearing to act as a bully in its dealing with the states, and on its need to court favour with the states to enable it to pass legislation through the Senate.

NOTES

1. The Trans-Tasman Mutual Recognition Arrangement (TTMRA), signed on 14 June 1996 by the Prime Minister, Premiers and Chief Ministers, extends internationally the 1992 Australian Mutual Recognition Agreement, which reduced regulatory barriers to the movement of goods and service providers between Australian jurisdictions. For details, see Commonwealth of Australia.

2. The High Court, in *Victoria v The Commonwealth* 1996, declared that treaty objectives that are regarded as 'aspirational', such as an obligation to promote full employment, lack sufficient specificity to qualify for legislative action under the external affairs power. For further discussion of the limitations on the use of the external affairs power see Parliament of Australia (1995) and Ravenhill (1990).

3. Exceptions to this generalization were the Fraser Coalition government's actions in using Commonwealth powers over foreign trade to block (on environmental grounds) sand-mining on the world's largest sand island, Fraser Island, off the Queensland coast, and to attempt to ensure that 'equitable' prices were achieved for the country's mineral exports.

4. The six states – New South Wales, Queensland, South Australia, Tasmania, Victoria, and Western Australia – each have 12 representatives in the Senate; there are also two representatives from the Northern Territory and the Australian Capital Territory. The system grossly over-represents the states that have relatively small populations, such as Tasmania.

5. A constitutional amendment has to be subjected to a referendum. It is carried only if approved by a majority of all voters, and by a majority of voters in a majority of the states.

REFERENCES

Commonwealth of Australia, Department of Foreign Affairs and Trade, Japan Secretariat (1981) 'The Commonwealth–State Relationship: Its relevance to Australia's Relations with Japan'. Canberra: Department of Foreign Affairs and Trade, Research Paper CCRJ/25/81, October.

Commonwealth of Australia, Department of Prime Minister and Cabinet (1996) 'Trans-Tasman Mutual Recognition Arrangement.' [http://www.nla.gov.au/pmc/trans.html].

Harris, Stuart (1993) 'Federalism and Australian Foreign Policy' in Brian Hocking (ed.), *Foreign Relations and Federal States* (London: Leicester University Press), pp.90–103.

Hocking, Brian (1984) 'Pluralism and Foreign Policy: The States and the Management of Australia's External Relations', *Yearbook of World Affairs*, London.

Parliament of Australia, Report by the Senate Legal and Constitutional References Committee (1995) 'Trick or Treaty? Commonwealth Power to Make and Implement Treaties' [http://senate.aph.gov.au/committee/legcon_ctte/4chapt5.html].

Ravenhill, John (1990) 'Australia' in Hans J. Michelmann and Panyotis Soldatos (eds), *Federated States in International Relations* (Oxford: Oxford University Press), pp.76–123.

Taylor, W. (1996) 'Trick or Treaty: An Australian Perspective.' [http://www.aph.gov.au/house/committees/jsct/1SPEECH.HTM].

The Quebec Experience: Success or Failure?

LOUIS BALTHAZAR

Quebec is probably the most advanced case of international involvement for a non-sovereign state.[1] There are many factors that led the French-speaking province of Canada to become internationally active by the mid-1960s. A good number of these factors are pertinent to the general rise of transnational relations during the same period as well as other motivations that are common to many non-sovereign international actors (Hocking, 1994; 1997). I have myself insisted elsewhere that most Quebec international operations are much more related to adaptation and necessity than reflecting a search for a special status both within Canada and on the international level (Balthazar, 1992; 1993 a, b). There are however other factors that make the Quebec case unique and do account for the particularly intense level of international involvement on the part of this non-sovereign state. This article will attempt to show that Canada's foundation and evolution made it more legitimate (if not easier) for one of its provinces to play an international role as well as Quebec's deep-rooted political identity. This provided for an interesting compromise arrangement between Ottawa and Quebec allowing the latter to acquire a certain status. But the advent of a government formed by a sovereigntist party made things somewhat more complicated, especially since the 1995 Quebec referendum on sovereignty. Parallel to these developments, the growth of Pan-Canadian nationalism made it much more difficult for Quebec to conduct international relations. Thus the case of Quebec may show that the equilibrium between a unique centralized foreign policy and the diverse international relations of a heterogeneous modern state is a fragile one. Central governments will allow their constituent parts to play an international role as long as this does not threaten the interests of the former and the image they wish to project abroad.

CANADA'S GENESIS AND EVOLUTION

Canada is a country that is particularly susceptible to give way to centrifugal diplomacy. First, by its very origin, it was not bound for a long time to develop a nationalism of its own. If there is a Canada today, it is due mainly to the refusal of its original population to take part in the American Revolution and, consequently, its determination not to build a nation as the United States had done. French Canadians were the first to refuse the

American Revolution in exchange for their own recognition by the British Crown through the Quebec Act of 1774. The Loyalists fled from the new country and settled in what was left of the British Empire to the North. They swore to remain different from their former compatriots by not creating a nation and rested their political identity on their allegiance to King and Empire (Bell, 1992). Thus for a long time Canada may be said to be a 'non-nation', basically a component of the British Empire, the antithesis of the American Republic which claimed to be greater than the sum of its parts. If this claim was challenged for some time by the Southern states, it became undisputed after the Civil War. Thus, while the American Constitution was proclaimed by the ringing words 'We the people', Canada's Constitution – the British North America Act, adopted by the Westminster Parliament ... began with the word 'whereas'. The founding fathers of Canadian Confederation may have created a new country but, in spite of their pretensions to build a nation, Canada was not a real fully-fledged nation-state.

In fact, for quite some time, officially until 1931 but a little earlier in practice, the government of Canada did not control its foreign relations. In such a context, provinces could be considered as capable as the central government to conduct international relations. This is not to say that Ottawa did not play a role at the international level and that provinces were as active as the Canadian government. Of course the latter became more and more involved, within the framework of British imperial policy, in all sorts of international activities. A Department of External (not Foreign) Affairs was created in 1909, mainly to deal with the United States but also to organize Canada's growing international role. But it was so important to let Great Britain prevail that there was strong opposition even to the creation of a mission in Washington in 1927. For R.B. Bennett, then the Conservative leader of the Opposition in the House of Commons, this amounted to unacceptable separatism: 'It is but the doctrine of separation, it is but the evidence in many minds of the end of the connection with the empire... If we are a sovereign state, we cannot belong to the British Empire' (Mahant and Mount, 1989: 127).[2]

Of course, Canada became fully sovereign but in a gradual way. Canadians never made a great case of the Statute of Westminster which granted Canada its complete autonomy as a Dominion of the British Commonwealth. One could safely assert that the British umbilical cord was not cut until the 1960s. In fact, Canadian citizenship was not instituted until 1947. The Canadian Supreme Court did not rule in final appeal before 1949. A proper Canadian flag was not adopted until 1965 (while Quebec had had an official flag since 1948) and a national anthem became official only in 1979.

Canadian provinces, for their part, claimed to be autonomous bodies, entirely responsible in their own large areas of jurisdiction. According to certain theories of Canadian federalism, provinces were equal partners with the central government, not to be subordinated to the latter. This was not accepted by everyone of course and was challenged by the federal government. But, as long as the judicial committee of the Privy Council in London was the ultimate Court of Appeal in constitutional matters, it tended to rule in favour of a large provincial autonomy. These judgements will be later interpreted by Quebec officials as granting the provinces the right to conduct international agreements in the matters under their jurisdiction.

As a result of both its early involvement within the large context of the British Empire and its reluctance to national assertion, when Canada found itself a middle-power after the Second World War, its natural tendency was to confer great value to its participation in international organizations. Canada's foreign policy was deliberately multilateral, and its officials were at ease in any of these groups. In fact, Canada is probably the country with membership in the largest number of international institutions. Again, Canada did not make itself known for its nationalism but for its internationalism. Such a stance prevailed at least until 1968 and it created a climate within the country that allowed for a loose and decentralized conception of the national interest, if there was such a thing as a unique Canadian national interest.

Moreover, as a small country with no strong national tradition, with a superpower as a neighbour and the inevitable stewardship that this entailed, Canada did not play a major role in international politics as such. It did not and could not have a very original foreign policy, that is, politically speaking. As a consequence, when priorities are defined, they almost invariably pertain to economic interests and the need to be better known. Canada is a rich country and devotes quite a large portion of its economic production to foreign exports. Hence the importance of foreign trade. But, here again, provinces come to the fore since they hold important jurisdiction over natural resources (of which Canada abounds) and they often express their own economic interests. As for the need to project a good image abroad, a province like French Quebec is obviously keen on its own distinctive features.

Finally, Canada is a multicultural and bilingual country. Quebec, being the only province with a French-speaking majority, may easily claim to be better equipped to embody the French essence of Canada, even though there are some French-speaking populations in other provinces. Quebec may even claim to have its own multicultural policies, since integrating immigrants and foreign cultures into distinctive French Quebec entails a different process and generates specific immigration policies.

As a consequence of all these factors, in 1965 when Quebec made its case for the right to have its own external policies and to sign international agreements in fields of its jurisdiction, it met with a fragile opponent. Canadian foreign policy was still a young and relatively unsure institution, but at the same time Canadian foreign affairs officials were all the more proud of their recent achievements and eager to assert their authority and preponderance over a provincial government. In particular, those French-speaking diplomats from Quebec, who had painfully found their way into what had been a very select English-speaking club in the department of External Affairs, were naturally quite shocked at Quebec's efforts to promote *sui generis* international relations. This was indeed a new phenomenon, and the claims that were made then had been unheard of before. It was obviously a reflection of the great modernization movement that had been taking place in Quebec since 1960, the so-called 'Quiet Revolution'. But, at the same time, Quebec officials could rely on the particular history of a political entity that was at least two centuries old.

QUEBEC: A DEEP-ROOTED POLITY

The province of Quebec can truly trace its origins to long before the Canadian Confederation. A specific colony called 'New France', and soon 'Canada', was settled on the Quebec territory in the mid seventeenth century and gave rise to a political organization. The French Empire went much beyond the present borders of the province of Quebec but there was a particular political settlement on the banks of the St. Lawrence on what is now the Canadian province. When the British displaced the French with the Treaty of Paris in 1763, they called this part of the newly acquired territory the 'Province of Quebec' and soon recognized it as a distinct society to be ruled by its own laws inherited from the French regime and shaped by the Catholic religion which was practised by the overwhelming majority of its inhabitants. In 1791, a new relatively uninhabited territory was carved from the old Province of Quebec to allow the settlement of newly arrived Loyalists. It was called 'Upper Canada' while French Quebec was called 'Lower Canada'. The two colonies could enjoy some form of political representation embodied in Houses of Assembly but the colonial government was still not responsible to them.

This obviously did not allow these political entities to conduct international relations since they were entirely subservient to British imperial policy. Nonetheless some members of the Lower Canada Assembly sought to establish relations first with the British Parliament and eventually with the United States. An agency of Lower Canada was established in the imperial metropolis from 1816 to 1833. The Speaker of the House, Louis-Joseph Papineau, travelled to London, won the sympathy of some members of the House of Commons and, after he unsuccessfully led a rebellion in 1837, went south to try to obtain support from American politicians and, after vain efforts, lived in exile in France where he could establish a few connections. This is not foreign policy, of course, not even really official international relations, but it was already a look abroad coming from Quebec as such.

In 1840, as a consequence of the troubled eras of 1837–38 in both Upper and Lower Canada, the two colonies were united in an effort to assimilate the French-Canadians into one British Canada. This did not take place. Even if Quebec had ceased to be a political entity of its own, it kept a solid identity to the point that, in practice, a duality was established in political institutions divided into Canada East and Canada West, corresponding to the former separated colonies. The 1867 Confederation created a larger ensemble but Ontario and Quebec became two distinct provinces with a large degree of autonomy. In Quebec, Confederation was always understood by the elite as a pact between two nations allowing the French Canadians to design their own political institutions according to the interests of a population in which they were the majority.

Again foreign policy was not a prerogative of the provinces. But neither was it the responsibility of the federal government, as we have seen above. Thus Quebec could appoint a representative in Paris in 1882 before Canada as such had opened any mission abroad. Some Quebec premiers crossed the Atlantic to visit France in their official function. Eventually the Quebec delegate became the Canadian minister. But Quebec also created a mission in London in 1908, another one in Brussels in 1915. These missions were all closed in the 1930s during the Depression. In 1940 an office was opened in New York mainly for economic purposes, for the promotion of trade and tourism. Already one could witness the effect of transnational relations between the United States and Quebec.

Thus when a delegation was opened in Paris in 1961, at the call of President De Gaulle who had visited Canada the year before, it was nothing new in itself. Quebec was responding to what had been wished by many among its growing community of young intellectuals and artists who had frequently been in France, especially since the end of the Second World War. To balance these new relations with the old mother-country, a general delegation was also created in London, and the mission in New York was upgraded in 1962. Later on, offices were opened in Milan, Brussels, Düsseldorf, in other American cities and in many places throughout the world.

While Quebec was simply doing what had been done before, it was undoubtedly doing it in a new assertive spirit. This corresponded to

modernization and to a newly understood role for the government of the
province. It was realized that the Quebec government was the only
institution where French-speaking Canadians could be in majority and in a
capacity to exert control. The territory of Quebec was the only one in North
America where a network of institutions and communication could be
established in the French language. The French-speaking majority of
Quebec would no longer identify itself as 'French Canadian'. It would, from
then on, refer to itself as Quebecker. All of this was conceived within the
federal structure. Some separatist movements were formed but they
remained marginal until the late 1960s. Yet, as loyal as Quebeckers
remained to Canada, they could not continue to see themselves as being part
of a Canadian province like the others. Frequent references were made to
the State of Quebec instead of the Province (a word with pejorative
connotations in the French language).

This could not but be reflected abroad. The Quebec government could
take advantage of new transnational realities, of the increasingly blurring of
the differences between domestic and external politics, of the developing
international role of federated units, including other Canadian provinces.
But its goal was not and could not be limited to low politics. It had to seek
to project a particular image abroad that Canadian missions were not yet
projecting adequately: that of a vibrant and dynamic French-speaking
society wishing not only to maintain its language and culture but to make it
grow and flower by opening wide windows on the world at large and by
establishing as many international links as possible. In other words, it
wanted to become a fully-fledged international actor.

This is why Quebec's growing international relations could soon be seen
as a threat to the Canadian government. All the more so in the year of 1965
when a 'doctrine' was formulated to justify the signing of international
agreements with France without Ottawa's supervision. This doctrine was
nothing but the expression of full autonomous responsibility of a provincial
government in the fields under its jurisdiction. It was expressed in two
speeches made by Mr Paul Gérin-Lajoie who was then minister of
Education. The language was blunt enough:

> Quebec is not sovereign in all matters: it is a member of a federation.
> But it constitutes, in a political sense, a state. It possesses all elements:
> territory, population, autonomous government. It is also the political
> expression of a people that is distinct in many ways from the English-
> speaking communities inhabiting North America.

> In all matters that are completely or partially under its competence,
> Quebec intends from now on to play a direct role that conforms to its
> personality and its rights... Quebec is determined to take its proper

place in the contemporary world and to make sure it has, externally as well as internally, all the means necessary to realize the aspirations of the society it represents (Bernier, 1996: 39: my translation).

The minister went on to make the point that there was no reason why the fact of implementing an international convention should be dissociated from the right of negotiating and concluding such a convention. He also considered it not acceptable that Ottawa would practise surveillance and control over Quebec's international relations.

Ottawa did not waste any time. It responded immediately through the voice of its minister of External Affairs, Paul Martin, with a strong assertion of the one and only international Canadian personality within the community of nations and of the exclusive power of the federal government to conclude and sign treaties. The debate went on and Quebec never accepted fully Ottawa's claim, although it could not but yield to it in practice. To this day the 'Gérin-Lajoie doctrine' is considered as the official foundation of Quebec's international activities. If not on the doctrine, at least on an international status for Quebec, the federal and provincial government could nonetheless achieve a compromise.

ARRANGEMENT AND COMPROMISE

With the help of France, Quebec had already secured a formal international presence. In the beginning the Canadian government, following its tradition of decentralization and tolerance, had not only approved but applauded and facilitated the opening of a delegation in Paris. In fact, the first delegate was a former federal official, the man who had just been director of the House for Canadian students in the French capital. Ottawa did not seem overly concerned with the special treatment offered by the DeGaulle government. At the same time, in London, the Quebec delegate general (or 'agent general') enjoyed diplomatic immunity. But Canadians had always received special consideration in the United Kingdom as members of the Commonwealth and, until recently, as British subjects. The British government had traditionally given much consideration to the provincial units of its Dominions, at least to the Canadian ones.

By 1965 however the situation was taking another turn and Ottawa began to react negatively, as we have just seen. To make things worse, an experienced French Canadian diplomat had just left the Canadian diplomatic service to accept the functions of delegate-general of Quebec in Paris. Jean Chapdelaine, former Canadian ambassador to Brazil, Sweden and Egypt, was treated by the French government with the same protocol as if he were still representing a sovereign country. This was particularly offensive to one of his old colleagues, Marcel Cadieux, who was appointed at the same time deputy-minister of External Affairs, the first French Canadian to receive this honour. It is in such a context that a treaty was signed by the French and Quebec officials on educational co-operation without the presence and approval of Canadian representatives. Ottawa hurried to conclude a framework agreement with France first in education, then in matters of culture to cover the Quebec agreement which would be called an 'entente' as well as another one on cultural exchanges.

In spite of Ottawa's stance, the DeGaulle government continued to encourage and foster Quebec's international endeavours especially in French Africa, much under the aegis of France. DeGaulle went as far as showing sympathy for the secessionist movement when he shouted 'Vive le Québec libre' from the Montreal city hall balcony on 24 July 1967. This created a diplomatic incident which was soon to be followed by another offence to Canadian prerogatives, when France was instrumental in having Gabon invite Quebec to participate alone to a conference on education for French-speaking countries in 1969. Ottawa immediately reacted vigorously by breaking relations with Gabon. It did not take long before the small African country offered excuses to the Canadian government which resumed relations and offered generous co-operation.

But Quebec was still in search of a status in the institutions of French-speaking countries, especially in the Agence de co-operation culturelle et technique (ACCT: agency for cultural and technical co-operation) that it contributed to create. Quebec claimed to be the sole representative for the French-speaking population of Canada as it was its only really Francophone government and was presiding over the only elaborate network of communications in the French language in Canada. But Ottawa, on its part, could rest its case on its being the only depository of sovereignty, holding responsibility for international relations and being able to represent all the French-speaking people of Canada, some of whom lived outside the province of Quebec. After all Canada was a bilingual country and was making renewed efforts, with the proclamation of the Official Languages Act in 1969, to foster the use of the French language in all government services throughout the country.

After much debate and bitter exchange between the two capitals, an agreement was reached that would allow Quebec to be a 'participant member' of ACCT but in the framework of the Canadian delegation. This status, in spite of its limitation, was considered as a real success for Quebec, having achieved with it its first membership in an international multilateral organization.

Quebec would naturally wish to become a member of a larger political organization that was to be called 'Francophonie'. But the Ottawa government was adamant. If an international organization was to be created (and Prime Minister Trudeau favoured its creation for as long as he was in office, 1968–79, 1980–84) it could not but be composed of sovereign countries on the model of the Commonwealth. Ottawa therefore would be the only representative for Canada. The Province of Quebec would have no business there. France opposed the setting of Francophonie, partly because of this exclusion of Quebec but also because it preferred to pursue its privileged relations with its former colonies in a bilateral way. The situation had changed, however, by 1985. There was a new Conservative government in Ottawa, much more inclined to compromise with the French-speaking province and, in Quebec, a federalist party was elected at the helm of the province. The Quebec Liberals were also more disposed to negotiate with Ottawa. All the more so since it was Robert Bourassa who returned as premier, the same man who had patiently presided over the 1971 compromise on the ACCT and who discreetly pursued and enhanced Quebec's international relations without confrontation with Ottawa. Brian Mulroney, the Canadian Prime Minister (1984–1993), was also a man of the centre. Moreover, the French government had become much less jealous of its bilateral relations with French-speaking countries. As a result, an agreement was reached in 1986 for the first meeting of the countries of Francophonie. The terms were similar to the one relating to ACCT. But since there were to be some political discussions among the participants, on topics dealing with world politics, in fields that were the obvious responsibility of a sovereign state, Quebec had to be excluded from these discussions. Therefore the agreement contained the following provision:

> On issues relating to the world political situation, the Premier of Quebec is present and behaves as an interested observer. On issues relating to the world economic situation, the Premier of Quebec could, after dialogue and with the ad hoc agreement of the Prime Minister of Canada, intervene on those of interest to Quebec… On issues relating to co-operation and development, the government of Quebec participates in debates and proceedings in full part, according to modalities and practice already followed at ACCT (Morin *et al.*, 1992: 519; my translation)

Beside these formal agreements, one could observe over the years a real *modus vivendi* between Quebec and Ottawa in matters of international relations. In spite of all the debate related above, on a practical basis – on the ground, so to speak – the representatives from the two capitals had generally harmonious relations. Quebec often benefited from the much more elaborate settings and instruments of Canadian diplomacy, especially in countries where Quebec either could not afford to be represented or could keep only a small office. Canadian diplomats often welcomed this heterogeneous extension of their work as a positive asset for the country. Moreover it has to be stressed that Quebec and Ottawa rarely conflicted on issues of substance or on political matters. It is interesting to point out that the entire debate about Quebec representation dealt almost uniquely with process. What made it much more difficult and sensitive is the advent of a government of the Parti Québécois (PQ) in 1976, to remain until 1985 and to come back in 1994 and remain to the present day.

PARADIPLOMACY OR PROTODIPLOMACY

Protodiplomacy is a word generally used to designate the diplomatic efforts of representatives who want to obtain recognition for an eventual sovereign state. This is to be distinguished from the diplomacy of a non-sovereign entity not specifically seeking a sovereign status (paradiplomacy). As the party that was in power in Quebec from November 1976 onwards aimed at achieving the independence of Quebec (the first article of its programme), most observers expected that the PQ government would practise protodipomacy and would work incessantly to promote the proposed objective of Quebec sovereignty throughout the world.

This was not so and for good reasons related to the ambivalent nature of the Quebec population and of leaders who were connected to public opinion. Let us say first that the founder of the PQ, René Lévesque, was a man who well reflected this ambivalence. For some time, he worked to achieve a better status for Quebec in the Canadian federation and when he had recourse to the sovereignty project, he would not do so without attaching to it a plan for economic association with the rest of Canada. At many times in his career, especially as Premier of Quebec, he gave the impression that he would have been satisfied with a renewal of the federal system that would account for greater autonomy for Quebec.

Moreover, the PQ had not been elected with a mandate to bring about the sovereignty of Quebec. It had campaigned on a platform of 'good government' and had kept quiet about its main project, except to promise that a referendum would be held during its mandate on whether or not sovereignty-association should be realized. Therefore, without a specific mandate for sovereignty, Quebec officials were in no position to promote it.

There was another factor that rendered Quebec diplomacy low-key and not much different from previously. Ironically enough, PQ leaders spent so much time convincing their followers that Canadian federalism was a failure and, during the campaign, on politics as usual – that is, provincial politics – that they had not developed much sophistication on issues of foreign policy, much less on problems of international security. For instance, they had been naïve enough to adopt a quasi-neutral platform on matters related to the Cold War, like participation in NATO and the North American Defence Organisation (NORAD), overlooking the fact that they would never get away with it while remaining a friendly neighbour of the United States. In this context, Premier Lévesque made a trip to New York two months after his election to reassure the Wall Street business community about his government's intentions. Lévesque had a penchant for the Americans. He had good memories of his service in the US forces as a journalist during the Second World War. Thus he was sincere when he thought he could attract sympathy for his cause with a speech at the Economic Club of New York in January 1977. While insisting that his government was social-democratic, not socialist by any means, he tried to compare the Quebec sovereignty movement with the American Revolution. He failed lamentably, not taking into account the fact that Americans tended to consider Canada as a successful and democratic state, a peaceful and accommodating neighbour (in spite of frequent quarrels on trade matters), a country quite similar to their own where individual liberties were protected. Thus what came to their mind, when they were suddenly informed of the secessionist movement, was the comparable move on the part of the Confederate states in the nineteenth century. To them, it was the Civil War, not the Revolutionary War. And the Civil War had silenced the secessionists. Lincoln, the president who began the war for the sake of unity, had become a hero, a second founding father. American unity is something to be celebrated. Why would it not be the same in Canada? Consequently, they had nothing but polite applause for the Quebec Premier.

Returning home, Lévesque understood that any big talk on sovereignty in the United States would be totally counterproductive. He was also pragmatic enough to realize that Quebec's priority should be to maintain sound economic relations with American investors and shareholders as well as those who were floating Quebec government and Hydro-Quebec bonds on the American market. Quebec should also continue to seek better access for its exports in the United States, by far its number one trade partner. Therefore, Quebec's continued paradiplomacy sought to reassure Americans, but did little to explain to them the rationale for secession. At best, the objective sought was to obtain benevolent neutrality from the US government in the referendum debate. For that purpose there was no need to appoint officials of strict sovereigntist obedience to represent Quebec. Some federalists, commissioned by the preceding Liberal government, were left in office and, in some cases, new appointments did not reflect the party's nationalist stance.

I have documented elsewhere that, far from becoming more political, the PQ's international policies of that era were even more oriented towards the economy than it was the case for its predecessor (Balthazar, 1993b). This happened to be true even for relations with France, where sympathy could be expected to be higher. The atmosphere of this special relationship had changed after the departure of General DeGaulle and French officials remained prudent, as they stated an official policy of' 'non indifference, but non intervention'. Quebec officials in Paris did not actively work for the promotion of sovereignty.

The Canadian government however, understandably enough, became worried by the presence of the PQ in power and by its international activities. As a consequence, the climate of confidence and collaboration was somewhat perturbed abroad. Ottawa became intransigent, not allowing a Quebec presence in key posts, such as Washington, where Quebec was permitted only a tourism office and some monitoring on the part of its political minister posted in New York. But, by and large, especially after the PQ was defeated in its referendum by a large margin, it was often 'business as usual' between Ottawa and Quebec representatives.

Co-operation between Ottawa and Quebec was much more affected by the return of a PQ government to power in Quebec in the fall of 1994. Jacques Parizeau, the man who was then PQ leader and became premier in late September was more radical than René Lévesque in his conception of sovereignty. He promised a referendum in the coming year and had no qualms about his intention to bring about full sovereignty for Quebec as soon as possible. He eventually became more moderate under the influence of public opinion and other political leaders who joined his project so that the question addressed to the population in October 1995 included necessary negotiations with Ottawa and a formal offer of political and economic partnership. But his resolute and confident stance was enough to cause great concern in Ottawa and in the rest of the country, let alone the Quebec federalists who were opposed to Quebec's secession.

There was however no all-out mobilization of Quebec representatives abroad. But the climate was tense enough to give the impression that Quebec had moved towards protodiplomacy. The new minister of International Affairs, Bernard Landry, was not yet talking about preparing for Quebec sovereignty abroad but he defined Quebec's external relations in terms of a 'nation' seeking to be heard and recognized. In a speech delivered in Montréal on 14 December 1994, he defined a modern concept of the nation as 'the place where democracy is practised, where social relations and arbitration are played and where the citizen has the greatest opportunity to take part in decisions that affect him or her.' (Bélanger, 1997: 49–50; my translation). This idea of a Quebec nation could be understood of course in the context of the Canadian federation but, as it was developed by a sovereigntist leader, it indicated a move towards an active diplomacy involving the promotion of a sovereign Quebec nation-state. Nonetheless there was no concerted effort to call for the eventual recognition of a sovereign Quebec by international partners. Quebec officials knew well enough that such an operation would be totally counterproductive: first, because Canada already enjoys such international standing that there are few who do not wish it to stay united; and second, because Ottawa has the means to retaliate to a Quebec offensive to the point of quasi-annihilation.

The atmosphere remains even more tense in the aftermath of the October referendum. Contrary to 1980, the result was terribly close (49.4 per cent voted 'yes' to the proposal of sovereignty with a formal offer of political and economic partnership with the rest of Canada) and, as a consequence, the Quebec government, still controlled by the PQ and enjoying good public support (especially under a new leader, the charismatic Lucien Bouchard), is determined to call another referendum early in the new century.

Lucien Bouchard has not embraced explicit protodiplomacy. He even closed a good number of missions abroad, keeping only six general delegations in Paris, London, New York, Brussels, Tokyo and Mexico, in the context of a deficit-cutting programme. According to the Premier, the best way to prepare for eventual sovereignty is to re-establish sound public finance by reducing the budget deficit to zero in the year 2000. However the sheer fact that a government is preparing itself to become sovereign, even though its diplomacy is not geared towards obtaining support for this intention, is enough to give at least the appearance of protodiplomacy. This is certainly how the Canadian government reads the situation, with the support of the largest part of the Canadian public.

RECENT CANADIAN NATIONALISM AND INTOLERANCE

The Canadian government has become more intolerant than ever of Quebec's international relations. Canadian diplomacy is mobilized everywhere to counter almost every effort of Quebec to play a distinctive role and assert its unique character. This of course takes place as a reaction to the presence of sovereigntists in the Quebec government and is natural enough. However this is more than a reaction. It may be seen as a trend predating the sovereignty movement. In fact one can see Quebec nationalism as an effect of a new Canadian nationalism as much as the other way around. The tragedy of the contemporary Canadian conundrum can be defined by the mutual reinforcement of these two nationalisms.

I have described Canada above as a non-nationalist country bent on gradualism, moderation, tolerance, heterogeneity and decentralization. In other words, Canada was the exact opposite of the Jacobean nation-state. A movement has taken place however, beginning with the 1930s – the period when Canada gained its total autonomy (at least in a formal way) and the welfare state was imposing itself in the context of economic depression. Thanks to that movement, quite strong among English-speaking intellectuals and civil servants, Canada would be gradually conceived as a nation-state by its elites, including its foreign policy elites. The rise of the country to prominence and prosperity after the Second World War helped to reinforce this new mood. Quebec has resisted however for the good reason that decentralized federalism was essential to the French-speaking province. The resistance was first passive and traditional, which only contributed to the Canadian nationalists' success as they could identify themselves with progress and modernity. But by the 1960s and the Quiet Revolution, Quebec's resistance became positive and more threatening to the new concept of Canada as one nation first and foremost. This was the time when a new international role for Quebec was conceived and promoted. The 1960s were also years when Canada seemed to adjust to Quebec's insistence on autonomy in the old Canadian spirit of compromise. The idea of the one and only Canadian nation, represented by an old stubborn leader who moved from the government to the opposition (John Diefenbaker) did not register much progress until the end of the decade. Lester Pearson, prime minister between 1963 and 1968, epitomized by his attitudes and policies the Canadian tradition of conciliation, compromise and internationalism.

Things would change considerably in 1968 with the advent of Pierre Elliott Trudeau who promoted a more nationalist and assertive foreign policy and did everything he could to have his fellow French-speaking Quebeckers reconciled to the idea of one bilingual Canadian nation and consequently to a unique foreign policy based on Canada's national interests, defined in Ottawa. This did not fit at all with Quebec's new international role, and it is only with great reluctance that Trudeau accepted the compromise and arrangement mentioned above.

Trudeau finally achieved his goal of having Canada shaped into a national mould by bringing about the patriation of the Canadian Constitution and proclaiming a new fundamental law with an annexed Charter of Rights and Freedoms. This was done in 1982 over the objections of Quebec's National Assembly, including its federalist members. The tragedy of this move is that it isolated Quebec as a whole from the constitutional process, not only the PQ government of the time (which had given up on sovereignty for an indefinite period) but also the federalist Liberal Opposition. As I indicated above, with Mulroney in Ottawa and Bourassa in Quebec by the end of 1985, there was a mood of conciliation that was reflected internally as well as externally. But all efforts to have Quebec endorse the new constitution eventually failed.

The new conception of Canada as one nation and the decline of a federalism based on two independent levels of government was greatly reinforced by the new constitution, by what was called the Charter spirit (Cairns 1991: 166). According to this new spirit Canadians see themselves less and less as belonging to a province and more and more as members of groups calling for their rights or simply as individuals. This phenomenon may be called the 'defederalization' of Canada.

Such a mood understandably prevails more within the department of External Affairs than elsewhere. For people already devoted to working for Canada abroad and inevitably less aware of internal tensions within their country, the definition of Canada as one tight-knit nation is welcome. Moreover, as Canada is always intent on practising cultural diplomacy and presenting a good image abroad, promoting one national culture (or a mosaic of subcultures, which is not that different) is a much simpler endeavour than reflecting asymmetry and accepting an important role for the provinces.

This new tendency is well projected in the 1995 government statement of foreign policy entitled *Canada and the World*. The paper sets three goals for Canadian foreign policy: the promotion of prosperity and employment, the projection of our security within a stable global framework and the projection of Canadian values and culture. It is under this third heading that that the new conception of Canada appears more clearly. Notice that 'culture' is always written in the singular. The immediate implication is that there is no distinctive Quebec culture. Moreover the document goes on to refer to 'our educational system' (p.11): singular again. No mention is made that education is one of the most important provincial jurisdictions in Canada. The promotion of 'Canadian culture and learning' is defined as 'a way to create an identifiable image for Canada and its goods and services'. It is recommended therefore 'to make better use of Canada's artists and scholars as part of a fundamental re-thinking of the way we promote ourselves and our products abroad'. Such utterances make it quite clear that Ottawa intends to monopolize cultural diplomacy for its own purpose.

But what about multilateral diplomacy? What about Quebec's status in Francophonie. Here again much is made of Canada's presence in multilateral organizations. Francophonie is mentioned along with the Commonwealth, with no reference to Quebec's role. Canada is always defined in singular terms. True, the uniqueness of the country is detailed into its being 'bilingual, multicultural and deeply influenced by its Aboriginal roots, the North, the oceans, and its own vastness' (p.37). But one who would read the document without previous knowledge of Canada would not know that there is a French-speaking province. One would hardly even discern that Canada is a federation. The only mention of provinces is in the following passage: 'We will work closely with the provinces, the

private sector, universities, colleges and all intended stakeholders to
promote Canadian institutions of higher education' (p.38).

With such a definition of Canadian foreign policy, there is not much
room for a Quebec diplomacy. Let us note that this policy statement was
published before the referendum of October 1995 and was prepared
previous to the return of the PQ in power. The referendum only reinforced
the nationalist offensive from Ottawa. The distribution of Maple Leaf flags
became part of Canadian actions abroad. I personally saw a senior diplomat
in an important embassy offering flags to a crowd attending a cultural event.
In February 1997, Lloyd Axworthy, Canadian minister of Foreign Affairs,
issued new directions for the promotion of Canadian culture. Artists would
be helped to perform abroad as long as they contribute to the promotion of
Canadian values and would project a certain image of Canada as defined by
the department of Foreign Affairs. This policy provoked such negative
reactions, especially in Quebec, that it was finally withdrawn. But it is
typical enough of the new aggressive nationalism that is displayed in
Canadian foreign policy.

It is true that Quebec does not help its cause when some of its officials
envisage international relations as a way to promote sovereignty. But there
are many Quebec representatives who do not act in such a way, just giving
the image of Quebec as a distinctive province, and they are either ignored
or discreetly side-tracked by Canadian officials. The case of the partial
presence of the New York councillor in Washington for the purpose of
monitoring is a good example of this attitude. In 1998 this official was, for
practical purposes, considered by the Canadian embassy as *persona non
grata*. One cannot but conclude that even paradiplomacy would be
extremely difficult in the present context.

CONCLUSION

Canada had all the features as a country to allow an important exercise of
paradiplomacy and even be a model of asymmetric federalism and
decentralized foreign policy. Quebec is the one Canadian province with
more reason to play an important international role, hence the co-operation
and arrangements that could have prevailed between Quebec and Ottawa in
those matters. These arrangements may be considered as exemplary. Two
distinct developments contributed to weaken if not destroy this spirit of co-
operation. One is the slow evolution of Canada towards a unitary image of
itself and the promotion of that image abroad. The other is the growth of the
sovereignty movement in Quebec, which can be seen as a direct
consequence of the rise of Canadian nationalism. Even if a secessionist
government in Quebec intends to continue its international relations in the

context of the federation, it provides a good pretext for Canadian foreign policy to claim a unique and exclusive presence abroad.

If the Quebec experience serves as a lesson, it shows that central governments will tolerate an international presence for some of its regions only as long as it is not too meaningful.

NOTES

1. I prefer to use this phrase 'non-sovereign' as opposed to 'subnational', for the very reason that many so-called subnational actors pretend to be nations in a limited sense.
2. It is interesting to compare this unwillingness to 'separate' from Great Britain to the current Quebec sovereigntists' reluctance to use the word 'separation'.

REFERENCES

Balthazar, Louis (1993a) 'Quebec's International Relations: A Response to Needs and Necessities', in Brian Hocking (ed.) *Foreign Relations and Federal States* (London and New York: Leicester University Press) pp.140–52.

Balthazar, Louis (1993b) 'Les relations Québec-Etats-Unis', in L. Balthazar *et al.*, *Trente ans de politique extérieure 1960–1990* (Sillery, QC: Les Editions du Septentrion), pp.65–105.

Balthazar, Louis (1992) 'The Other Side of Canada–U.S. Relations', in John English and Norman Hillmer (eds), *Making A Difference? Canada's Foreign Policy in A Changing World Order* (Toronto: Lester Publishing Ltd), pp.15–33.

Bélanger, Louis (1997) 'Les enjeux actuels de la participation du Québec à la francophonie multilatérale: de la paradiplomatie à la protodiplomatie', *Politique et société* (Société québécoise de science politique, Montréal), Vol.16, No.1.

Bell, David V.J. (1992) *The Roots of Disunity, A Study of Canadian Political Culture* (Toronto: Oxford University Press).

Bernier, Luc (1996) *De Paris à Washington. La Politque Internationale du Québec* (Québec: Les Presses de l'Université du Québec).

Cairns, Alan (1991) *Disruptions: Constitutional Struggles from the Charter to Meech Lake* (Toronto: McClelland and Stewart).

Government of Canada (1995) *Canada in the World: Government Statement* (Canada Communication Group-Publishing, Public Works and Government Services, Ottawa).

Hocking , Brian (1994) 'Les intérêts internationaux des gouvernements régionaux: désuétude de l'interne et de l'externe', *Études internationales (*numéro spécial sur *Les politiques extérieures des États non souverains* sous la direction de Ivan Bernier), Vol.xxv No.3, pp.409–20.

Hocking, Brian (1997) 'Regionalism: An International Relations Perspective', in Michael Keating and John Loughlin (eds), *The Political Economy of Regionalism* (London and Portland, OR: Frank Cass).

Mace, Gordon *et al.* (1996) 'Canadian Foreign Policy and Quebec', in Maxwell Cameron and Maureen A. Molot, *Canada Among Nations 1995:Democracy and Foreign Policy* (Ottawa: Carleton University Press).

Mahant, Edelgard and Graeme Mount (1989) *An Introduction to Canadian–American Relations*, 2nd edition (Toronto: Nelson Canada).

Morin, Jacques-Yvan *et al.* (1992) *Droit international public: Notes et Documents, tome II: Documents d'intérêt canadien et québécois* (Montréal: Éditions Thémis).

The International Relations of Basque Nationalism and the First Basque Autonomous Government (1890–1939)

ALEXANDER UGALDE ZUBIRI

THE FOREIGN AFFAIRS OF BASQUE NATIONALISM AS AN OBJECT OF STUDY

This contribution examines from a historical perspective the background to the present-day Basque presence abroad, namely, the international relations of Basque nationalism (1890–1936) and the first Basque autonomous government (1936–39). The presence of the Basque Country in contemporary international society, its role as another actor on the international scene, is a very topical subject. This can be observed in the fact that Basque foreign action grew more and more intense, taking shape in all sorts of events – political, economic, social, cultural – as well as in other activities showing 'features of internationality' (Truyol, 1987). I am referring to the foreign action promoted by the Basque government (bilateral and multilateral co-operation among regions, co-operation across nations, co-operation for development, activities promoting the economy and culture, attention to Basque communities living abroad, trips, offices in other countries, the creation by the Basque government of the General Secretariat for Foreign Affairs), and to the activities carried out by social organizations, such as political parties, non-governmental organizations and municipal councils. It is not a recent phenomenon we are dealing with; there are some antecedents to be considered. This is why my study about the presence of Basque nationalism abroad is made from a historical perspective. This requires us to employ the expression 'international actor' in the broad sense in line with the trend in international relations from state-centred formulae to more modern approaches which underline the existence, alongside the state and international or supranational organizations, of a series of 'transnational forces' (Merle, 1988) or which consider the presence of unofficial actors within the 'plurality of members' of International Society to be significant (Arenal, 1990; García, 1993).

This aspect of Basque nationalism must be placed within the frame of reference of a broader international phenomenon captured in concepts such as 'non governmental diplomacy' (Zorgbibe, 1982) and 'protodiplomacy'

(Duchacek, 1986). These concepts are used to explain the role of nationalist movements, national minorities and ethnic groups not dominant within International Society as actors in international relations (Esman, 1990 and 1995; Mayall, 1990; Heraklides, 1990; Smith, 1991; Chazan, 1991; Schechterman and Slann, 1993; Moynihan, 1993; Ryan, 1995; Esman and Telhami, 1995). This subject is arousing more and more interest both in the field of historiography (Núñez, 1996) and in the theory of international relations (Cornago, 1996) and it also appears in other studies dealing with nationalism in general (Beramendi, Maiz and Núñez, 1994).

The year 1995 was the centenary of Basque Nationalism, if we take as a point of reference 31 July 1895, when the first *Bizkai-Buru-Batzar* (General Council of Biscay), the embryo of the Basque Nationalist Party (*Partido Nacionalista Vasco*), was constituted. From this date it gradually consolidated its doctrinal, programme and organization, gaining social influence and electoral presence to become an essential component of the Basque contemporary history; today it remains part of the complex Basque socio-political reality, albeit divided into several ideological and political formations.

There are some outstanding studies of Basque nationalism.[1] The centenary has brought a further wave of studies (Granja, 1994 and 1995; Pablo, 1995; Pablo, Granja and Mees, 1998). Yet the international aspects of Basque nationalism have been rather neglected, with some notable exceptions. Granja (1989) covers the *Galeuzca* pact and the agreement of its signatories to combine their efforts in pursuit of 'propaganda and international action'. Estévez (1991, 1992) deals with relations among the peripheral penninsular nationalisms, one of whose features was that they thought of their alliances as 'international', and with nationalist presence in European congresses. Núñez's (1992a) doctoral thesis is about the nationalities in Europe between the wars and the Catalan, Galician and Basque 'protodiplomacy' at the Congress of European Nationalities. The same author has written on the repercussion of Irish nationalism on the Iberian nationalisms (Núñez, 1992b) and on the international relations of Basque nationalism (Núñez, 1995a, 1995b). Conversi (1993) deals with the consequences of the international events on Basque and Catalan nationalism, and Lorenzo (1992) with the influence of Irish nationalism on Basque nationalism. San Sebastián (1991) is a compendium of the materials of the Basque Delegation in New York. With regard to international relations, we can note Aguirre (1987), who has studied historical models of an integrated Basque space and its articulation with other international spaces.

This article focuses on the crucial period from 1890 to 1939 and asks whether Basque nationalism followed a definite model for its action abroad during the these years, looking both at the theoretical basis for the policy, and its practical application. Three broad conclusions emerge:

- First, Basque nationalism as a political and social movement, structured through several political organizations in different phases, took its first steps in the last decade of the nineteenth century, and its action abroad increased until the late 1930s. Its activities were in the beginning weak and irregular but they reached a considerable level during the years of the Republic.
- Second, projection abroad is something inherent in Basque nationalism. Its doctrine, its sustaining principles, its goals and its platform made it establish its project of a Basque political space in relation to the European frame and the international context. Basque nationalism had to establish itself in the Basque country, both as an organization and also as regards political, social and electoral aspects; it had to raise its demands before the central government and it had to make itself a place on the international scene following, to a great extent, the path of other nationalist movements. All things considered, I think that the activities of Basque nationalism abroad are consistent with its doctrine.
- Third, we can identify several indicators which, both separately and as a whole, show that the foreign action performed by Basque nationalism conformed to a well defined pattern with its corresponding chronological evolution. In this respect, it was the sort of foreign action typical of a political movement, that is to say, it consisted of diplomatic relations of a non-governmental character which aimed at achieving the international recognition of nationalism itself as a political movement and, in future, the international recognition of the Basque nation.

The constitution of the first Basque government in 1936 brought about a significant, qualitative advance as regards foreign action, since it meant the beginning of institutional, governmental action. Insofar as it had its own government, the Basque country became an actor within international society, and its government, as a representative of the Basque people, played a prominent role on the international scene. The activities carried out by the Basque government between 1936 and 1939 not only have historical value, they also provide a precedent for the international activities of sub-state actors which are nowadays becoming so important (Duchacek, Latouche and Stevenson, 1988; Duchacek, 1990).

INDICATORS OF THE MODEL OF FOREIGN ACTION AND THEIR APPLICATION

The problem of processing and interpreting all the material gathered, basically coming from nationalist periodicals and texts written by nationalist leaders, is solved by applying a number of indicators which enable us to identify and specify the pattern followed by nationalism with regard to foreign action. These fall into three types: doctrinal (sustaining principles); platform (aims pursued); and instrumental and auxiliary. In all, there are ten indicators:

Historical Context

In order to examine the foreign action it is essential to make reference, in each phase, to the triple Basque, Spanish and international frame. For instance, the consequences of the First World War influenced the thought and the activity of the Basque nationalists, which makes the relation between local and worldwide events evident.

The International Context and Events

Finding out how and with what intensity and regularity Basque nationalism followed and kept a record of what happened abroad, mainly by means of its periodicals, it emerges that Basque nationalism was not a self-centred movement, but followed international processes such as the European nationalities movement.

Sustaining Principles

Foreign action is usually based on ideological-political guidelines of a more or less generic nature, which set the framework for concrete decisions and activities. The founder of nationalism himself, Sabino Arana, demanded an independent Basque Confederation (*Euskadi*) with its own frontiers and international relations. Later on the official doctrine based on the recovery of the old Basque *fueros* (statutory privileges) and subject to a number of interpretations ranging from autonomy to independence, implied that such independence should be attained in foreign affairs too.

The Goals of Foreign Action

These were established little by little and by the 1930s they had been fully elaborated. Among them we can underline: relations with other nationalist movements; presence at the international organizations of nationalities and minorities; contacts with embassies and consulates; the establishing of relations with governments; the tightening of the bonds of friendship with Basque communities living abroad; foreign propaganda and, finally, the presentation of the Basque 'national problem' on the international scene.

International Alliances

The fact that they did exist and that they involved reaching agreements and acting in co-ordination with other interlocutors shows that international links became highly developed. Some plans for activities abroad were never fulfilled. Thus, Sabino Arana in 1901 thought of achieving the Basque independence 'under British protection' and his brother, Luis Arana, put a personal project to the British Foreign Office in 1938 for the establishment of a British Protectorate in the Basque country. In 1924 a project was outlined for a 'League of Oppressed Nations', an alternative to the League of Nations, composed of the Basque country, Catalonia, Ireland, Egypt, Morocco, India and Philippines. Furthermore, the agreements signed by the Basque, Galician and Catalonian nationalists ('Triple Alliance' in 1923 and 'Galeuzca' in 1933) were considered by their signatories as 'international'. Membership in international organizations is included under this heading, the two most important events being attendance at the Third Congress of the *Union des Nationalités* (1916) and participation in the Congress of European Nationalities (1929–30). There was also a trade union, Basque Workers' Solidarity, which joined the International Confederation of Christian Trade Unions.

Means and Instruments

It was when foreign action had already completed its initial phase that Basque nationalists started to set the appropriate means and instruments to reach their goals. Their achievements depended on how conscious they were of the need to start some really effective devices and also on whether they had at their disposal the organization, and human and economic means necessary to support them. Such means did not appear in a proper, stable way until the 1930s and in relation to them we must underline the creation of a Basque General Secretariat by the Basque Nationalist Party, in charge of 'international propaganda'.

Foreign Delegations

These are concrete proof of international presence and denote their interest in keeping permanent links and relations with other countries. Although it was never done, in 1902 Sabino Arana thought of sending 'representatives to other nations'. From 1904–06 onwards nationalist delegates were appointed in Latin-American countries (Argentina, Cuba, Mexico) and in Philippines, and later on in Europe (Dublin and Paris). Nevertheless, the great step forward was taken with the institutional delegations of the Basque government during 1936–39, which represented not only nationalists but also other republican and left-wing political tendencies.

Activities and Ways of Showing Their Presence Abroad

Under this heading I have gathered several concrete initiatives and activities (for example, trips and tours; communiqués and manifestos; relations established with other movements, diplomatic corps, governments and international organizations; propaganda). Among many examples, we can cite: a telegram from the *Sociedad Euskalerria* to William Edwart Gladstone, British Prime Minister, in 1894; the telegrams from Sabino Arana to Theodore Roosevelt, president of the USA, and to Lord Salisbury, British Prime Minister (1902); the trip to Rome of a delegation which held interviews with the Vatican Secretary of State and with Pius X (1911); the nationalist official position for the Allies in the First World War (1914); bilateral relations with other delegations (Lithuanian, Albanian, Caucasian) during the Third Congress of the *Union des Nationalités* in Lausanne (1916); a telegram from several deputies and senators to Woodrow Wilson, president of the United States, acknowledging his doctrine (1918); demonstrations in support of the Irish republican movement (1920); support to the Riffean rebellion in Morocco (1921); the establishment of formal relations with the Sinn Féin (1922); a document sent to the League of Nations (1926); support for the Pan-European movement (1926 and 1929); memorandum to the representatives of the League of Nations (1929); the visits of Ewald Ammende, secretary of the Congress of European Nationalities, to the Basque country (1931 and 1933); regular contacts with national groups such as Bretons and Flemish (1932); a tour of Argentina and Uruguay (1934); a trip to Geneva during which some interviews were held with the President of the Council of the League of Nations and with the Abysinian representative (1935); another trip to the Vatican (1936).

Geographical Area

In order to evaluate the presence of Basque nationalism abroad, one must bear in mind the areas at which its action was aimed and explain the reasons why some areas had priority over others. For reasons of geographical proximity, historical links and political decisions, most contacts took place within Western Europe and with America.

We now need to consider how these factors operated over time, as Basque nationalism consolidated its position with regard to foreign affairs, from its formative years, until its culmination in the Spanish Civil War.

THE EVOLUTION OF FOREIGN ACTION

During the five-decade period chosen, the nationalist activities abroad went, in summary, through five important moments:

• It was between the end of the nineteenth century and the beginning of the twentieth, at the time when Basque nationalism was born and started to expand, that its action abroad took its first steps, but nationalist foreign action was slow at the beginning. We can see some of the indicators already: the attention paid to international events; activities such as trips or sending telegrams; the impulse given to extra-territorial affiliation or the designation of delegates of the Basque Nationalist Party (PNV) in America. Yet starting international relations was a secondary task, as there were more fundamental needs to meet regarding both political and organization matters. The *euskalerriaco* (moderate nationalist) Eduardo de Landeta pointed it out in the weekly *Euskalduna* in 1909: 'Nobody took the trouble to establish relations with the world outside'. It is, therefore, too early to talk about a pattern of foreign action.

- In the late 1910s and early 1920s, coinciding with the First World War and the postwar period, foreign action underwent a considerable advance. The nationalist leaders became aware of the need to go abroad, and this involved a theoretical effort as well as a number of initiatives. There were the first attempts to achieve international recognition, as can be deduced from the attendance of the Basque Nationalist Party to the Third Congress of the *Union des Nationalités* (Lausanne, 1916), asking to be 'recognized as belligerent in this great fight of small nationalities'. There were greetings and relations observed after the war; and the claims for a space on the international scene and even for a place at the League of Nations. In this respect José Vilallonga talked about the 'international personality' of the Basque people, declaring that they cannot give up their relations with other countries (*Hermes*, 1918). Luis de Eleizalde said: 'we must manage to take the Basque Nation, respected by everybody, into the assembly of the cultivated people of Europe' (*Hermes*, 1919).

- In spite of the split between the two nationalist parties, *Comunión Nacionalista Vasca* (CNV) and PNV, on a more *aberriana* political line, that is to say, more radical and secessionist, foreign policy activity increased in the early 1920s with, for example, contacts with the Irish republicans and expressions of solidarity with the Moroccan Rif, although it suffered a temporary interruption during the Primo de Rivera dictatorship. Nevertheless, there were some notable events in the second half of the 1920s, such as the assumption of Pan-Europeanism by the *comunionistas* (Ugalde, 1994) and the sending of some memoranda to the League of Nations by the *aberrianos*.

- Nationalist foreign action recovered and consolidated from the early 1930s, and into the Spanish Second Republic (1931–36), reaching almost complete consolidation in all respects. Despite the peculiarities of the different nationalist parties (PNV and ANV –*Acción Nacionalista Vasca*) and groups (*Jagi-Jagi*), the internationalist conscience and doctrine were well established. Foreign affairs began to occupy a prominent place and there developed a variety of relations and activities worldwide. In 1931

José Antonio Aguirre predicted such a process: 'Today we are proceeding toward a foreign life for our country'. Numerous articles were written in the nationalist press focusing on the international facet of the Basque problem. The PNV created a Basque Secretariat General, for propaganda abroad. There were trips to other countries. The PNV joined the Congress of European Nationalities and attended their annual meetings, according to Ramón Bikuña this gave 'worldwide character to our case'. A new motto 'Euzkadi-Europa' was coined.

- The final phase commenced in 1936 with the establishment of the autonomous Basque government and the simultaneous outbreak of the Spanish Civil War. Foreign action took a further step culminating the process that began some decades before. It can now be described as Basque and institutional, going beyond international relations of a merely nationalistic nature and between political parties. For Basque nationalism this was the culmination of its most deeply felt aspirations, and for the rest of the Basque republican parties it involved contributing, despite disagreements, to a historical moment for the Basque Country with regard to its presence abroad. The new way of managing foreign affairs was the basis for the policy that the Basque cabinet would follow in the 1940s and 1950s.

THE FOREIGN ACTION OF THE FIRST BASQUE GOVERNMENT FROM 1936 TO 1939

The first Basque government was constituted in October 1936 after the Statute of Autonomy for the Basque country was passed. The cabinet, headed by José Antonio Aguirre, included a variety of political representatives, all of them loyal to the Spanish Republic and opposed to Franco's party, including the Basque Nationalist Party (*Partido Nacionalista Vasco*) and the Popular Front (*Partido Socialista Obrero Español, Partido Comunista de Euskadi, Acción Nacionalista Vasca* – left-wing Basque nationalist party, *Izquierda Republicana* and *Unión Republicana*), with diverse ideological and political positions.

It developed its activities mainly in two fields: the Spanish Civil War and the complex international situation previous to the Second World War. It governed under special circumstances due to the military confrontation, so most of its means were put in the service of the needs raised by the conflict. In juridical terms, international relations were the exclusive competence of the Spanish central government, according to the Spanish Constitution of 1931 and the Statute of Autonomy of the Basque country of 1936. However, the political and military circumstances of the period brought about the assumption by the Basque government of further responsibilities in several matters (army and war direction, autonomous police, issue of currency, passports, foreign trade, Basque Red Cross, enterprises of its own), surpassing what was provided by the law. In the same way, it was also able to establish international relations.

The foreign action of the Basque government pursued several objectives:

- the defence on the international scene of the legitimacy of the Republic, faced with Franco's rebellion, and the denunciation of foreign military intervention – German and Italian – in the Basque territory, which broke the non-intervention agreements;
- the implementation of a number of measures aimed at meeting the basic needs arising from the location of the Basque territory, which was partly isolated from the other republican areas – in this regard, there were a number of activities involving foreign trade matters, provisioning, air and sea transport, evacuation and sheltering of refugees, which doubtless had a foreign aspect;
- the proclamation before the International Society that formally the Basque country was already an autonomous region within the Spanish state, despite the war situation;
- seeking a foreign presence for the Basque country, mainly in the political and cultural spheres;
- and, finally, the aspiration of the Basque country and its government to be recognized by other states and international organizations.

Within the Presidential Department, a Secretariat for Foreign Relations was created which was in charge of co-ordinating the foreign relations of work carried out by the different departments of the government, and of guiding the work of the Basque delegations in other countries. That Secretariat was directed by Bruno de Mendiguren, whom George Lowter Steer, a South African journalist working for the British newspaper *The Times*, called the 'Mr. Eden of Euzkadi' in his book *The Tree of Gernika: A Field Study of Modern War* (published in London, 1938).

The international activites performed by the Basque government between 1936 and 1939 can be summarized under twelve headings:

Contacts with embassies and consulates.

The most important were those with diplomats from Great Britain (Ambassador Henry Chilton), France (Ambassador Jean Herbette), the United States of America (Ambassador Claude G. Bowers), the Soviet Union, Argentina and the Vatican.

Agreements through the International Red Cross

These were for the humanization of the war and the exchange of prisoners.

Contacts with governments through messages and interviews

These included messages to French leaders Léon Blum and Edouard Daladier, President Franklin Delano Roosevelt of the Unitet States, British Prime Minister Arthur Neville Chamberlain, and Czechoslovak leader Edvard Bénés.

Economic initiatives with a foreign scope

These included the purchase of arms, sending business agents to buy products, control of the foreign currency deposits, managing the activities of the Basque merchant navy, the regulation of international airlines and the setting up of enterprises in other countries, for instance, the 'Mid-Atlantic Shipping Company Limited' in London and the 'Société Finances et Entreprises' in Paris.

Control of the international sea frontiers, immigration services, evacuation of the civilian population and control over the Diplomatic Corps

This included the dismantling of the Francoist spy ring, in which the consuls of Austria, Hungary and Paraguay were involved, and expulsion of the German, Italian and Portuguese consuls.

Granting of diplomatic asylum in the offices of the Basque delegations in Spain, which acted as foreign legations.

Visits to the Basque country of foreign personalities, political representatives, delegates, writers, religious authorities and journalists.

These included Reverend Helwett Johnson, Dean of Canterbury, and Leah Manning of the British organization 'Spanish Medical Aid'. There were notes of support such as those sent from London by David Lloyd George and Clement Attlee.

Solidarity from other countries.

This can be seen in the statements signed by French personalities, *Pour le peuple basque. Un appel à tous les hommes de coeur*, and one by American personalities, 'An appeal to the conscience of humanity'. Incidents such the bombing of Guernica stimulated overseas interest and committees were founded to deal with refugee issues, for example The American Board of Guardians for Basque Refugee Children.

The work of the delegations of the Basque government.

These were appointed in the Spanish cities of Madrid, Barcelona, Valencia and Alicante; in Europe, in Paris, Bordeaux, Brussels-Antwerp and London; and in the Americas, in New York, Boise, Buenos Aires, Mexico, Santo Domingo, Caracas and La Havana.

Activities of propaganda.

Books and magazines were published, such as *Euzko-Deya*. Official spokesmen were located in the Basque delegations in Paris, London and Buenos Aires. There was a Basque section in the Spanish Pavilion at the Universal Exhibition in Paris. Tours were arranged for the *Euzkadi* football team and folk groups all over Europe and America.

Initiatives of a diplomatic nature.

These included attempts to mediate with several foreign interlocutors, including diplomats from several countries, during the war.

The creation of institutions.

These included the Basque Red Cross, International League of Friends of the Basques, Pro-Basque Inmigration to Argentina Committee, and a proposed Basque Worldwide Association.

THE QUALITATIVE CHANGE: FROM THE FOREIGN ACTION OF BASQUE NATIONALISM AS A POLITICAL MOVEMENT TO THE GOVERNMENTAL INTERNATIONAL ACTION OF THE FIRST BASQUE GOVERNMENT

So during the 1936–39 phase, foreign action underwent a qualitative change with the first Basque government under the presidency of José Antonio Aguirre. Yet, although this entailed a positive qualitative and quantitative change for the Basque country as regards its presence abroad; it built on the foundations laid in the earlier period and represented a development of earlier trends.

Until 1936, with regard to specifically nationalistic foreign action, what we have is a political movement with a concrete ideology, which managed foreign affairs according to its sustaining principles, goals, alliances – that is to say, according to its own political criteria. Between 1936 and 1939, however, what we have is a legal government with an institutional character and which, because of the historical situation, had to assume its responsibility as a sort of 'acting state' and, therefore, exercised a shared sovereignty with the Republican government. The Basque government was forced, given such exceptional situation, to perform sovereign functions reserved for the state. Besides, the cabinet, widely supported both socially and politically, was representative of the Basque people of the time, which undoubtedly had decisive consequences as regards foreign affairs, since the claim for legality and for democratic legitimacy would contribute to give content to the Basque government's foreign policy arguments right from the beginning.

A decisive change was effected in the scope of international action, the tasks undertaken and the structure of the Basque government. The contacts and relations established, the official or semi-official recognition of the delegations and wider spread of propaganda represented a huge advance on what had been achieved before by nationalism as a political movement.

Euskal Herria (the Basque country), as a nation, with the first Basque government of its history, entered international life by right. This course could be pursued in the following years, since the Basque government in exile did not dissolve or break up. The Basque country continued to be present on the international scene as a nation without a state but with a government that could still represent it abroad. This lasted for as long as the circumstances, conditions and configuration of international society, among other reasons, allowed it.

So we can see in this historic experience the antecedents of the present external policy of the Basque nationalist movement and government.

ACKNOWLEDGEMENTS

The author wishes to thank Professor Michael Keating for his methodological advice, so helpful for the elaboration of this article, and Miren Villa for the translation of the same.

NOTE

1. See Larronde, 1972; Payne, 1974; Solozabal, 1975; López Adán, 1976; Apalategi, 1977 and 1985; Elorza, 1978 and 1981; Corcuera, 1979 and 1991; Azcona, 1984; Douglass, 1985; Granja, 1986; Letamendia, 1987; Pablo, 1988; Martínez, 1989; Heiberg, 1989; Waldmann, 1990; Mees, 1991 and 1992; García de Cortázar and Azcona, 1991; Meer, 1992; Ugalde, 1993; Beobide, 1993; Chueca, 1996; Zabalo, 1996).

REFERENCES

Aguirre, Iñaki (1987) 'Nacionalismo vasco y relaciones transnacionales en el contexto de la frontera hispano-francesa: cuatro modelos históricos', in C. del Arenal (ed.), *Las relaciones de vecindad* (Bilbao: Universidad del País Vasco), pp.73–101.
Apalategi, Jokin (1977) *Nationalisme et question nationale au Pays Basque 1830–1976* (Bayonne: Elkar).

Apalategi, Jokin (1985) *Los vascos, de la autonomía a la independencia. Formación y desarrollo del concepto de la nación vasca* (San Sebastián-Donostia: Txertoa).
Arenal, Celestino del (1990) *Introducción a las relaciones internacionales* (Madrid: Tecnos, 3rd edition).
Azcona, Jesús (1984) *Etnia y nacionalismo vasco: una aproximación desde la antropología* (Barcelona: Antrophos).
Beobide, Ignacio María (1993) 'Nacionalismo vasco: nación y poder', *Estudios de Deusto*, Vol.41, No.1, pp.9–98.
Beramendi, Justo G., Ramón Maiz and Xosé M Núñez (eds) (1994) *Nationalism in Europe. Past and Present* (Santiago de Compostela: Universidad de Santiago de Compostela, 2 volumes).
Camino, Iñigo and Luis de Guezala (1991) *Juventud y nacionalismo vasco. Bilbao (1901–1937)* (Bilbao: Fundación Sabino Arana).
Chazan, Naomi (ed.) (1991) *Irredentism and International Relations* (Boulder: Lynne Rienner).
Chueca, Iosu (1996) *El nacionalismo vasco en Navarra durante la II República* (Doctoral Thesis, Universidad del País Vasco/Euskal Herriko Unibertsitatea).
Conversi, Daniele (1993) 'Domino Effect or Internal Developments? The Influences of International Events and Political Ideologies on Catalan and Basque Nationalism', *West European Politics*, Vol.16, No.3, pp.245–70.
Conversi, Daniele (1997) *The Basques, the Catalans and Spain* (London: Hurst & Company).
Corcuera, Javier (1979) *Orígenes, ideología y organización del nacionalismo vasco (1876–1904)* (Madrid: Siglo XXI).
Corcuera, Javier, Oribe, Yolanda and Alday, Jesús María (1991) *Historia del nacionalismo vasco en sus documentos* (Bilbao: Eguzki, 4 volumes).
Cornago, Noé (1996) *Acción exterior y paradiplomacia: la proyección internacional de los mesogobiernos* (Doctoral Thesis, Universidad del País Vasco/Euskal Herriko Unibertsitatea).
Douglass, William A. (ed.) (1985) *Basque Politics: A case study in Ethnic Nationalism* (Reno: University of Nevada).
Duchacek, Ivo D. (1986) *The Territorial Dimension of Politics: Within, Among and Across Nations* (London: Westview Press).
Duchacek, Ivo D. (1990) 'Perforated Sovereignties: Towards a Tipology of New Actors in International Relations', in H.J. Michelmann and P. Soldatos (eds), *Federalism and International Relations. The Role of the Subnational Units* (Oxford: Clarendon Press), pp.1–23.
Duchacek, Ivo D., Daniel Latouche and Garth Stevenson (eds) (1988) *Perforated Sovereignties and International Relations. Trans-Sovereign Contacts of Subnational Governments* (New York, Greenwood Press).
Elorza, Antonio (1978) *Ideologías del nacionalismo vasco, 1876–1936* (San Sebastián-Donostia: Haranburu).
Elorza, Antonio (1981) *Nacionalismo vasco, 1876–1936 (temas)* (San Sebastián-Donostia: Haranburu).
Esman, Milton J. (1990) 'Ethnic Pluralism and International Relations', *Canadian Review of Studies in Nationalism*, Vol.XVIII, No.1–2, pp.83–93
Esman, Milton J. (1995) 'Ethnic Actors in International Politics', *Nationalism and Ethnic Politics*, Vol.1, No.1, pp.111–125.
Esman, Milton J. and Shibley Telhami (eds) (1995) *International Organizations and Ethnic Conflict* (Ithaca: Cornell University Press).
Estévez, Xosé (1991) *De la Triple Alianza al Pacto de San Sebastián (1923–1930). Antecedentes del Galeuzca* (San Sebastián-Donostia: EUTG-Mundaiz).
Estévez, Xosé (1992) 'El nacionalismo vasco y los Congresos de Minorías Nacionales de la Sociedad de Naciones (1916–1936)', by several authors *XI Congreso de Estudios Vascos* (San Sebastián-Donostia: Sociedad de Estudios Vascos), pp.311–22.
García de Cortázar, Fernando and José Manuel Azcona (1991) *El nacionalismo vasco* (Madrid: Historia 16).
García, Caterina (1993) 'La evolución del concepto de actor en la teoría de las relaciones internacionales', *Papers*, No.41, pp.13–31.
Granja, José Luis de la (1986) *Nacionalismo y II República en el País Vasco: Estatutos de*

Autonomía, partidos y elecciones. Historia de Acción Nacionalista Vasca, 1930–1936 (Madrid: Siglo XXI).

Granja, José Luis de la (1989) 'La alianza de los nacionalismos periféricos en la II República: Galeuzca', in J.G. Beramendi and R. Villares (eds), *Actas Congreso Castelao* (Santiago de Compostela: Universidad de Santiago de Compostela), Vol.1, pp.321–47.

Granja, José Luis (1990) *República y Guerra Civil en Euskadi* (Oñati: IVAP).

Granja, José Luis de la (1991) *Bibliografía de Historia Contemporánea del País Vasco* (Vitoria-Gasteiz: Eusko Bibliographia).

Granja, José Luis de la (1994) 'La historia del nacionalismo vasco en la bibliografía más reciente', *Notas* (Frankfurt), No.2, pp.2–12.

Granja, José Luis de la (1995) *El nacionalismo vasco: un siglo de historia* (Madrid: Tecnos).

Heiberg, Marianne (1989) *The Making of the Basque Nation* (Cambridge: Cambridge University Press).

Heraklides, A. (1990) *The Self-Determination of Minorities in International Politics* (Londonand Portland, OR: Frank Cass).

Larronde, Jean-Claude (1972) *Le nationalisme basque. Son origine et son idéologie dans la vie et l'oeuvre de Sabino Arana Goiri* (Bordeaux: Université de Bordeaux).

Larronde, Jean-Claude (1977) *El nacionalismo vasco: su origen y su ideología en la obra de Sabino Arana Goiri* (San Sebastián-Donostia: Txertoa).

Letamendia, Pierre (1987) *Nationalismes au Pays Basque* (Bordeaux: Presses Universitaires de Bordeaux).

López Adan, Emilio 'Beltza' (1976) *El nacionalismo vasco, 1876–1936* (San Sebastián-Donostia: Txertoa).

Lorenzo, José María (1992) 'Influencia del nacionalismo irlandés en el nacionalismo vasco, 1916–1936', by several authors *XI Congreso de Estudios Vascos* (San Sebastián-Donostia: Sociedad de Estudios Vascos), pp.239–47.

Martínez, Araceli (1989) *Antecedentes y primeros pasos del nacionalismo vasco en Navarra, 1878–1918* (Pamplona: Gobierno de Navarra).

Mayall, James (1990) *Nationalism and International Society* (Cambridge: Cambridge University Press).

Meer, Fernando de (1992) *El PNV ante la Guerra de España (1936–1937)* (Pamplona: Universidad de Navarra).

Mees, Ludger (1991) *Entre nación y clase. El nacionalismo vasco y su base social en perspectiva comparativa* (Bilbao: Fundación Sabino Arana).

Mees, Ludger (1992) *Nacionalismo vasco, movimiento obrero y cuestión social (1903–1923)* (Bilbao: Fundación Sabino Arana).

Merle, Marcel (1988) *Sociologie des relations internationales* (Paris: Dalloz, 4th edition).

Moynihan, Daniel Patrick (1993) *Pandemonium: Ethnicity and International Conflicts* (New York, Oxford University Press).

Núñez, Xosé Manoel (1992a) *El problema de las nacionalidades en la Europa de entreguerras. El Congreso de Nacionalidades Europeas (1925–1938)*, Doctoral Thesis, European University Institute of Florence, see also a summary in (1994) *Bulletin d'Histoire Contemporaine de l'Espagne* (Bordeaux), No.19, pp.122–7.

Núñez, Xosé Manoel (1992b) 'El mito del nacionalismo irlandés y su influencia en los nacionalismos gallego, vasco y catalán (1880–1936)', *Spagna Contemporanea* (Torino), No.2, pp.25–58.

Núñez, Xosé Manoel (1995a) 'Relaciones exteriores del nacionalismo vasco (1895–1960)', in S. De Pablo (ed.), *Los nacionalistas. Historia del nacionalismo vasco, 1876–1960* (Vitoria-Gasteiz: Fundación Sancho el Sabio), pp.381–417.

Núñez, Xosé Manoel (1995b) 'Protodiplomacia exterior o ilusiones ópticas? El nacionalismo vasco, el contexto internacional y el Congreso de Nacionalidades Europeas (1914–1937)', *Cuadernos de Sección. Historia-Geografía. Sociedad de Estudios Vascos*, No.23, pp.243–75.

Núñez, Xosé Manoel (1996) 'Minorías nacionales y relaciones internacionales en las historiografías anglosajona y centroeuropea: algunas reflexiones' (Communication at the I Congress of History of the International Relations, Madrid, 1994) in *La historia de las Relaciones Internacionales: una visión desde España* (Madrid: Comisión Española de

Historia de las Relaciones Internacionales), pp.315–52.

Pablo, Santiago de (1988) *El nacionalismo vasco en Alava (1907–1936)* (Bilbao: Ekin).

Pablo, Santiago de (ed.) (1995) *Los nacionalistas. Historia del nacionalismo vasco, 1876–1960* (Vitoria-Gasteiz: Fundación Sancho el Sabio).

Pablo, Santiago de, José Luis de la Granja and Ludger Mees, (eds) (1998) *Documentos para la historia del nacionalismo vasco. De los Fueros a nuestros días* (Barcelona: Ariel).

Payne, Stanley G. (1974) *Basque nationalism* (Reno: University of Nevada Press).

Ryan, Stephen (1995) *Ethnic Conflict and International Relations* (Aldershot: Dartmouth Publishing, 2nd edition).

San Sebastián, Koldo (1984) *Historia del Partido Nacionalista Vasco* (San Sebastián-Donostia: Txertoa).

San Sebastián, Koldo (ed.) (1991) *The Basque Archives. Vascos en Estados Unidos (1938–1943)* (San Sebastián-Donostia: Txertoa).

Schechterman, Bernard and Martin Slann (eds) (1993) *The Ethnic Dimension in International Relations* (New York: Praeger).

Smith, Paul (ed.) (1991) *Ethnic Groups in International Relations* (New York: New York University Press).

Solozabal, Juan José (1975) *El primer nacionalismo vasco: industrialismo y conciencia nacional* (Madrid: Túcar).

Truyol, António (1987) *La Sociedad Internacional* (Madrid: Alianza, 6th edition).

Ugalde, Alexander (1994) 'Nacionalismo vasco y europeísmo', *Muga* (Bilbao), No.89, pp.6–11.

Ugalde, Alexander (1995a) 'La acción exterior del nacionalismo vasco (1890–1939): historia, pensamiento y relaciones internacionales', *Bulletin d'Histoire Contemporaine de l'Espagne* (Bordeaux), No.21, pp.122–9.

Ugalde, Alexander (1995b) 'Acercamiento a los vínculos pasados y presentes vasco-africanos (conclusiones de una investigación)', *Estudios Africanos* (Madrid), Vol.9, No.16–17, pp.77–91.

Ugalde, Alexander (1996a) 'La actuación internacional del primer Gobierno Vasco durante la Guerra Civil (1936–39)', *Sancho el Sabio* (Vitoria-Gasteiz), No.6, pp.187–210.

Ugalde, Alexander (1996b) *La acción exterior del nacionalismo vasco (1890–1939): historia, pensamiento y relaciones internacionales* (Oñati: Instituto Vasco de Administración Pública).

Ugalde, Alexander (1997a) 'Entrada del nacionalismo vasco en el Congreso de Nacionalidades Europeas, 1929–1930 (siguiendo la documentación del Fondo Apraiz)', *Revista Internacional de Estudios Vascos* (San Sebastián-Donostia), No.42, No.2, pp.403–21.

Ugalde, Alexander (1997b) 'Les relations internationales du nationalisme basque depuis son apparition jusqu'à la Guerre Civile espagnole (1890–1939)', *Lapurdum* (Bayonne), No.2, pp.359–65.

Ugalde, Mercedes (1993) *Mujeres y nacionalismo vasco. Génesis y desarrollo de Emakume Abertzale Batza (1906–1936)* (Bilbao: Universidad del País Vasco).

Waldmann, Peter (1990) *Militanter Nationalismus im Baskenland* (Frankfurt am Main: Vervuert).

Zabalo, Julen (1996) *Euskal nazionalismoa eta nazio lurraldea* (Bilbao: Udako Euskal Unibertsitatea).

Zorgbibe, Charles (1982) *Sur l'état de la Société Internationale* (Paris).

Making Sense of Paradiplomacy?
An Intertextual Enquiry about a Concept
in Search of a Definition

IÑAKI AGUIRRE

ONLY A MATTER OF FASHION?

This enquiry arises from a personal dissatisfaction with those academic trends in International Relations, which endow certain buzz-words with a mysterious success in specialized literature, even though their analytical definition is not clear. Because its meaning has, academically, evolved in a random way, this might be the case with the term *paradiplomacy,* initially related to the international involvement of non-central governments (NCGs).[1]

The 'paradiplomacy' neologism appeared in the early 1980s in a rather innocent and basically empirical way, within the field of the comparative political analysis of federal states and the renewed theory of federalism, specifically in North American literature about recent forms of federalism or 'new federalism' and the puzzling international activities of federated constituencies.[2] Since then, the term 'paradiplomacy' has experienced a strange detour through recent academic literature about NCG international involvement and the latest 'postmodern' critical analysis of diplomacy.

In such a case, the methodology of our enquiry must be an appropriate one – that is, a methodology able to deal with subtle intellectual moves in academic literature. In the first place, we should have to analyze the academic discourse that invented and promoted the term 'paradiplomacy'. Further, as the meaning of this term varies throughout literature, we could probably not avoid a *semiological* approach to the intellectual contexts in which the re-invention, semantic metamorphosis, later criticism and final dismissal of the neologism came about. Such a critical and literary, rather than empirical, approach to the matter will probably not be appreciated by all scholars in the research field of federalism and regionalism, but it is almost unavoidable. Politics is, even if we do not always acknowledge it, also a matter of *semantics,* an art that implies the *power* to give a certain meaning to things such as complex political processes through *words.* We shall, therefore, have to ask ourselves where, how and why the word 'paradiplomacy' appeared in the academic literature.

Indeed, the emergence, in the 1980s, of the neologism 'paradiplomacy' in the writings of Ivo Duchacek and Panayotis Soldatos on the international involvement of federated states, must be identified, localized and questioned *according to the texts* and the economic, political, ideological and literary conditions of their production. But we shall also have to elucidate how and why the meaning of the term 'paradiplomacy' experienced a subtle semantic shift – becoming one of the most volatile 'paradigms', or 'transparadigms', of a provocative postmodern *deconstruction* of diplomacy, operated, almost at the same time, by James Der Derian.

We shall, finally, have to recall the harsh theoretical criticism this kind of buzz-word has recently suffered, including a certainly convincing – but not totally successful – attempt made in the 1990s, by Brian Hocking, to remove, definitively, such hasty neologisms from the latest academic discourse about the involvement of NCGs in foreign affairs.

Meanwhile, the word 'paradiplomacy' has been definitively enriched by the hazardous *intertextuality* that grew around it, becoming a definitively polysemic, suspicious, criticized – but also fashionable – concept.[3] Can we, still, try to make sense of 'paradiplomacy'?

Any attempt at 'making sense of paradiplomacy' will, necessarily, have to sketch its *genealogy*,[4] tracking the various strategic and tactical manipulations of a multipurpose neologism which has been idly moved as if it was a joker good for almost any theoretical piece of play. This 'genealogical' enquiry will, perhaps, help us understand how and why unexpected (re)interpretative shifts can occur in the academic destiny of an apparently innocuous analytical neologism. If this intertextual enquiry could, in the meanwhile, indirectly afford us some insight into the puzzling scenery of contemporary theories of diplomacy, whether central or non-central, private or public, the attempt will have been worthwhile.[5]

THE INVENTION OF 'PARADIPLOMACY': THE TRANSNATIONAL APPROACH

In a text published after his death, Duchacek seems to endorse the use, proposed by Soldatos, of the 'paradiplomacy' neologism instead of Duchacek's previous term, 'microdiplomacy'. This is one of the rare mentions we have found in the literature of the rather obscure paternity of the term 'paradiplomacy' or, at least, one of the few commentaries about its analytical function in academic literature regarding NCG international involvement.[6]

But what is more important for us is to recall the general intellectual and political North American debate, within which both Duchacek and Soldatos inserted the notion 'paradiplomacy' as an operative analytical concept that seemed to fit a new political phenomenon: the increasing international involvement of NCGs. This academic debate focused on the changes which occurred during the 1970s and 1980s in federal states (the so-called 'new federalism') and, particularly, in the relations between federal governments and federated states in matters of foreign policy. The political tension between the two main poles, central and non-central, of any federal structure, seemed to be even more acute in the field of international relations, since foreign policy had been, historically, the preserve of central government. This tension between central government's 'diplomacy' and the international involvement of federated states was interpreted as a particularly interesting symptom of the dynamic internal process of centralization/decentralization in federal states.

Meanwhile, the theoretical framework needed to interpret and analyze the increasing international involvement of federated states – sometimes, inappropriately, called 'subnational political units' – was to be found in Keohane and Nye's early 'transnational' approach and international 'complex interdependence'. 'Paradiplomacy' was used as the twin of the previous neologism 'microdiplomacy' created by Duchacek, when speaking of 'regional microdiplomacy', that is, transborder regional relations between federated states belonging to different federal states such as the United States and Canada, or the United States and Mexico.

We will have to check these successive definitions, ranging from 'microdiplomacy' and 'paradiplomacy', to 'protodiplomacy' and 'macrodiplomacy', proposed by Duchacek and Soldatos, in order to understand the original tentative, but, analytically, creative, intellectual native ground of the concept of 'paradiplomacy'.

One of the first mentions of 'paradiplomacy' in Duchacek-edited writings appears in *The Territorial Dimension of Politics: Within, Among, and Across Nations* (Duchacek, 1986a).

> The forms, goals, intensity, frequency and importance of noncentral governments' entries onto the international stage vary greatly. They depend on various intervening variables such as coordinating mechanisms, as well as self confidence of the national center; radical, revolutionary or moderate political climate; the quality and skill of provincial/state elites; ethnic/lingual heterogeneity; and, of course, the nature of the political system – non centralizing federal, centralizing federal, decentralized unitary, or centralized (as well as the corresponding political cultures, ranging from confederal to 'Jacobin-centralist')...
>
> The various initiatives taken by noncentral governments on the international scene have so far assumed four distinct yet

interconnected forms: (1) transborder regional microdiplomacy, (2) transregional microdiplomacy, (3) global paradiplomacy, and (4) protodiplomacy (Duchacek, 1986a: 240).

Further, the main concepts are more precisely defined:

> Global paradiplomacy consists of political contacts with distant nations that bring noncentral governments into contact not only with trade, industrial, or cultural centers on other continents...but also with the various branches or agencies of foreign national governments (Duchacek, 1986a: 246–7).
>
> Global protodiplomacy is a term that may be used to describe those initiatives and activities of a non central government abroad that graft a more or less separatist message onto its economic, social and cultural links with foreign nations. In such a context, the regional/provincial parent authority uses its trade/cultural missions abroad as protoembassies or protoconsulates of a potentially sovereign state. Such missions may be sometimes viewed and treated by the recipient foreign government in a similar fashion (Duchacek, 1986a: 248).

In a contemporary text, Duchacek, confusingly, uses, without any distinction, the two neologisms ('microdiplomacy' and 'paradiplomacy').[7]

> The projection of subnational needs and interests onto the international scene has so far assumed two distinct, though quite often interlaced forms: *global microdiplomacy* (or *paradiplomacy*) and transborder regionalism. The first reflects the subnational awareness of global interdependence, whereas transborder regionalism represents a geographically circumscribed response to the risks and opportunities for cooperation arising from contiguity (Duchacek, 1986b: 13).

In the same text, speaking of 'Two Concepts in Search of Pre-Theories' (Duchacek, 1986b: 23), that is, 'transborder regionalism' and 'microdiplomacy', these two notions merge under a more general category: 'paradiplomatic activities'.

> Transborder regionalism and global microdiplomacy are concepts that still remain to be correlated to the working and crises of national and international systems. Our ability to provide these relationships with explanatory coherence is at present outpaced by new developments in domestic and international politics that attract non-central governments to play significant, though clearly secondary, roles on the international scene.

One obvious difficulty is our habit of viewing the nation states – speaking with one legitimate voice to other nation states – as the primary units of analysis in both international and comparative politics. At the opposite pole, although more rarely, is the effort to explain national behavior by international systemic constraints and impulses. What is needed are improved theoretical tools to analyze, correlate, and explain the regional and global paradiplomacy in which so many noncentral governments now engage.

The initial search for a more suitable analytical framework has so far proceeded along the lines of the Nye/Keohane 'world paradigm'. Our study has expanded and changed the paradigm, however, by emphasizing the opposition party and noncentral governments in addition to Nye/Keohane list that consists of such nonstate actors as transnational corporations, ideological movements, churches, and international pressure groups (labor, managers, professionals, artists and intellectuals). I suggest the concept of a nation state as a multivocal (polyphonic) actor which, on the international scene, speaks with more than one central-government legitimate voice: the audible voices of noncentral governments can be heard, as well as the often strident voice of the potential government of tomorrow, the opposition party or the ethnic community aiming at independence. Diagramatically, the nation state *qua* multivocal actor could be illustrated in the form of a stepped Saqqara pyramid, with its separate yet interconnected points of entry on the international scene, in contrast to the neat, single apex of the Cheops pyramid.

It is evident that global and regional microdiplomacy poses some research questions which neither our research data nor our present theoretical tools can answer. A set of additional concepts and pre-theories is required to introduce some order for the purpose of explaining paradiplomatic activities, especially their causes and consequences (Duchacek, 1986b: 23–7).

The taxonomy, nevertheless, becomes more assured in later literature about NCG 'trans-sovereign activities'.

Three types of trans-sovereign activities initiated and maintained by noncentral governments should be briefly identified at this point.
Cross-Border Regionalism or *Regional Paradiplomacy*, which often leads to transborder regional 'cooperative regimes', refers to regionally confined interactions between peripheral local and provincial, state, cantonal, or Länder governments...
Transregional paradiplomacy refers to trans-sovereign, usually institutionalized, contacts between noncentral governments which are

not geographically neighbors but whose national governments are...
Global paradiplomacy involves direct contacts between noncentral
governments in one nation with their subnational counterparts in other
distant (non-contiguous) nations (such as prefectures in Japan or
provinces in China), central governments (inevitably so in socialists'
countries), or private groups in foreign capitals...
Subnational participation in international relations may also take the
form of so-called co-location, that is, the appointment of provincial
personnel to national embassies or consulates abroad (Duchacek,
1988: 12–13).

The same thing occurs, in the same study, with the opposite term of
'protodiplomacy'.

This study applies the term '*proto*-diplomacy' to the conduct of
international relations by a noncentral government that aims at
establishing a fully sovereign state. This is in contrast to
*para*diplomatic activities abroad, primarily concerned with economic,
social, and cultural issues. Protodiplomacy represents diplomatic
preparatory work for a future secession and for the international
diplomatic recognition of such an occurrence (Duchacek, 1988: 22).

In the latest texts of Duchacek, seemingly under the influence of Soldatos,
the term 'paradiplomacy'[8] seems to have, definitively, won the lexical battle
around NCG international activities.

The direct and indirect entries of non-central governments into the
field of international relations vary greatly in form, intensity,
frequency and goals, which are dominantly technical and economic
and only partly political – except in the case of secessionist provinces.
As to their geopolitical dimensions, three categories of negotiating
lines may be distinguished: (1) transborder regional paradiplomacy
(2) transregional (or macroregional) and paradiplomatic contacts, and
(3) global paradiplomacy.
    If by diplomatic negotiation we mean processes by which
governments relate their conflicting interests to the common ones,
there is, conceptually, no real difference between the goals of
paradiplomacy and traditional diplomacy: the aim is to negotiate and
implement an agreement based on conditional mutuality. Both sides
pledge a certain mode of future behaviour on the condition that the
opposite side act in accordance with its promise. In contrast to
domestic law, in international relations (whether on a micro- or a
macro- diplomatic level) no common superior authority can be
invoked in case of violation. Yet, as we know from international

relations, such unenforceable bargains are generally observed, since both sides continue to have a very similar interest in preserving the assumed advantage assured by the initial bargain; in adhering to their pledges as a reaffirmation of credibility, an essential ingredient for future bargains; and in reconfirming the principle of good will.

If, as this study basically argues, paradiplomacy by non-central elected officials and their aides is here to stay – here complementing, there challenging, and often duplicating the macrodiplomacy conduct by central governments – several quite practical questions should be posed. Should foreign-service officers, who manage the nation's macrodiplomacy, be better informed about the problems and management of the various forms of paradiplomacy? ... Should, on the other hand, non-central 'paradiplomacy' have some exposure to centre-to-centre macrodiplomacy before they are assigned abroad? (Duchacek, 1990: 15–16).

Soldatos, in his study 'An Explanatory Framework for the Study of Federated States as Foreign-policy Actors' (1990), developed some of Duchacek's most acute insights about NCG foreign involvement in federal states, and focused on the rationalizing process implied in the process.

The foreign-policy activity of a federated unit, in the setting of an advanced industrial society, involves a whole array of concepts, the 'hard core' of which could be reduced to the following, presented in the subsequent rubrics as part of a few taxonomies on *segmentation, paradiplomacy, paradiplomatic actions, segmentation of actors and activities*. The purpose of such conceptualization is to allow for more precision in the definition of the dependent variable that we are trying to explain in this study, i.e., the *paradiplomacy of federated states*.

Although in our previous writings we used the term 'fragmentation' within the context of Canadian and US politics, we decided to adopt here the term of segmentation, proposed by I. Duchacek's work. Such conceptualization could be more appropriate in indicating that segmentation is not always, within the above context, a disintegrating phenomenon (as the term of fragmentation may imply), but could, in many instances, be part of a rationalization process in external relations...

Actor and policy segmentation are two constituent elements of federated units' *paradiplomacy*, i.e. direct and, in various instances, autonomous involvement in external–relations activities. We have two main categories of paradiplomacy: first, *global paradiplomacy* (using the adjective global in a functional rather than in geographic sense, the latter use being proposed by I. Duchacek), where federated units deal with issues concerning the whole international system (e.g. peace and war, liberalization of international trade)...

Such a global paradiplomacy is not common, since federated units usually deal with issues of 'low politics' and matters of regional relevance. Our second type of paradiplomacy is *regional*, where the issues involved are of a regional relevance to the communities taking part in a subnational activity (e.g. issues involving relations between the province of Quebec and New York State).

There are two kinds of regional paradiplomacy: first, *macroregional*, which takes place when actors are dealing with issues concerning communities which are non-contiguous (e.g. Quebec–France); and second, *micro-regional*, where the issues concern communities that have a geographical contiguity (e.g. Quebec–New England states). Micro-regional paradiplomacy can be *transborder* or *transfrontier* (when the contiguity implies common boundaries).

Whereas micro-regional paradiplomacy usually generates minimal controversy, macro-regional paradiplomacy, normally involving actors of different regional systems, can become politicized, even if it refers to a 'low-politics' issue (Soldatos, 1990: 34–8).

The last words of this study summarize the position of Soldatos regarding what he calls 'the paradiplomacy of federated units in advanced industrial societies'.

As a final conclusion, we could formulate the following statement: the paradiplomacy of federated units in advanced industrial societies is here to stay for the foreseeable future; more and more it will take on the aspect of rationalization with less emphasis being placed on conflict. It will increasingly be a co-operative rather than a parallel paradiplomacy; but, although co-operative, it will continue to pose problems for federal governments' foreign policy in terms of harmonization and global coherence; it will make greater use of transnational channels...in conjunction, however, with transgovernmental channels (including the cities' network of international relations). More and more it will be nourished by external causes, mainly by interdependence; more and more it will develop its macro-regional range (Soldatos, 1990: 51).

What is most significant, in these texts, is the main proposition of the overall analysis. The core of the enquiry is not about the international involvement of NCGs, *as such*. The main question is to articulate a critical discourse about *federalism*, stressing the newest challenges faced by 'new federalism', and their diplomatic consequences – such as the 'fragmentation' or 'segmentation' of central diplomacy, and, eventually, of the federal state itself, as a political system.

The main question being about the nature of late federal state's diplomacy and not properly about the federal constituencies' new capability in foreign affairs, the reflection will progress along the axis of an endless *dialectic of centralization/decentralization.* What can happen if 'diplomacy' is no longer the monopolistic captive market of central government? Is it good or bad? Constitutional or unconstitutional? Rational or irrational? The main worry becomes to distinguish between 'good' and 'bad' non-central foreign activity.

In the words used by Duchacek and Soldatos, the main opposition is between 'paradiplomacy' – a new, perhaps a 'good' form of decentralized, complementary and seemingly innocuous kind of 'diplomacy', and 'protodiplomacy' – an older,[9] surely a more dangerous form of non-central foreign activity, always suspected by central governments of 'secessionist' aims.[10]

What is interesting to notice at this stage of the enquiry, is that a neologism such as 'paradiplomacy' *does not appear alone.* It has to be understood as one more link of an analytically endless semantic chain. It has, therefore, to be understood, jointly, with other linked but nevertheless, opposed twin concepts, such as 'micro'-, 'macro'- or 'proto-diplomacy'. The 'transnational' approach to the phenomenon of 'paradiplomacy' results in the analytical 'invention' of a chain of interrelated concepts within a *semantic continuum* or, what is the same, the 'deconstruction' of a main concept (*diplomacy*) into a series of opposite or alternative concepts. This is taken even further by the 'postmodernist', properly 'genealogical', approach to the complex historical phenomenon of 'diplomacy'.

THE RE-INVENTION OF 'PARADIPLOMACY': A NEOCLASSICAL APPROACH

The postmodernist reading of diplomacy dramatically alters the previous meaning of the words 'protodiplomacy' and 'paradiplomacy', which we have been dealing with in the literary context of the 'invention' of these neologisms by the transnational approach. Surprisingly, thanks to Der Derian, we are now pulled back to the most classical intellectual atmosphere of 'realism'. Here the modern 'nation-state' is again in the fray, as main historical reference for the enquiry. Der Derian's 'genealogy' of diplomacy (1987) is an interesting and learned enquiry about the centuries-old international – *diplomatic,* thence, *symbolic* – process of construction of the Western modern nation-state. The focus on state diplomacy is consistent with Der Derian's 'neoclassical' approach to International Relations, as he himself acknowledges (1995). Indeed, this enquiry on 'diplomacy', even though it is methodologically and epistemologically 'postmodern', is intellectually indebted to Hedley Bull,[11] a member of the so-called 'English school' of International Relations, a school of thought in which the 'state' is the main international actor and the 'society of states', the real international arena for diplomacy.[12]

Even if the 'neoclassical' approach of this 'postmodern' International Relations 'master in the making'[13] could, partially, explain his strange heuristic blindness, when speaking of diplomacy, towards so non-conventional a political phenomenon as the increasing involvement of NCGs in foreign affairs, it would nevertheless still be amazing.[14] Indeed, the 'paradiplomacy' neologism appears, rather shyly, in the text of Der Derian's 'genealogy of Western estrangement' (1987), but with a quite different meaning. It is as if the word 'paradiplomacy' had suddenly emigrated *backwards*, from the 'New World' of 'transnationalism', 'complex interdependence', and 'new federalism', back to the 'Old World' of 'anarchical society' of 'states', and Machiavellian secret 'diplomacy', the well-known, quarrelsome, and bloody, 500-year-long process of European nation-state building. This is a surprising ideological and semantic *exodus*, indeed, full of disturbing consequences for the academic destiny of the neologism.

However, the 'genealogical' method of enquiry requires us to quote the *texts* in order to show how the concept of 'paradiplomacy' could now function within a different discourse: the sophisticated 'semiological' framework of diplomatic 'paradigms' constructed by Der Derian.

> The first strategy, a paradigmatic one, is necessary to articulate the vast amount of material in a coherent way. In this case, a paradigm is a shorthand reference to a number of related changes in the principles and practices of diplomacy. It represents something less than Thomas Kuhn's uncompromising scientific 'concrete puzzle-solutions' and something more than Martin Wight's categorical 'traditions'. It resembles Kuhn's in that it is an analytical tool which provides a framework for understanding the period it addresses. However in contrast to Kuhn's original scheme in which no two paradigms can coexist simultaneously, I suggest a multiparadigmatic approach, as does Wight, in recognition of the multiplicity of discourses subsumed in the study of diplomacy. Therefore, I will put forward six interpenetrating paradigms to analyse the origins and transformations of diplomacy: mytho-diplomacy, proto-diplomacy, anti-diplomacy, neo-diplomacy and techno-diplomacy. Other categories which cut

across the major paradigms ('transparadigms', if the neo-realists do not mind) will also be used. Three such categories are crypto-diplomacy, para-diplomacy and, fully earning its quotation marks, 'macho-diplomacy'. I am sure that opinions will vary as to whether these paradigms are insightful reconstructions or inciting deconstructions of the past (Der Derian, 1987: 5).

Unfortunately, the references to 'paradiplomacy' afterwards become so scarce, throughout the witty text of *On Diplomacy,* that the intriguing status, and function of 'transparadigm' allowed to it by Der Derian remains basically unexplained. The new meaning of 'paradiplomacy' seems, nevertheless, clear. Der Derian (re)interprets it in a quite strictly etymological way, as *para*, that is, 'beside', 'along', or 'in opposition to', 'diplomacy'. It seems clear that this kind of 'abnormal' diplomacy is definitely not a new version of *governmental*, albeit non-central, international involvement. On the contrary, it is a politically 'eccentric', democratically uncontrolled, private or corporate, religious or mediatic, strictly *non-governmental* 'diplomacy'. Hence, it can correctly be called 'paradiplomacy' by Der Derian, since this kind of 'diplomacy' moves sideways in relation to the main referential 'diplomacy', the only 'diplomacy' admitted by traditional political discourse: the diplomacy of the central government of the state.

The precise historical examples of contemporary 'paradiplomacy' further proposed by Der Derian, even if quite inappropriate in some cases,[15] are expressive enough of this 'postmodern' shift in the interpretation of the neologism.

> To make some sense of the way states and non-state organizations now communicate and interact at the international level, I would like to suggest that a *techno-diplomacy* is operating. In a general sense, this refers to the global communication processes by which scientific or other organized knowledge is being systematically applied to and inscribed by power politics...
> Not to be overlooked are the parallel forms of mediation generated by techno-diplomacy itself. To avoid confusion with earlier paradigms, these terms would probably best be described as different expressions of a *para-diplomacy*. The expansion of and challenge posed by a global peace movement is one powerful example. Another is the individual response to an apparently depersonalized techno-diplomacy, as demonstrated by Jane Fonda in Hanoi, Armand Hammer in Moscow, Jesse Jackson in Damascus, Bob Geldof in Addis Ababa, and Pope John Paul just about everywhere. Here we see celebrities or, at the very least, elevated personalities, going around

and over the heads of state when techno-diplomacy appears to be at an impasse. Interdependent with celebrity or inspirational diplomacy is another form of para-diplomacy, perhaps the most significant form: media diplomacy. Certainly the methods of media diplomacy are compatible with techno-diplomacy – instantaneous communication, imagery over substance, an instrumentalist, non-teleological approach to global problems – but media diplomacy sits uncomfortably with the official practitioners of techno-diplomacy, who would prefer, especially in crisis situations, monopoly control over the management and perception of events (Der Derian, 1987: 202–3).

No interpretation could be further from the previous meaning of 'paradiplomacy' and from the original academic and political context of the invention of the neologism.

Even 'protodiplomacy' has a different meaning in Der Derian's very personal taxonomy. Its position as *one* moment in the long historical building process of the modern nation-state, and, consequently, of 'diplomacy' itself makes it definitely inappropriate to express any contemporary outbreak of virtually secessionist, non-central diplomacy, oriented towards an international recognition of a future sovereign state, as in Duchacek's and Soldatos's taxonomies.[16] So this ambitious 'semiological' resetting of diplomacy-related categories ignores the most interesting analytical proposal made, some years earlier, by Duchacek and Soldatos: that is to insert the concepts of proto- and para- diplomacy in the complex *inside/outside* and *centralization/decentralization* merging dialectical processes of contemporary federal systems' foreign policy-making.

Nevertheless, Der Derian's disruptive semantic (re)interpretation of 'paradiplomacy', is interesting because it provides a new, and, perhaps, a more appropriate, meaning to the neologism. This meaning could partly explain its ambiguous and ongoing success in specialized literature and in modern casual journalistic jargon. 'Paradiplomacy' could then mean any kind of *non-governmental international activity of non-state actors*, including transnational corporations, international labour organizations, religious communities, NGOs, international lobbies, mass-media industry, transcultural artistic movements, scientific associations, outstanding individuals, which could be broadly labelled 'diplomatic' because they actually operate, to use Der Derian's key philosophical concepts, a 'mediation' between mutually 'estranged' or 'alienated' realities such as civil societies and international governmental organizations, artists and foreign policy-making, scientists and international public opinion. This non-state 'diplomacy' will, of course, essentially be a *non-governmental* 'diplomacy', even if it will have to cope with *states* in the international arena.

'Paradiplomacy' will, nevertheless, be more innocuous than Der Derian's diplomatic 'paradigm' of 'antidiplomacy', because its purpose will not be so politically subversive, the central aim of 'antidiplomacy' being to *subvert* 'diplomacy' and thus the 'state', and replace it by something new such as the 'modern diplomacy' – another paradigm of Der Derian's – promoted by the *Bolsheviks* once they reached power *and* government.

If our main scientific curiosity is, really, to wander around these more or less obscure 'borderlines' of marginal forms of 'diplomacy', no doubt that the 'semiological' approach of Der Derian can, intellectually, be a quite stimulating one, mostly for young International Relations students. But what happens, then, with NCG involvement in international affairs? Here our dissatisfaction appears again, for several reasons.

The first and disturbing problem is about *diplomacy* itself. An interpretation of diplomacy understood as a dialectical and historical process, both of 'estrangement' and 'mediation', is no more than a Hegelianized version of 'political realism'. The 'reality' which lies at the heart of Der Derian's 'genealogy of Western estrangement', is the Hobbesian myth of *Leviathan*, that is, the modern nation-state, understood as a unique and homogeneous international actor, with its random behaviour throughout the centuries in a foreign 'anarchical' arena. This is one more consequence of the 'neo-classical'/'postmodern' sophisticated intellectual stance of this author. The problem is that, if the *suspicion* is founded, the 'genealogy' written by this author would not really be a disturbing Nietzschean 'genealogy'. Instead, it would rather be an erudite but, at once, quite *conservative* 'archaeology' of 'diplomacy', despite all the acknowledgements to 'master in thinking' French philosopher and historian Michel Foucault.

In a time in which classical diplomacy seems to be losing some of its former prestige, and, thence, a good deal of its traditional function, it is impossible to be blind to the present 'multilevel' subversion of the principles of traditional diplomacy, a 'subversion' which is not to be understood, only, in political terms, because it is, also, a quite generalized, if often dubious or conflictive, contemporary social and cultural stance regarding international relations. This is one more result of the continuous overlapping, or bypassing of central governments' classical foreign policy by quite a number of new *non-governmental* actors, but also by fully *governmental,* even if non-central, actors.

Here, in my opinion, lies the key question: what do we really mean by *government* in contemporary politics, both domestic and foreign? An appropriate understanding of the external dimension of the political,

economic, social and cultural, root issues, any 'government', whether
'central' or 'non-central', 'macro' or 'micro', 'local' or 'global', is expected
to deal with, is of course, unavoidable. The lack of a sound theoretical
interpretation of today's diverse 'governmentality' can explain the numerous
semantic, ideological, and constitutional, contradictions spread throughout
the literature about NCG international involvement.[17] As we shall see now,
Hocking's criticism of 'protodiplomacy' and 'paradiplomacy' neologisms,
will help us understand that it is because they *are* governments that the
NCGs are impelled to make some kind of 'foreign policy', as naturally as
they promote, locally, employment, educational or housing policies.

THE DISMISSAL OF 'PARADIPLOMACY': THE 'MULTILAYERED DIPLOMACY' APPROACH

With the analytical proposals articulated by Hocking we are again in a
'global international society' perspective. Hocking studies the impacts of
globalization on contemporary diplomacy and sees one of these impacts
precisely in NCG involvement in international affairs. This analytical
approach will look for a compatibility between central diplomacy and non-
central foreign activities, two kinds of foreign involvement which do not
necessarily have to be in endless competition or conflict. Hence the
proposed alternative concepts of 'multilayered diplomacy', first, and, more
recently, 'catalytic diplomacy', handled by this author in order to explain
the changes which have occurred in international relations and
contemporary diplomacy.[18] Once again, the main question is to cope with
the changes in the nature and function of contemporary, mostly, but not
exclusively federal, states' external activities in an increasingly globalized
world market. To put it shortly, it is the concept of *diplomacy* itself which
is, here, in need of a new definition.

If we really wanted to find one plausible 'postmodern' approach to NCG
international involvement, this approach would be found, surely not, as we
already have seen, in the writings of the 'postmodernist' Der Derian, but
rather in those of Hocking, even though the intellectual approach of the
latter, cannot, of course, seriously be labelled 'postmodernist'. Once again,
throughout our 'intertextual' enquiry, we discover some of the heuristic
virtues of more epistemologically classical approaches to contemporary
inside/outside political processes. Nevertheless, does not Hocking's concept
of 'catalytic diplomacy', sound strangely 'postmodern'?[19] What is more
interesting, the core question becomes, lately but fortunately, thanks to
Hocking, an *ontological* problem: the classical anthropomorphic 'monism'
of the state is, definitively, replaced by a far more sophisticated
understanding of complex, continuously overlapping and essentially

'pluralistic' nature of contemporary political systems. In brief, the question is of the international 'actorness' of NCGs.

Indeed, what is really important to understand, now, is how and why Hocking, since the beginning of his analytical approach to foreign involvement of NCGs, vigorously rejects the 'paradiplomacy' and suchlike neologisms. The reasons given are clear, and have apparently nothing to do with Der Derian's conceptual 'genealogies' – even if it has, now, become impossible, for us, not to bear them in mind, as 'intertextuality' obliges. It would be worth discussing extensively the overall theoretical approach of Hocking. Nevertheless, we shall limit our enquiry to some insights into one text: *Localizing Foreign Policy. Non-Central Governments and Mutilayered Diplomacy* (Hocking, 1993).

> It has become increasingly clear that the growing international interest demonstrated by NCGs is but part of a broader process whereby foreign policy is becoming 'localized'.... The growth of international interests and activity at the local level is subject to differing interpretations. For some it represents a highly desirable democratization of the foreign policy processes, traditionally the preserve of the executive; even, perhaps, an opportunity to restructure the international order towards more just and peaceful goals. For others, localization is a dangerous derogation from governments' power to conduct a coherent foreign policy, providing the opportunity for other state and non-state actors to profit from internal divisions. Furthermore, on the surface there appears to be a contradiction between the forces of globalization and enhanced economic interdependence between national communities on one side and development of localization on the other. What appears to confront us are not so much well-defined developments marking the predominance of any one political arena, but a bewildering network of linkages between those arenas through which actors relate to each other in a variety of ways... Partly because of this, the traditional distinction between domestic and foreign policy is becoming harder to sustain... In this sense, what was regarded traditionally as a phenomenon of international politics – diplomacy – has assumed a domestic dimension which, as trade negotiations demonstrate, is crucial to its success (Hocking, 1993: 2–3 *passim*).

This new and more comprehensive theoretical approach allows Hocking to reject some of the first conceptual attempts at defining NCG international involvement.

> The picture has been clouded further by the emphasis in the literature of international interdependence on change at the systemic level and

the relative inattention to the changing character of the foreign policy processes which accompanies it. Consequently, the impact of the image of NCG international activity thus created has been to set it apart from the patterns of traditional diplomacy, to seek new terms to describe it (such as 'paradiplomacy' and 'protodiplomacy') which serve to reinforce the distinction, and to emphasize the elements of conflict between the national and subnational governments which have accompanied its growth (Hocking, 1993: 3–4).[20]

Further, Hocking explains why neologisms like 'paradiplomacy' have to be replaced within a larger analytical approach to NCG involvement in international politics.

Instead, NCGs are located in a complex diplomatic milieu which does not recognize the exclusive territories of the domestic and international but blends both together in various ways at the behest of a range of forces located at differing political levels. Here, international diplomacy is regarded not as a segmented process presided over by undisputed gatekeepers but as a web of interactions with a changing cast of players which will interact in different ways depending on the issue, their interests and capacity to operate in a multilevel political environment. The idea, then, of NCGs as engaged in 'new forms' of diplomacy – whether these be termed 'microdiplomacy', 'protodiplomacy' or whatever – is replaced by an attempt to fit them into the changing patterns of world politics (Hocking, 1993: 36).

Finally, Hocking's dismissal of Duchacek's categories is based on the existing 'imperatives of cooperation' between 'central and subnational levels' (Hocking, 1993: 47).

The emphasis on Duchacek's various categories of NCG international activity, such as 'paradiplomacy' and 'protodiplomacy', whilst helpful in distinguishing between different types of relationship, tend to emphasize separateness from national policies and to reinforce the image of conflict between centre and region projected into the international environment. The factors determining the involvement of NCGs in the forms of multilayered diplomacy ... are more likely to stress patterns of linkage between levels of political authority and activity (Hocking, 1993: 46–47).

I am ready to welcome the reasons given by Hocking in order to reject the rather unfortunate neologism 'paradiplomacy', especially since, in doing so, this author explicitly refers to a number of internationally relevant political issues linked with contemporary 'governmentality' of NCGs *as such.* The analytical approach proposed by Hocking takes seriously into account the political nature of NCGs. In fact, this 'multilevel' and theoretically more comprehensive approach, operates a Copernican revolution in relation to former approaches to NCG behaviour in foreign activities, since these activities are no longer studied from a purely 'state-centric' point of view, from outside and from the top, as they previously were, but from their own position. In the comprehensive framework of Hocking's 'multilayered' or 'catalytic' diplomacy, the NCGs actually *are* fully international 'actors', even if as complex and 'plural' as the 'state' to which they belong.

The only difficult point with this quite positive approach to the problem of NCG international involvement, is that it seems to offer too easy, fashionable and sophisticated a global theoretical *solution* to an essentially political problem: the *compatibility* between the foreign activities of NCGs and the 'central diplomacy' of the 'state'. It does so before having analyzed *all* different sorts of international activities of *all* different kinds of NCGs, within *all* structurally complex political systems, whether federal or not. I am conscious that this kind of criticism is rather easy, mostly since we know that it is really difficult to fulfil, in practice, a truly exhaustive comparative enquiry, before starting the necessary intellectual task of theorization. Nevertheless, in more recent writings, Hocking stresses the historical and political *heterogeneity* of NCGs, as is unavoidable when widening the scope of the enquiry, from federal to non-federal decentralized politic systems.

This recent theoretical awareness of the irruption, in the international arena, of a number of non-central autonomous governmental 'actors', due, only in part, to the pressures economic globalization imposes to NCGs, as *non-central*, but, nevertheless, *governmental*, and increasingly active and influential participants in multiple inside/outside overlapping issues, is certainly, to be welcomed. This is especially so since contemporary international economic and political issues are, as Hocking rightly stresses, mainly a matter of access to information, a struggle for the access to networks. There is no doubt that Hocking's theorization about 'multilayered diplomacy', or 'catalytic diplomacy', is a descriptively accurate, intellectually exciting, and basically optimistic answer to puzzling problems. It helps us demythologise an increasingly complicated, and, apparently, conflicting political situation that is at once, internal and external, central and non-central. But do things, really, work like this?

Diplomacy is no longer the exclusive monopoly of a monistic 'self', the central state. This is true, of course, if we are speaking of decentralized democracies. This could be even more true if we spoke of the European Union and its common foreign policy, which could rarely, if ever, become a 'univocal' foreign policy but is bound to become a new version of truly

postmodern 'catalytic diplomacy'. A 'catalytic diplomacy' in which
international 'actorness', sometimes referred at as a matter of European
identity – should be strictly defined as a *singularity*, that is an international
political phenomenon at once 'unique' and 'plural'.[21] Nevertheless, some
problems still remain, probably because our enquiry is, in fact, endless, and
because the literature we have handled about the users of the concept of
'paradiplomacy' and their critics is not yet exhaustive.

'PARADIPLOMACY' AND BEYOND

The historical context in which the concept of 'paradiplomacy' appeared in the
literature was that of institutional crisis of federal states, globalization of
economy, and increased interdependence in international relations. The
dramatic irruption of a 'postmodernist' discourse in the literature about
'paradiplomacy' only had an *archaeological* effect: the discourse on
contemporary diplomacy was paradoxically re-centred on the classical issue of
sovereign, homogeneous, exclusive, nation-state diplomacy. Though offering
new and interesting insights about marginal and, sometimes, abnormal forms
of late twentieth century 'diplomacy', this posmodernist discourse was unable
to focus on the main target of the enquiry: the contemporary nature and
meaning of the NCG international involvement, *as such*.

Less 'postmodernist', and more empirical approaches, have in the
meanwhile proved more capable of genuine, if analytically questionable,
heuristic achievements. At the end, they have been more successful in
coping with the puzzling inside/outside contemporary complex linkage than
more aesthetically disruptive or theoretically up-to-date methodological
proposals. Nevertheless, our initial dissatisfaction remains. Why is it so?

Throughout the literature, the scope of the enquiry still focuses too much
on the *state*, its 'central' government and its 'central' diplomacy, and too
little on the new reality of the *non-central,* but, nevertheless, *governmental,*
'actorness' of NCGs in international relations. The classical paradigm of the
'central' state is, epistemologically and ideologically, so powerful that the
most fearless attempts to widen the scope of analytical discussion are in
danger, as we have seen throughout this 'intertextual' enquiry, of being,
once again, tamed. This could suggest that we should change our analytical
strategy and try to start from the bottom, that is, from where NCG
international involvement historically starts. But, if we actually focus on
historical, cultural, and political, circumstances of some very specific
NCGs, our theoretical conclusions will have to be extremely cautious, even
more, if our approach is a comparative one. In any case, we shall, certainly,
have to face a disturbing historical, political and sociological diversity.

Historically, the case of the Canadian province of Quebec has played, throughout North American academic literature, the role of a unique and outstanding internationally 'centrifugal', or secessionist, *paradigm* inside the intensively studied field of federal political systems foreign policy processes. The scope of comparative enquiry has since, fortunately, been widened, so as to include, besides Canada, the United States and Australia. The enquiry became, consequently, more interesting, and a certain degree of less irrelevant generalization became possible. When specifically European federal cases, such as Germany, Belgium, Austria or Switzerland, were, progressively, included within the enquiry, some new comparative forms of NCG foreign behaviour began to appear. Nevertheless, the research was, still, tightly bounded to federal systems.

More recently, the scope of the enquiry about NCG international involvement has been widened enough so as to take into account constitutionally decentralized and structurally complex states which, nevertheless, are not genuine federal systems, such as contemporary democratic Spain. This broader and more ambitious research programme had, then, to cope with a series of historically, culturally and politically rather heteregeneous forms of NCGs, set in complicated and subtle political systems, such as the so-called Spanish 'state of the autonomies', a still largely unknown, and, indeed, exciting scenery for a political scientist. Some of these 'autonomous communities' encompass economically, politically and culturally extremely vigorous local civil societies, as is the case in Catalonia and the Basque Country – two outstanding paradigmatic 'historical nationalities' ruled by internally solid and externally influential NCGs. In both cases, despite their historic differences, the degree of *governmentality*, as measured by exclusive competencies is, without any doubt, especially relevant not only politically, but also theoretically. In both cases, a non-central vigorous foreign activity has emerged recently, thanks to democracy, but also to a previously existing particularly high degree of private, and often clandestine, plural political involvement of civil society in foreign affairs. The whole internal and external activity of both Catalonia and the Basque Country could not be properly understood without taking into account the long-standing political nationalist feelings existing in both societies. Such nationalist feelings have strong roots in a frequently forgotten, often distorted and tragic history.[22]

Indeed, when the proper names are used, the incipient theory of NCG involvement in international relations becomes theoretically even more puzzling, and hasty generalization even more dangerous. Nevertheless, what is really relevant is the 'governmentality' of these new 'autonomous' non-central international actors.

By 'governmentality' I mean two things:

- first, that these new 'autonomous' international non-central governmental actors are not only structurally and, now, constitutionally, 'fragments of state' or as Georg Jellinek (1896) called them a century ago, 'Lands' or 'Countries', as in the original pre-federal and pre-constitutional meaning of the German word (*Land/Länder*). They are also territorialized and 'localized' representations of a constitutionally 'plurinational' state;
- second, at a purely factual and political level, 'governmentality' means that these NCGs are in charge of public administration in a very large scope of 'exclusive' constitutional legislative competencies, which means that they have to deal with matters – such as industrial, commercial, cultural, educational, social, housing, tax or even security – that are increasingly *internationally conditioned*. This is something clearly foreseen by the first explorers of the international involvement of NCGs as one more consequence of the globalization of the economy, but whose overall political, constitutional and international consequences are still to be extensive and intensively analyzed.

In today's post-Amsterdam European Union, purely economic issues are no longer the issues that matter. The daily concerns of the lives of European citizens have become relevant and – in the case of unemployment, immigration and socially related problems – politically extremely sensitive. It is clear that – even if the 15 central government bureaucracies of the present member states of the Union still fight vainly to maintain the prestige of the central governments' monopoly of 'diplomatic' sovereign relations with the supranational structures of the European Union – more and more, the day-to-day practical 'external' policies of European NCGs have to cope with 'communitarized' policies, because these policies directly affect their local vital interests.

The same phenomenon occurs, on a larger scale, in the world-wide process of globalization/localization of international economic relations and the increasing competition between regional NCGs in order to capture foreign investment and access to international markets. But this global process does not have the same political *constituent* meaning, because, in the end, even if it is for some of the 15 present member states ideologically difficult to acknowledge it, the European Union is a new, unknown, political federal 'supranational' building process in the making.

If today's 'diplomacy' is mostly a matter of access to international networks, what can happen if a NCG, based in a strategically developed region of the European Union, manages to have much more efficient access to international investments and markets than the central government's centralized, bureaucratic and rather old-fashioned diplomacy? This might happen, either because regional/international targets of some NCGs are strategically more precisely defined than those of the central governments, or because needs are more clearly perceived by the local population, or even, in some cases, because a certain know-how – be it industrial, technological, commercial, educational or even political, cultural or 'diplomatic' – has been developed through generations at a mostly local level. Once again, we are facing some of the well-studied problems we have been dealing with throughout our 'intertextual' enquiry about the nature and theoretical interpretation of NCG international involvement in Anglo-Saxon literature about federal political systems. But we are coping with them within a wider comparative framework – more global, more heterogeneous and, probably, heuristically more rich.

But what about 'paradiplomacy', then?

To tell the truth, I think we could hardly speak of 'paradiplomacy' in any of the cases of NCG involvement in international relations referred to. The highly relevant international activity of NCGs – the really dynamic and highly motivated, day-to-day, international/regional merging of modern democratic governance – is definitely not an 'abnormal', not even a 'parallel', form of 'diplomacy'. It is, perhaps, not even 'diplomacy' at all, especially if we refer to Der Derian's (post)modern Hegelian interpretation of 'estrangement' and 'mediation' as the essence of 'classic' or 'central' diplomacy. Opportunities seem to be, nowadays, scarce for old-fashioned 'protodiplomatic', and rather tortuous, separatist strategies, because the highly institutionalized democratic internationalization process of NCG seems unstoppable.

Never mind. If words matter, as I personally believe they do, then the international involvement of NCGs could much more properly be labelled 'postdiplomatic', because it is a process that moves beyond the nation-state, that is, 'beyond diplomacy'.[23]

At the end of the twentieth century, it has become obvious that a wide range of extremely diverse and sometimes quite relevant autonomous international activities *do* exist, which are directly connected with, and politically legitimated by, the day-to-day political responsibilities of local democratic governmental authorities and people's vital interests. Their multiple voices express, in the international arena, the main contemporary economic, social, ecological, cultural and normative issues of modern democracies, much more clearly than do 'national' security or defence bureaucratic spokesmen (the late public servants of classical 'high politics' sovereignty issues of states). This is one more consequence of the increasingly complex and diverse internationalization of local public policies, those policies which are closer to the citizens. Or, to put it dialectically, it is one more consequence of the local international response to the unavoidable challenge of the contemporary process of localization of international relations.

NOTES

1. We prefer the expression 'non central governments' (NCGs) rather than 'subnational units', an expression which does not stress the 'governmental' nature of the international actors we focus on. 'Subnational' in the United States does not imply any subordination of smaller 'nations' to a larger one, as it would do in Europe, where the word 'nation' is used both for 'nation-states' and for historical smaller 'nations' included in a larger 'nation-state'. These historical political units are, nevertheless, on their one behalf, 'nations' too (generally previous to the 'nation-state'). A translation of 'subnational units' could be 'substate units', another quite confusing expression, for instance in a federal state where the word 'state' is polysemic. Some authors have also proposed the neologism 'mesogovernments', a term which – apart from other more or less negative connotations – is not correctly constructed linguistically.

2. 'Federated constituencies' or 'constituent states' are the expressions used by John Kincaid.

3. The avoidance of giving a more accurate definition of 'paradiplomacy' entitles the user to use it freely with all its diverse and contradictory connotations (for example non-governmental, corporate or private), and, in particular, to apply it to the case of the international involvement of NCGs.

4. James Der Derian (1987) explains what is meant by 'genealogy' when used to refer to the method proposed by French philosopher and historian Michel Foucault: 'a genealogy is a history of the present, in the sense of a Nietzschean (and Foucauldian) method of analysis in which specific cultural practices are historically related to the exercise of power to disclose modern discursive practices. What concerns this genealogy are the symbols, rules, norms, and conventions of a diplomatic culture and the political configurations of power which were mutually interdependent to the extent that they might be said to organize and constitute paradigms of diplomacy'(ibid.:69–70). Genealogy, as Der Derian further reminds us, is 'intended to disrupt some commonly held beliefs about the origins of diplomacy. This function of a genealogy has been most aptly described by Michel Foucault: "The search for descent", he says, "is not the erecting of foundations; on the contrary, it disturbs what was thought unified, it shows the heterogeneity of what was imagined consistent with itself.' (ibid.: 199–200). Elsewhere, Der Derian develops the effects of the genealogical approach upon 'narrow definitions of terms': 'Almost by definition, a genealogy shuns narrow definitions of terms. If a single definition could capture the essence of a phenomenon, then there would be no purpose for a genealogy. In fact, it would negate a genealogy, for its very rationale is to refute the existence of a defining essence. Moreover, the high level of ambiguity in international relations can defeat attempts at exact definition.' (ibid.: 211, n.14).

5. We shall first try to expose the process of invention, definition and re-definition or criticism of the concept of 'paradiplomacy' in a purely *chronological* way. Nevertheless pure chronology will soon be subverted by the underlying wandering of *meaning*, the shift of the signified under the signifier. The approach to the concept-building process will have to take into account not only the epistemological differences between the analytical frameworks (and political discourses), but also the *intertext* created between them. Our hope is that this 'intertextual' puzzle, far from clouding the meaning of the concept of 'paradiplomacy' will, on the contrary, help us to avoid an uncritical use of it. The textual occurrences of the word 'paradiplomacy' are, in any case our Ariadna's thread throughout literature.

6. 'Initially, I used the colloquial "microdiplomacy"; since a derogatory sense could be read into it, I gladly accept Professor P. Soldatos's much better term "paradiplomacy". Not only has it no derogatory sound, but "para" expresses accurately what it is about: parallel to, often co-ordinated with, complementary to, and sometimes in conflict with centre-to-centre "macrodiplomacy"' (Duchacek, 1990: 32, n.11). This enquiry cannot pretend to reach an exhaustive 'historiographic' accuracy while re-constructing the genealogy of the neologism.

The main purpose is to sketch the context in which the neologism was 'invented'. Hazard also plays its part in literature (the *texts* put together) and in the 'intertextual' connections/disconnections. The *context* we want to interpret is in fact enclosed *within* the literature we are analyzing. In this sense – to use the terminology of literary criticism – our reading will apply the method of 'internal criticism', not that of 'external criticism', since what is under examination is an academic (thence *political*) discourse.

7.   The same thing occurs in other parts of this text: 'The term global "microdiplomacy" or "paradiplomacy", as used here, refers to processes and networks through which subnational governments search for and establish cooperative contacts and compacts on a *global* scale, usually with foreign central governments and private enterprises. The aims of such subnational activities beyond the national borders are mostly export trade, reverse investment, cultural exchanges, environmental protection, and tourism as major sources of income. The actual forms of global microdiplomacy in which local and regional governments in North America engage range from short-term fact-finding missions abroad to promotional trips undertaken by subnational leaders (Canadian premiers, mayors of major cities, and US state governors), to hosting foreign dignitaries and corporate or business leaders, and to establish foreign trade zones. Other microdiplomatic activities include trade and investment shows featuring local and provincial/state manufacturing and technological skills' (Duchacek, 1986b: 14).

8.   'The term "paradiplomacy" seems appropriate indeed; the term "para", in fact, indicates not only something parallel, but also, according to Webster's Dictionary, something "associated in a subsidiary or accessory capacity",' Duchacek comments, in a different context of this posthumous study (Duchacek, 1990: 25).

9.   Not only because the phenomenon of 'protodiplomacy' seems to have existed throughout history but also because the concept itself appeared earlier than other ones in historiographic literature in order to describe the different features and phases of 'secessionist' or 'separatist' nation-building processes.

10.   The word 'secession', often used in US literature and in particular in the writings of I. Duchacek, becomes 'separatism' when this author is published in the UK. These two words probably belong to different political cultures and, of course, different political systems. Do they really mean the same thing?

11.   The 'neoclassicism' of Der Derian is not only a circumstance of his personal academic 'genealogy', it seems to be a personal intellectual stance as it appears in *International Theory. Critical Investigations* (Der Derian, 1995: vii–viii).

12.   No use stressing how far intellectually, and politically, this picture stands from recent 'global' approaches to international economic and political 'interdependence', and from the increasing doubts about the nature and functions of the 'state', as a 'unique' diplomatic actor.

13.   De Derian is one of the 'masters in the making' studied in Iver B. Neumann's and Ole Waewer's *The Future of International Relations: Masters in the Making?* (London, Routledge, 1997).

14.   It is even more amazing if we take into account the later enquiry made by Der Derian on several kinds of abnormal 'diplomacies' such as the 'antidiplomacies' of spies, terrorists and 'narcos' in *Antidiplomacy* (1992).

15.   One of these inappropriate examples is certainly that of Pope John-Paul II's supposedly 'paradiplomatic' international travels. Isn't Vatican diplomacy – as it has been acknowledged by historians – one of the oldest diplomacies of all? 'Genealogically', isn't 'archeodiplomacy' ('God's diplomacy') one of Der Derian's main 'paradigms'? Wasn't the Vatican known as one of the best schools of diplomacy in the world – a school of *modern* 'state diplomacy', of course, because the Vatican is still a sovereign 'state'.

16.   In Der Derian's interpretative scheme, the role played by 'protodiplomacy' with the meaning given to this concept by Duchacek and Soldatos – as a 'separatist' version of non-central diplomacy – seems to be transferred to 'antidiplomacy', a new concept created by the author of *Antidiplomacy* (Der Derian, 1992), a meaning which seems to have absorbed all the subversive ('secessionist'/'separatist') connotations of the former 'protodiplomacy'. 'Antidiplomacy' is, in fact, in Der Derian's mind, the sinister and restless 'paragovernmental' empire of spies, terrorists and 'narcos'.

17. Perhaps a truly 'postmodernist' approach could have been of some help here: *la gouvernementalité*, a neologism invented by Michel Foucault – a concept which is a kind of French mixture of the two concepts of 'government' and 'governance' – correctly expresses what we want to stress. In this sense, we could say – besides some Foucauldian negative connotations of the term *gouvernementalité* – that contemporary everyday life is being – for the best or for the worst – intensely 'governementalized', as it is, on the other hand, increasingly internationalized. Nevertheless, the notion of 'governmentalization of human societies' early used by John Kincaid is not very different from the idea we want to express. In 'Constituent Diplomacy: US. State Roles in Foreign Affairs', a paper presented at the World Congress of International Political Science Association, Paris, 15–20 July 1985, Kincaid grouped the main reasons for the increased participation of the US states in international relations into four 'causal' categories: '(1) desire for constituent (federal components) autonomy (2) global interdependence (3) international complexity, and (4) the governmentalization of human societies'(quoted by Duchacek, 1986a: 254, n.2).
18. Significantly enough, the first field studies made by Brian Hocking in this matter will be on federal political systems (see 1993a).
19. Brian Hocking acknowledges his conceptual debt with 'Lind's suggestion that the integral state, the product of an evolutionary period lasting several centuries, is being replaced by the "catalytic" state which is better able to cope with new challenges by entering into coalitions comprising other states, private sector interests and transnational organisations' (Hocking, 1996: 41). On the other hand, we cannot forget that the overall inside/outside debate in IR theory was extensively discussed in 'postmodernist' Rob Walker's *Inside/Outside: International Relations as Political Theory* (1993).
20. This overall picture can be compared with further developments in the same study (Hocking, 1993: 31–3), and in later texts (Hocking, 1994: 411–2; 1996: 38–9).
21. As it has been insightfully defined in the PhD dissertation of Cristina Churruca, *Génesis y desarrollo de la política exterior común (1991–1996). Origen de la Unión Europea como actor singular en la sociedad internacional* (Leioa, Universidad del País Vasco/Euskal Herriko Unibertsitatea, 1997, unpublished).
22. The complex and heterogeneous Western 'national' phenomenon studied by Michael Keating through the cases of Catalonia in Spain, Quebec in Canada and Scotland in the United Kingdom.
23. Our proposal meets Hocking's rejection of the 'state-centric image of the international systems', and, consequently, this dismissal of the language of the 'state system' when referred to NCG international activities (Hocking, 1996: 38–9).

REFERENCES

Der Derian, James (1987) *On Diplomacy: A Genealogy of Western Estrangement* (Oxford: Basil Blackwell).

Der Derian, James (1992) *Antidiplomacy: Spies, Terror, Speed and War* (Oxford: Basil Blackwell).

Der Derian, James (1995) *International Theory: Critical Investigations* (Basingstoke and London, Macmillan).

Der Derian, James and Michael Shapiro (eds) (1989) *International/Intertextual Relations: Postmodern Readings of World Politics* (Lexington, MA: Lexington Books).

Duchacek, Ivo D. (1986a) *The Territorial Dimension of Politics: Within, Among, and Across Nations* (Boulder and London: Westview Press).

Duchacek, Ivo D. (1986b) 'International Competence of Subnational Governments: Borderlines and Beyond' in Oscar J. Martinez (ed.), *Across Boundaries: Transborder Interaction in Comparative Perspective* (The University of Texas at El Paso: Texas Western Press).

Duchacek, Ivo D. (1988) 'Multicommunal and Bicommunal Polities and Their International Relations', in Ivo D. Duchacek, Daniel Latouche and Garth Stevenson (eds), *Perforated Sovereignties and International Relations: Trans-Sovereign Contacts of Subnational Governments* (New York and London: Greenwood Press).

Duchacek, Ivo D. (1990) 'Perforated Sovereignties: Toward a Typology of New Actors in International Relations', in Hans J. Michelmann and Panayotis Soldatos (eds), *Federalism and International Relations: The Role of Subnational Units* (Oxford: Clarendon Press).

Dyment, David K.M. (1993) 'Substate Paradiplomacy: The Case of the Ontario Government' in Brian Hocking (ed.), *Localizing Foreign Policy: Non-Central Governments and Mutilayered Diplomacy* (New York: St. Martin's Press).

Hocking, Brian (1993a) *Foreign Relations and Federal States* (London and New York: Leicester University Press).

Hocking, Brian (1993b) *Localizing Foreign Policy: Non-Central Governments and Mutilayered Diplomacy* (London and New York: Macmillan and St Martin's Press).

Hocking, Brian (1994) 'Les intérèts internationaux des gouvernements régionaux: désuétude de l'interne et de l'externe?', *Revue Etudes Internationales*, Vol.XXV, 4.3.

Hocking, Brian (1996) 'Bridging Boundaries: Creating Linkages: Non-Central Governments and Multilayered Policy Environments', *Welt Trends*, n.11.

Jellinek, Georg (1896) *Über Staatsfragmente* (Heidelberg: Verlag von Gustav Koester).

Kincaid, John (1990) 'Constituent Diplomacy in Federal Polities and the Nation State: Conflict And Cooperation' in Hans J. Michelmann and Panayotis Soldatos (eds), *Federalism and International Relations: The Role of Subnational Units* (New York: Oxford University Press).

Michelman, Hans J. and Panayotis Soldatos (eds) (1990) *Federalism and International Relations: The Role of Subnational Units* (New York: Oxford University Press).

Philip, Christian and Panayotis Soldatos (eds) (1996) *Au-delá et endeça de l'Etat-nation* (Bruxelles: Bruylant).

Smith, Patrick J. (1993) 'Policy Phases, Subnational Foreign Relations and Constituent Diplomacy in the United States and Canada: City, Provincial and State Global Activity in British Columbia and Washington', in Brian Hocking (ed.), *Localizing Foreign Policy: Non-Central Governments and Mutilayered Diplomacy* (London and New York: Macmillan and St Martin's Press).

Soldatos, Panayotis (1990) 'An Explanatory Framework for the Study of Federated States as Foreign-policy Actors', in Hans J. Michelmann and Panayotis Soldatos (eds), *Federalism and International Relations: The Role of Subnational Units* (Oxford: Clarendon Press).

Walker, R.B.J. (1993) *Inside/Outside: International Relations as Political Theory* (Cambridge: Cambridge University Press).

Abstracts

Regions and International Affairs: Motives, Opportunities and Strategies
Michael Keating

Recent years have seen an increasing involvement of regional governments in the international arena, a phenomenon sometimes known as paradiplomacy. The reasons lie both in changes at the level of the state and international system, and in political and economic developments within regions themselves. Globalization and the rise of transnational regimes, especially regional trading areas, have eroded the distinction between domestic and foreign affairs and by the same token have transformed the division of responsibilities between state and sub-national governments and pitched regions into competition in the international market. To these functional reasons are added political reasons, where territorial elites are engaged in a process of region- or state-building.

Patrolling the Frontier: Globalization, Localization and the 'Actorness' of Non-Central Governments
Brian Hocking

The growing extranational involvement of regional and local governments has provided a growing focus of interest from a variety of disciplinary perspectives. Consequently, we have a good deal of analytical and empirical material from which to draw conclusions regarding the meaning and significance of this phenomenon. Diversity is accompanied by disagreement and NCG internationalization has provided sustenance for very different approaches to understanding world politics, from realist to post-modern analyses, from arguments concerning neo-medievalism to territorial 'debordering'. Frequently, however, the processes of NCG internationalization have been isolated from their broader contexts, imposing on them assumptions derived from the concerns and language of foreign policy, and focusing on the boundaries separating actors rather than the linkages binding them together. This is reinforced by a tendency to locate NCGs within the traditional, and increasingly uninformative, categories of state and non-state actor rather than seeking to appreciate their defining characteristics. As with other entities, the analysis of the qualities inherent in NCGs as actors in world politics – their 'actorness' – helps us to move beyond evaluations of their role and significance rooted in these assumptions of separateness, discontinuity and exclusivity.

Diplomacy and Paradiplomacy in the Redefinition of International Security: Dimensions of Conflict and Co-operation
Noé Cornago

This article analyses the role of paradiplomacy in international security. The problems raised by its articulation with state diplomacy, both the conflictive and the co-operative dimensions, are also considered. First, on the basis of varied experiences, the article discusses the possibilities which the promotion of certain forms of sub-national foreign action can offer as instruments for the reduction of transnational ethnic tensions. Then, different forms of paradiplomacy are considered as an instrument, limited but worthy of consideration, for the promotion of confidence and regional security. The article then concentrates on the most complex expression of the sub-national dimension of international security: the difficulties of the politically-centralized management of some of the most important issues of our time, such as ecological problems and migration and the effect this has on the power and competences of regional governments, imposing the need to rethink the conventional methods of diplomacy as a whole.

The European Union and Inter-Regional Co-operation
Kepa Sodupe

In the academic literature, it is often claimed that the process of European integration has been accompanied by a reaffirmation of regional identity. Considerations of a cultural or linguistic nature, which are generally associated with regionalism, are not wholly responsible for this development. New factors, which have emerged in recent decades, must be taken into account. To a certain extent, it is possible to say that a new regionalism has appeared which constitutes a response to increasing levels of interdependence. These are a consequence of the elimination of protectionism, the creation of the internal market and the move towards monetary union.

Towards Plurinational Diplomacy in the Deeper and Wider European Union (1985–2005)
Francisco Aldecoa

This article puts forward a case for the exploration of new forms of sub-statal participation in the formulation and implementation of foreign policy in those states which have a complex structure in the context of the European Union. It suggests the need to adopt a new approach. Referring to the genesis and evolution of European integration and of the political recognition of the regions as two parallel processes which respond to a common logic, the concept of plurinational diplomacy is presented, as the necessary reformulation of the ways of understanding and practising diplomacy from the recognition of legal and political reality of a shared sovereignty within the European Union. Plurinational diplomacy implies the development of a double loyalty: on the one hand, the incorporation into the foreign agenda of the state of specific attention to the needs of the international scope of regional governments; on the other hand, attention to and development of a certain dimension of state politics in the foreign activities of regional governments.

The Other Dimension of Third Level Politics in Europe: The Congress of Local and Regional Powers of the Council of Europe
Jose Luis de Castro

Recently, and with the positive effect the Treaty of the European Union had on the regional question, the Committee of Regions has occupied researchers with the relevance of the European Union and the importance derived from its policies. However, in the *other* Europe, in the Great Europe which is represented by the Council of Europe, there have also been important advances and interesting innovations regarding the regional phenomenon. This article focuses on a different aspect of growing international relevance, which has different profiles and objectives but which has equal importance, or potential, than other developments of the regional phenomenon in the European continent.

The International Competence of US States and Their Local Governments
John Kincaid

US states and their local governments possess limited international competence derived from constitutional authority, political freedom and governmental capacity. Although states have always played some roles in US foreign policymaking and international affairs, their current, more active roles began to emerge during the late 1950s. As such, states, and often local governments, can be said to play a number of roles in foreign affairs, namely they serve as partners in foreign policy development; pressure points in foreign policymaking; self-governing political communities; promoters of area interests; proxies for the nation; parties to agreements with foreign governments; public education and opinion forums; problem solvers on the world scene; patrons of democracy; and serving as practitioners of goodwill. For the most part, state and local governments do not unduly intrude upon or oppose the federal government's foreign-affairs prerogatives, and the federal government's responses to state and local international affairs activities have been tolerant, supportive and often co-operative. To date, however, state and local governments have not plunged deeply into the international arena. Their international activities still constitute small portions of their budgets and personnel.

Federal-State Relations in Australian External Affairs: A New Co-operative Era?
John Ravenhill

External affairs have intruded on relations between the states and the Commonwealth (federal) government in Australia in the last three decades, principally through two sets of issues. The first is the international diplomatic activities conducted by the states. The second is the impact that the Commonwealth government's negotiation and entry into international treaties has had on the division of powers established by the constitution. Both dimensions have caused considerable tension between the states and the Commonwealth. This article reviews how, in the 1990s, collaborative relations on both sets of issues have emerged as the states and the Commonwealth reached a new *modus vivendi*.

The Quebec Experience: Success or Failure?
Louis Balthazar

Quebec provides an interesting case of paradiplomacy (international activities of a non-sovereign state that does not seek to be recognized as sovereign). Its legitimacy in this respect is rooted in its own distinctive character and in Canada's history as a federation. Although Quebec's claim to an international presence has created tensions between this provincial and the Canadian federal government, a compromise was achieved. But inasmuch as Quebec did seek to realize its sovereignty, it can be said to have practised some form of protodiplomacy and thus met with the opposition of Canadian diplomacy. However the Quebec sovereignty movement may be seen as an effect of the failure of the Canadian political system to recognize Quebec's distinctive character.

The International Relations of Basque Nationalism and the First Basque Autonomous Government (1890–1939)
Alexander Ugalde

This article focuses on the crucial period from 1890 to 1939 and asks whether Basque nationalism followed a definite model for its action abroad during these years, looking both at the theoretical basis for the policy, and its practical application. Three broad conclusions emerge. First, the international relations of Basque nationalism as a political and social movement, structured through several political organizations in different phases, were at the beginning weak and irregular but they would reach a considerable level during the 1930s. Second, projection abroad is something inherent to the doctrine, principles and goals of Basque nationalism. Third, the foreign action performed by Basque nationalism conformed to a well defined pattern and evolution which aimed to achieve the international recognition of the Basque nation. The constitution of the first Basque government in 1936 brought about a significant, qualitative advance as regards foreign action, since it meant the beginning of institutional, governmental action. Insofar as it had its own government the Basque Country became an international actor, and its representative government played a prominent role on the international scene.

Making Sense of Paradiplomacy? An Intertextual Inquiry about a Concept in Search of a Definition
Iñaki Aguirre

The 'paradiplomacy' neologism first appeared within the field of comparative political analysis of federated states' international involvement. Since then, the term has experienced a strange detour through empirical literature, 'post-modern' critical deconstruction of diplomacy, and finally recent theoretical dismissal. Meanwhile, the word paradiplomacy was enriched by the *intertextuality* which grew around it, becoming a polysemic concept. Nevertheless, if words still matter, the international involvement of non-central governments, in structurally complex modern states, should be more properly labelled 'post-diplomatic'. This is one more consequence of non-central governmental response to the contemporary process of the localization of international relations.

Notes on Contributors

Francisco Aldecoa is Professor of International Relations and Jean Monnet Professor of Political Science at the University of the Basque Country. He has published extensively on European and Latin-American integration, and Spanish foreign policy. He has edited among other books: *De la Comunidad a la Unión: una visión desde Euskadi* (1993) and *Euroelecciones: Un parlamento para una legislatura constituyente de la Unión Europea* (1994). Recently he has published a number of articles on the European Union after the Amsterdam Treaty.

Michael Keating is Professor of Political Science at the University of Western Ontario and co-director of the European Consortium for Political Research Standing Group on regionalism. He previously taught at the University of Strathclyde and has held visiting positions at Virginia Polytechnic Institute and State University; Institut d'Etudes Politiques, Paris; European University Institute, Florence; University of Santiago de Compostela; Norwegian Nobel Institute; and Nuffield College, Oxford. He is currently visiting professor at the Universities of the Basque Country, Strathclyde and Sunderland. He is author of 11 and editor of seven books on urban and regional politics, nationalism and European politics. His most recent book is *The New Regionalism in Western Europe. Territorial Restructuring and Political Change* (Edward Elgar, 1998).

Brian Hocking is Professor of International Relations at Coventry University in the UK. Among his publications relating to the extra-national involvement and activities of non-central governments are: *Foreign Relations and Federal States* (ed.) (Leicester University Press, 1993); *Localizing Foreign Policy: Non-Central Governments and Multi-Layered Diplomacy* (Macmillan, 1993); *Beyond Foreign Economic Policy: The United States, the Single European Market and the Changing World Economy* (with Michael Smith) (Pinter, 1997).

Noé Cornago is Senior Lecturer in International Relations at the University of the Basque Country. He is interested in the sub-national dimensions of the international political economy and international regimes, as well as on the contemporary transformations of diplomacy.

Kepa Sodupe is Associate Professor of International Relations at the University of the Basque Country. His current work focuses on inter-regional co-operation in Europe and the relations among the European Union and the Eastern Europe Countries. He has recently written, in collaboration with E. Benito, *La Unión Europea y la Federación Rusa: La cooperación en el sector de la energía* (1997). He has also co-edited *Los Acuerdos de Asociación con Europa Central* (1994), y *La construcción del Espacio Vasco-Aquitano* (1998).

Jose Luis de Castro is Senior Lecturer in International Relations at the University of the Basque Country. He has published *La emergente participación política de las regiones en el proceso de construcción europea* (1994), and co-edited *Cooperación transfronteriza Euskadi-Aquitania* (1994), as well a number of articles on different topics related to the political participation of the regions in the European institutions.

John Kincaid is the Robert B. and Helen S. Meyner Professor of Government and Public Service and Director of the Meyner Center for the Study of State and Local Government at Lafayette College. He is the editor of *Publius: The Journal of Federalism.*

John Ravenhill is Senior Fellow in the Department of International Relations, Research School of Pacific and Asian Studies, Australian National University. He is also Chair of the Research Committee of the Australian Institute of International Affairs. His current research focuses primarily on inter-governmental collaboration in the Asia-Pacific region, and on the evolution of international production networks. His most recent book, *Asia-Pacific Economic Cooperation: The Construction of Pacific Rim Regionalism*, will be published by Cambridge University Press in 1999.

Louis Balthazar is Professor Emeritus of Université Laval, Quebec City. He has written extensively on Canada–United States relations, nationalism and US foreign policy. Among his publications are: *Bilan du nationalisme au Québec*) (with Alfred O. Hero Jr) (Montréal: L'Hexagone, 1986); *Contemporary Quebec and the United States: 1960-1985* (Cambridge, MA: Harvard Center for International Affairs and Lanham, MD: University Press of America, 1988); and (with the same author) *Le Québec dans la mouvance américaine* (Montréal: Québec-Amérique, 1999).

Alexander Ugalde is Senior Lecturer at the University of the Basque Country, and was formerly Professor of Contemporary History at the National University of Nicaragua. He has published *La acción exterior de lnacionalismo vasco* (1996), as well a number of articles dealing with different historical and international political aspects of Basque nationalism.

Iñaki Aguirre is Associate Professor of International Relations at the University of the Basque Country. His current fields of research are the critical and normative theory of international relations. Among his recent publications are *La teoría normativa de las relaciones internacionales, hoy* (1996) and *Voluntariado, solidaridades y teoría internacional* (1997).

Index

Books of Related Interest

The Political Economy of Regionalism

Michael Keating, *University of Western Ontario*, and
John Loughlin, *University of Wales, Cardiff* (Eds)

*'This is a very welcome addition to the literature. It comes at a
time of confusion and uncertainty where the basic notions and
concepts about power, legitimacy, allegiance and institutions are
challenged by the redefinition of their territorial dimension. This
book brings new insights and effectively blends theoretical
considerations with empirical case studies.'*
Yves Mény, European University Institute, Florence

This book examines the effects of economic and political restructuring
on regions in Europe and North America. The main theses are:
international economic restructuring and its impact on regions; political
realignments at the regional level; questions of territorial identity and
their connection with class, gender and neighbourhood identity; policy
choices and policy conflicts in regional development.

504 pages 1997
0 7146 4658 X cloth
0 7146 4187 1 paper
Regional & Federal Studies Series Volume 1

FRANK CASS PUBLISHERS
Newbury House, 900 Eastern Avenue, Ilford, Essex, IG2 7HH
Tel: +44 (0)181 599 8866 Fax: +44 (0)181 599 0984 E-mail: info@frankcass.com
NORTH AMERICA
5804 NE Hassalo Street, Portland, OR 97213 3644, USA
Tel: 800 944 6190 Fax: 503 280 8832 E-mail: cass@isbs.com
Website: www.frankcass.com

The Regional Dimension of the European Union

Towards a Third Level in Europe?

Charlie Jeffery, *University of Birmingham* (Ed)

The 1990s have seen intense debates about the role of regions in
European Integration. The significance of regional tiers of government
in EU politics has been boosted by changes in EU structural funding
rules, the innovations of the Maastricht treaty, and the growing
importance of federal and regional government within member states.
The effect has been to shift the balance of decision-making
responsibility within the EU to a third (regional) level of government
emerging in the EU policy process alongside the first (union) and
second (member state) levels. As a result, a system of multi-level
governance can increasingly be identified, in which different levels of
government adopt different roles in different fields or phases of the
European policy process.

240 pages 1997
0 7146 4748 9 cloth
0 7146 4306 8 paper
A special issue of the journal Regional & Federal Studies

FRANK CASS PUBLISHERS
Newbury House, 900 Eastern Avenue, Ilford, Essex, IG2 7HH
Tel: +44 (0)181 599 8866 Fax: +44 (0)181 599 0984 E-mail: info@frankcass.com
NORTH AMERICA
5804 NE Hassalo Street, Portland, OR 97213 3644, USA
Tel: 800 944 6190 Fax: 503 280 8832 E-mail: cass@isbs.com
Website: www.frankcass.com

Remaking the Union

Devolution and British Politics in the 1990s

Howard Elcock, *University of Northumbria at Newcastle* and **Michael Keating**, *University of Western Ontario* (Eds)

Devolution is firmly back on the British political agenda since a Labour government committed to its introduction was elected by a massive majority on 1 May 1997, and the Conservative Party was wiped out in both Scotland and Wales. This volume offers an exploration of debates about devolution in Scotland and Wales and the English regions, discussion of political issues such as electoral reform and increased representation for women; the changing balance of power between the European Union, the member states, and the nations and subnational units of those states.

240 pages 1998
0 7146 4876 0 cloth
0 7146 4430 7 paper
A special issue of the journal Regional & Federal Studies

FRANK CASS PUBLISHERS
Newbury House, 900 Eastern Avenue, Ilford, Essex, IG2 7HH
Tel: +44 (0)181 599 8866 Fax: +44 (0)181 599 0984 E-mail: info@frankcass.com
NORTH AMERICA
5804 NE Hassalo Street, Portland, OR 97213 3644, USA
Tel: 800 944 6190 Fax: 503 280 8832 E-mail: cass@isbs.com
Website: www.frankcass.com

Paradiplomacy in Action

The Foreign Relations of Subnational Governments

Francisco Aldecoa, *University of the Basque Country* and
Michael Keating, *University of Western Ontario* (Eds)

Paradiplomacy, while for the most part unspectacular, represents an
important and new dimension both to regionalism and to international
affairs and between national and regional matters. Tackling such issues
as the repercussions upon subnational autonomy of the progressive
constitution of diverse international regimes – the European Union,
NAFTA, APEC – or the complex relations between the growing
subnational foreign action and the contemporary conditions for the
formulation and implementation of foreign policy in federal and
quasifederal states, Paradiplomacy in Action represents an important
contribution to a better understanding of the growing subnational
involvement in foreign affairs.

232 pages 1999
0 7146 4971 6 cloth £37.50/$52.50
0 7146 8018 4 paper £17.50/$26.50
A special issue of the journal Regional & Federal Studies

FRANK CASS PUBLISHERS
Newbury House, 900 Eastern Avenue, Ilford, Essex, IG2 7HH
Tel: +44 (0)181 599 8866 Fax: +44 (0)181 599 0984 E-mail: info@frankcass.com
NORTH AMERICA
5804 NE Hassalo Street, Portland, OR 97213 3644, USA
Tel: 800 944 6190 Fax: 503 280 8832 E-mail: cass@isbs.com
Website: www.frankcass.com